The Book
of
Honor

Lawrence J. Dickson

ISBN 0-9666440-0-X

Printed in the U.S.A.

The Book
of
Honor

Lawrence J. Dickson

Fierce Press
P.O. Box 1371
La Jolla, CA 92038

Acknowledgments

Front cover photograph by Debra Denker. Used by permission of the Afghan Help Organization, which purchased from Debra the right to reproduce this photo to raise money for Afghan aid. In return, one seventh of the profits of this book will be given to help with mine clearing and other relief efforts in Afghanistan.

Family photo and car illumination on rear cover by Thomas Dickson. Billboard photo on rear cover from Dickson family archives. Cover design by Jeanne and Lawrence Dickson. LATEX typesetting by Thomas Dickson. Computer processing of cover art by Dickson and Reeves Graphic Design.

Extensive quotations from *The White Rose,* by Inge Scholl, are used by permission of University Press of New England. Short excerpts from many other authors are given credit where they are quoted, whether by permission or by fair use.

This book is deeply indebted to the art and thoughts of all my sources. Nevertheless, all the opinions expressed herein are solely the responsibility of the author.

My thanks go to my wife Jeanne, and to my children Thomas, Elizabeth and Alice, for their patience during the writing of this book, and for their many shared experiences and thoughts, with which the book is filled. There is simply no way it could have been done without them, or without the seminal input from my friends, starting with Jay Hoffman. My life and mind, alone, are not big enough.

Contents

Introduction

Spit on Pittsburgh

My personal formation began in the fall of 1956, around my ninth birthday. For the first time ever, I paid attention to a news story. Budapest was burning. The freedom fighters, betrayed by both East and West, were manning their barricades, exploding tanks, broadcasting hopeless pleas for help, fleeing, and dying. My mother's people are from Slovakia, across only one border from Hungary on the mosaic of Eastern Europe.

I wrote a speech about the Hungarian Revolt, which I kept delivering to my high school debate club years later. (They told me it was well written but poorly spoken.) I even went so far, at age 13, as to write a science fiction novel based loosely on the heroic events.

During my young adulthood I hoped that the "conservative" political movement would fight for the right. I joined Youth for Goldwater and subscribed to *National Review,* since they proclaimed that our appeasement of the Soviet Union was a dirty betrayal. I willingly submitted to the Vietnam draft physical in 1968, but was rejected because of asthma, which had nearly killed me a couple of times already.

The ultimate betrayal and unfair fight was the attack on babies, so I helped found the anti-abortion movement (*Youth United for Human Life,* Washington state, 1970) before most people were aware the issue existed. This occurred during a "political break" that many major universities (including Princeton, where I was studying for my doctorate in mathematics) declared in Autumn 1970 to allow students to campaign in the elections. There was a ballot issue to legalize abortion in my home state of Washington, more than two years before the *Roe vs Wade* Supreme Court decision.

Foul things happened during the 1970s: the legalization of abortion, the end of the moon shots, the fall of Saigon and ensuing mass murders. There was also a technology depression, made just for people like me. ("Will the last person to leave Seattle please turn out the lights?") After a decade spent here and there, with some foreign travels, I married in 1979 in Seattle.

Soon thereafter, Soviet tanks moved into Afghanistan. My wife Jeanne and I were founding a little magazine *November* (Jay Hoffman, editor), and we sought out a Seattle Afghan leader, Faizullah Kakar, to write for our first issue about his people's fight.

Long attention to the heroes of the world does bring about a gift of prophecy. It was a time of despair for most anti-Communists (the mass murders of Cambodia were the most recent trend) and everyone was predicting that the Afghans would last a few months at most. Dr Kakar's article, "Afghan Blood", was perhaps the first in English to foretell the ultimate failure of the Soviet "digestion" of Afghanistan. It also noted the threat this failure would pose to the USSR itself.

We never ceased our contact with the Afghan community, even when we moved to San Diego with our baby son Tom in 1981. With the aid of the Aronson family, Peace Corps veterans, we started the *Afghan Help Organization* to ship fruit to Afghanistan to relieve vitamin deficiencies. That failed but helped to start something much bigger.

Dr Robert Simon, a great medical hero of our century, sold his Malibu house around this time to finance an illegal trip, alone, to Afghanistan to bring medical aid and gather evidence. We were able to introduce him to the San Diego community, including the family of Congressman Duncan Hunter. They were bowled over, and pitched in to form the San Diego chapter of the International Medical Corps, which is the group Dr Simon founded to bring illegal medical aid to Afghanistan. These people also joined a community of congressmen who influenced President Reagan on the Afghanistan issue.

Thus it is possible that our tiny, failed attempt to ship limes to the Afghans ended up helping to topple the Soviet Union.

But history did not end with the fall of the USSR. What was happening on the abortion front—including rape and torture—hardly bore looking at. We never ceased our contact with the pro-lifers either, but the endless evil news and gloating began to tell on my wife's sanity. My personal time of prosperity was ending, and our family with three children started drawing the attention of those California authorities who hate any families with children.

By 1990, our income was decreasing, and cash-hungry people were sniffing around for excuses to sue us (our modest savings were mostly in cash). Educational experts were closing in on our middle child, Elizabeth, setting her up for "special" treatment, an atrocity which had already been done to my wife in her youth. We read the signs in time, and took refuge across the border, in Tijuana. That is where we live today. It's good for the wife, good for the children, and good for the pocketbook when paychecks are uncertain.

Seven years later we lift our heads and I write this book. Why just now? Three recent events have brought me to this.

The first event was a conversation I had with my son Tom, then 16. He goes to Saint Augustine, a boy's high school in San Diego. One day that spring he complained to me that he and his friends were feeling the lack of adventure in life. No more men on the moon, no more arming against the evil empire: they are reduced to fantasy role-playing adventures in a local game room. They are hungry for honor and would choose that over any amount of corporate careerist wealth.

This Saint Augustine High School is in the rough part of town, and the boys talk a kind of rap dialect in their recreational moments, though their studies are serious enough. They form part of a continuum that goes right through to the most "hopeless" gangbangers and young underclass males. The answer to Tom's complaint is also an answer to what ails them.

This book is therefore a father's advice to his family. Everything is grist for my mill. Things are mentioned that may be offensive to some, but please remember that it is a serious duty to offer a complete picture to my children.

The second event is an ending. We have followed the worst of those police rape cases, the so-called "Pittsburgh nightmare", for nearly a decade. The unrepentant authorities used every legal trick to avoid justice, and in May 1997 they finally won. Their sexual assault and torture were vindicated in court.

The authorities were afraid that any admission of wrongdoing would damage the law's legitimacy. But their victory—in collusion with all the state and Federal authorities who could have filed civil rights suits and the like—their victory totally wipes out the law's legitimacy.

If the rapist cops had been punished, they could pay their debt to society and be called reformed. They could be absolved. But they are obdurate and refuse to repent. So now Pittsburgh cops are rapists forever. Spit on Pittsburgh for me!

On top of all the law's other lies and offenses of the last thirty years, each more arrogant than the last, this final wad of cumm means it is time to abandon the conservative hope. American law has proved itself resolute in evil. It can no longer be honored by the honorable. American law is not worth the toilet paper it is printed on.

The consequences of this momentous judgement—which are simple and surprising—will be one of the main themes of this book. And that leads to the third event. By the courtesy of my friend, Jay Hoffman, I received a copy of *The Notebooks of Sologdin,* by Dimitri Panin, a Soviet labor camp veteran known in Solzhenitsyn's work as Sologdin.

Solzhenitsyn makes Panin's heroism and mental stature quite clear. But Solzhenitsyn's work is abstracted: he is like a historian or a journalist, giving the big picture. Panin's book is an intensely personal memoir. And as such it has a rare virtue, shocking to me as its meaning slowly filtered through. It is a virtue I intend to emulate.

Panin, far more than anyone else I know of, actually "makes up his own mind". Without casting glances over his shoulder or worrying about what anyone will think, he draws conclusions from what he sees. And he makes bold proclamation of each of them—no trimming!—often he assembles them into lists. Some sound obvious, some sound odd and dated or foot-in-the-mouth embarrassing. But that does not matter. They are all truly his, and he has a great mind, and they are all worth careful attention, every one.

More: Panin makes me bold to emulate him. No trimming here either, if I can avoid it (I have the same cringing, pussy-mouthed speaking habits that all Americans have, so avoiding it will take effort!) I will set it down flat: matters of honor after the law has fallen. I will make my logic clear, take it or leave it. I will even, on occasion, present lists.

My language will sometimes seem rough to my respectable friends. And it will seem stuffy and scholarly sometimes to my rough friends. But I am writing this book for everyone from George Soros to the homeboy in his colors. It is too wide a gap. All I can do is once again emulate the great zek authors like Panin and Solzhenitsyn: speak my own language, and hope to be understood.

One final note. I wrote the chapters of this book in order, from Spring 1997 to Spring 1998. I have chosen not to alter the present time of each part. The reader will therefore notice that observations current in any chapter may be past at the time of a later chapter.

Chapter 1

King Arthur's Law

The law has rotted. That ought to come as good news to young men (if you can believe it), since for over a century in America, the law has replaced justice and honor. Ordinary Joe is neither expected nor allowed to right any wrongs. No jobs for young princes or knights errant. Just wait for the experts.

Some of you, particularly if your families have money, will need a more detailed justification before discarding the rotted law. Indeed, discarding it will not be the conclusion—it is stranger than that. There is a chain of reasoning leading to the strange conclusion, and I will go through every link.

What the Law really Is

Start with the definition of law. There is only one that fits every place and every system. The law is the policeman.

An example of how this works. Traffic law touches all our lives frequently. But traffic law is really just the fact that a cop may pull us over for breaking the rules. And what are the rules? We and the cop have the same understanding of them: the state Driver's Handbook (available at your local DMV) applied to nearby signs and road markings, plus a lot of experience and good sense.

When the cop pulls you over, you usually know what you did wrong. If not, he tells you. Normally there is no real dispute, though there are marginal cases.

You may weasel out of the charge using some legal technicality. Conversely, the cop may use a technicality to "get" an unoffending motorist that he doesn't happen to like. Everybody understands that both of these are kinds of cheating.

There are statutes that supposedly govern all this, but neither you nor the policeman probably read many of them. It would take a lawyer to understand them, and that understanding would be likely to conflict with good sense.

Recently in California, an off-duty cop, speeding without siren or lights, killed some pedestrians when he went out of control. The survivors sued and lost because the speed limit, by statute, is only a *recommendation* and not a requirement.

So say the lawyers; but these loopholes are usable only by the wealthy and the powerful, who can afford a lawyer, or who are backed (like that cop) by an entity that commands legal clout. For most of us, the speed limit is a requirement, not a recommendation.

A believer in statutes and lawbooks will object that no policeman is a law unto himself. His actions are based, however crudely, on words passed by due legislative process, and he will be out if he violates them. Thus (says the lawyer) the real law is those words.

One answer is that those words are the regime, not the law. Nazi Germany had a complex system of well-reasoned (if evil) laws, but they vanished like a puff of smoke when Berlin fell in 1945. They had in turn replaced earlier lawbooks by Weimar, which in turn had replaced the Kaiser, etc. The policemen mostly remained the same through it all, shifting back and forth as the winds changed.

We in America have the unusual experience of statutory continuity for 200 years. That gives us a false notion of the power of legal parchments. But suppose some citizen wrote his own law book, and then somehow converted or replaced all the police so that the authorities all used his book. Then all the old Constitutions and statutes and case law would vanish like the morning mist, exactly as if we were a banana republic.

The second thing to remember is that I said the policeman *is* the law, not that he is the *master* of the law. That metal and vinyl and tubing all add up to *be* your car; but they do not drive your car. To know what your car will do for (or to) you, you must know all about that metal, how strong or brittle, and how in fact it is controlled.

For almost all of us, almost all of the time, the law is what the policeman understands it to be. The policeman has a firm idea of what he has to enforce and, in addition, has a clear idea of what constitutes an outrage that he should jump in against. He will not hesitate to stop a robbery in progress, even if he has never read any legal authority on the topic of robbery.

Also the policeman is aware of limits to his powers. There are things that he may not do, unless he wants to get in trouble himself. Sometimes it is more a notion of *who* he is not permitted to touch.

"The policeman" includes a complex authority behind the man you meet in the uniform. Somebody does actually police the police. A Poway, California cop a few years ago strangled a girl and dumped her body off the misnamed Mercy Road. When the other police worked this one out, they arrested and jailed him; he was convicted and now is serving a long sentence. Nobody needed to consult a law book on this one either.

More subtly, the reason not to cheat openly on your taxes is that the IRS will take away your liberty and property. The IRS does this, not only through arresting officers, but through agencies like your bank which, on demand, empties your bank account and forwards it to the IRS. Thus the banker acts as a policeman, because he understands that *he* will be himself policed if he does not follow the orders of the IRS.

The banker's understanding of the law is probably limited to a determination never to say "no" to an IRS officer.

A setup like this is called an "enforcement tool", and in it the legal words become more important. The authorities craft the statute to make the tool work (for instance, making clear that they will punish the banker harshly if he does not help the IRS). At the same time, people with clout have their say, so that the tool is designed *not* to be effective against them.

Both these opposing trends go to extremes, leading to three results:

1. Ordinary working people and poor people are punished more and more severely, caught by enforcement tools that are ever more arbitrary, for doing things that never used to be illegal.

2. At the same time, more and more exceptions are written into law to protect wealthy and influential persons from the consequences of their actions.

3. Struggling hopelessly to accomplish (1) and (2) at the same time, the word processors of lawmakers churn out "junk law" until the whole code becomes massive, complex and impossible to understand.

Just as a baseball fan keeps his eye on the ball, we can understand the meaning of these trends by examining their effect on the state of mind of a policeman.

(2) and (3) are a threat to the policeman. Since understanding is no longer possible, (3) means the policeman has to concentrate on following orders, instead of fighting crime. Even if the policeman's superior makes an error, "following orders" is a good personal defense for the underling.

This makes the police more like a military assault squad. (Think of agencies like the ATF, who carried out Janet Reno's massacre at Waco, Texas.) "To Protect and Serve," though still painted on the sides of police cars, no longer has much meaning.

(2) forces the police to become aware of pecking orders and privileged groups. Certain classes of people, like homosexual activists and abortion clinic escorts, are even permitted to carry out violent physical attacks with impunity. In *these* cases, the policeman who naively jumps in to protect the person being beaten up is in for a short career!

On the other hand, (1) gives the policeman more freedom of action than ever before. Where "tightening" or "cracking down" is announced, the policeman can plunge right ahead with actions that used to be illegal or even personally repugnant (an example is kidnapping small children). The only catch is that the policeman must be careful that he attacks only those who are *targeted* by an agency with clout. Normally those targeted are to be found among the poor or the working people, those lacking in political influence or living in unfashionable neighborhoods.

The new California smog tests, called "Smog Check II", include spot checks (called *butt sniffers*) at highway intersections, and automated reporting by smog check stations to the DMV. The purpose is to drive older model cars—common in lower class neighborhoods where people have to get to work but can't afford new cars—off the road. Soon after Smog Check II went into effect, an outcry arose because the butt sniffers were catching classic cars driven by residents of exclusive neighborhoods like La Jolla and Rancho Santa Fe.

This is an instance where the lawmakers, by error, did not calibrate their enforcement tool finely enough. It acted against the privileged as well as the poor, an oversight which is no doubt being corrected even as I write. There would have been no outcry if the enforcement tool had worked only on low-income car owners.

The Hunt for the Friendless

Among "good government" movements, the most famous and successful in the history of the world was the work of the Founding Fathers of the United States of America, who wrote the Declaration of Independence and the Constitution over two hundred years ago. It stood up to the usual legal trends for a century or more. People and nations imitated it all around the world.

But the Constitution ran up against another, more powerful worldwide trend moving in the opposite direction. That trend, the essence of twentieth century law, swamped other countries before it got to us. But it has the United States at last, and now we are even leading the charge to break down the last resistance to this second trend, which I label *the hunt for the friendless.*

The way to get ahead is to kick someone weaker than yourself. That kick then gets passed along, as in a rowdy classroom. Ultimately, in this world of selfish atheists, the whole crowd gets together against someone who is completely helpless, and stomps him into a bloody corpse.

Old-fashioned law would stop this before anything really horrible happened, but steps (1)-(3) transform the policeman to protector of the stomper. Most important is to make sure that the stomped one is not only helpless but *friendless.* Just review recent history, to see this more refined tactic in action.

The Soviet Union contented itself with driving the nobles out of Russia—they had friends in the West. Its great works of death focussed on the nameless peasants, in Eastern European villages unknown to anyone more than a few miles away. They killed these people by enforcing artificial famines at the same time as the Soviet Union was being "welcomed into the community of civilized nations" by our President Roosevelt. I won't go into the details of an artificial famine here. Try working them out for yourselves, to understand what an odd range of tastes our national leaders have.

Those who did the welcoming—the big money families of the United States—were fully aware that the artificial famines were going on. Through the *New York Times,* and a Pulitzer Prize reporter named Duranty who wrote puff pieces for the USSR, they arranged for this news to be suppressed (1932-3). The amount of money for them to make in the Soviet Union was slight, but the feeling of superiority over starving peasants must have been a great pleasure. By arranging for millions to die without making even a ripple of disturbance, they proved their power over the lowly crud people of the world.

Hitler, coming a little later, leaned on old communities of oddball minorities scattered through the master race's lands. Everybody knows how spectacularly that backfired, but think how safe it looked at the time. Funny looking old Jewish tailors and pawnbrokers shuffling along in dark suits: who could have foreseen that anyone would care if they were crushed?

Like our homosexual gangs, Hitler's homosexual gangs (the SA and SS) had the right to ravage at will without being stopped by police. Czeslaw Milosz, author of *The Captive Mind,* remembers a fleeing Jewish girl being slaughtered in the street—such a waste of life and beauty! (the young man's reaction.)

Normally a policeman would leap in to stop such a horror, but police

under the Nazis knew better. Trend (1), extreme severity, applied to the
Jews. Trend (2), the right to wreck without suffering any consequences,
applied to their persecutors.

The Jews were avenged in 1945 due to an accident of war and power
politics. The safe bet of the Soviets went bad more slowly. That is a great
tale of honor, which I will treat in more detail later.

Those who remembered the murdered villagers were humiliated and
rejected in the free countries. Names like "McCarthyite" were invented for
them. There were tenacious relatives in America, who in the end could join
with Lithuania and Solidarity and the Pope—and there were Afghans who
had heard tales they would never forget.

Faizullah Kakar, who grew up in northwestern Afghanistan, remembers
in "Afghan Blood" how it was in his apparently peaceful childhood:

> In teaching me how to handle a gun, my father stressed
> several rules. One such rule was that whenever I was playing
> with even an empty gun, I must turn it away from any human
> beings nearby, and if safe point it north toward the Russis...
>
> For it was known what the Soviets had done to the Ozbeck,
> Tadjik, Turkmen, and Kazakh Muslims whose lands the Rus-
> sians had seized...
>
> In the 1920's a special campaign was pressed by Stalin against
> these nations. It often assumed genocidal proportions... But
> their sufferings did not pass unnoticed.
>
> Thousands of refugees poured into Afghanistan and Iran,
> telling of the horrors they and their relatives had experienced.
> These eyewitness accounts spread into every corner of Afghani-
> stan, and have long since inoculated the Afghans against the
> Russians.

That was written in 1980, just after the Soviet invasion. The cries of
the friendless continued to echo for years to come, in Afghanistan. Those
guns that were aimed north: they really did fire, and they brought down
the monster.

Doomed Little Sister

Hitler and Stalin have fallen. Our own hunt for the friendless has learned
from their mistakes. Nobody is more helpless than a baby, and nobody
is more abandoned than a baby whose own mother has betrayed it. Thus
"Choice" was born, the free world's final and most refined bloody stomp.
Supported by the same people who were at home with the Nazis and the

Soviets—the Culture of Wealth—it has swept the law of nations almost everywhere.

To all appearances, this was not such a sure thing, when the issue became public knowledge in the mid-60s. Of course, it was well known before then that such activity went on, in the underworld of the Mafia and in foreign cesspools like Sweden. George Orwell's 1930s novel *Keep the Aspidistra Flying* has the protagonists considering abortion. C.S. Lewis' 1940s novel *That Hideous Strength* refers to the notion of "teaching abortion and perversion" to schoolgirls.

The 1950s led into our issue with a more general struggle, justice vs regime as source of the law. This was the Civil Rights movement which used the tactic of "civil disobedience" of a law manifestly unjust. The issue *seemed* to be decided in favor of justice, with the Brown vs Board of Education decision of the Supreme Court. Later skirmishes like Governor Wallace's schoolroom stand against integration, and Bull Connor's unleashing of his police dogs, were clearly failing twitches of a losing cause.

But the triumph of justice was a fatal misreading of that integration debate. The point is that nobody with real clout needed Bull Connor's version of oppression. Bull Connor was hopelessly outclassed and outdated and provincial. His petty tyranny could be crushed and never even inconvenience the real powers.

And the lesson drawn was not: Don't be unjust like Bull Connor was. The lesson drawn was: Learn from the mistakes Bull Connor made.

All law can be divided into two parts: *boring duty,* preventing harm, rightly settling disputes, protecting the innocent (the kinds of things that law-abiding citizens think of as proper functions of the law); and, *fun stuff,* where the law provides its masters with the juicy prizes its masters choose to take. They took away Bull Connor's fun stuff; that must not (so the lesson went) happen to us.

Such an attitude was not apparent back then (the 1960s) to ordinary citizens like me. We still believed in America. I was only 16 when I joined "Youth for Goldwater". What a trusting young idealistic fool I was! It has recently come out that Goldwater was buying an abortion for his daughter way back in the 1950s. If I had known that, I would have spewed all over his name.

So when the big push for abortion began (in the mid '60s, with the thalidomide trouble and Mrs Finkbine's abortion) many of us reacted with horror. We thought it was a fluke (we were so wrong). Surely if we just explained to these people exactly what it was they were doing, they would put on the brakes as quickly as Dad when he realizes he's backing over the neighbor's toddler!

This feeling (of appealing to people of good will over a misunderstanding) went on for a whole generation—thirty years. Only in the last year or two has it finally petered out.

You met the best kind of people there (in the anti-abortion movement): people with heart, who would not stand for blatant injustice against a helpless baby. In particular, you met the best kind of women (*that* was something a young man noticed). With enough courage to face the little mischances of life. Not afraid of having a baby, nor of anything this side of having a baby.

In case you are wondering, yes, I did marry one of them. A kind of insurrectionist at Seattle's doomed Lincoln High School. She got involved after one of her classmates put it to a vote in her homeroom whether her baby would live or die. (The vote was thumbs up, and the baby was spared.)

Meet a real woman like this, and you'll never again be interested in any silicone-breasted, airbrush-fleshtoned, dollar-sign-eyed commercial skin model. One Sydney, Australia prolife secretary (a devout ex-nun, near 40 but still beautiful) told me she thought men loved to fight for the right and to defend the underdog. Then why weren't there more men active for our cause? Not an easy question to answer.

Maybe this whole book is an attempt to answer it.

Well, I helped start the cause. In 1970 I was shepherding around groups of teenage boys and girls from good families, as they passed out leaflets protesting the Washington State abortion referendum. (When I say "good families," I do not mean "rich families," I mean "good families.") There were a couple of other leadership positions, but I (and, later, my wife) have long followed a vector that slants slowly away from this movement.

That does not ever mean that I find fault with their cause or their work. On the contrary. It leaves me angrier. It leaves me as one yelling at the graveside of a trusting, idealistic, murdered sister. Yes she made mistakes; she misjudged the forces. Nevertheless she always spoke the truth *and you all knew it*. By what it did to her, the law has condemned itself.

The anti-abortion civil disobedience pioneer, Joan Andrews, used to do things like chain herself to suction machines before that became popular. In the early 80s, when they sent her to jail, they used to take great delight in performing "full body cavity searches" on her. Of course they knew as well as I do that Joan Andrews was about as likely as Mother Teresa to smuggle cocaine or razors in her crotch!

The purpose of this action of United States law was solely to humiliate and punish opposition to the regime. The Bull Connor lesson was being learned. (Also of course, there is the "fun stuff" aspect of the law: a clean old fashioned Catholic single woman is finer and safer than the standard whores and drug addicts that normally come to hand.) But I have not forgotten this detail.

A man of honor needs clear memory. There are judgements that will need to be made. It is presumptuous to make them in snap fashion after one offense. But accumulating evidence must be let accumulate, to tip the scales in time.

A side note: Miss Andrews married at last, very late in life, and had a baby. (People like her make it a serious point of honor to marry first.) Unlike Frodo the Hobbit, she got to enjoy what she tried to save for others. And believe me, for someone as generous as her it is a joy. I wish her the best of it.

[Later news: Acting on a warrant activated by her attempt to adopt a baby found in a garbage can, a Pittsburgh judge recently jailed Miss Andrews, now Mrs Bell, for a protest of twelve years ago. She would not swear allegiance to unjust laws. Nevertheless they released her a few months later—she was converting half the convicts in her prison.]

In the meantime, the nature of the battle was getting clearer. Civil disobedience that tripped up unfashionable nigger haters in the Old South was one thing. Civil disobedience that threatened the personal cleanup tool of every wealthy lecher in the Capitol was quite another.

Nowadays we are used to this. The sex wallowing of the Packwoods, Clintons, Kennedys and all the rest is public knowledge now. Each of them obviously lives in need of his own personal backup abortionist. For those who are not too squeamish, this is such a great way of shutting up the witness and cutting costs. And it stretches as far as the Goldwaters!

Historical note: It turns out that the real author of *Roe vs Wade,* William O. Douglas, not only went through a Hollywood list of wives, but was well known as a party boy even before he dumped his first wife. "Jane Roe's" recent troubles of conscience have revealed that the whole case was in essence a fraud, publicized false as to fact, with the snickering (literally) connivance of High Court members who were in on the joke. One hand on the quill pen, the other hand in their pants.

I have a copy of this decision. It is junk! It is what any half-baked law student, with access to a good library, could produce for a term paper if assigned the job of coming up with a crooked argument based on one-sided selections from Cliffs Notes legal history. This same guy (Douglas) had previously openly mocked the Constitution by basing a decision on something "emanating from [its] penumbras" (that is, farting from its shadows). And he got away with it.

Well, Little Sister plowed ahead ignorant of all this corruption. (Should have been warned when Nathanson's ruthless movie, *The Silent Scream,* did not move them.) I guess the attempt had to be made, because otherwise they could say, "Nobody asked." So the attempt was made. The authorities had their answer. Torture.

The U.S. Department of Justice developed techniques of torture (officially called *pain compliance*) and taught them to local police departments in training sessions in the 1980s. The coincidence of dates with *Operation Rescue* activity is no coincidence at all. Suppression of political dissent is the prime goal of torture in regimes throughout the world and throughout history.

Listen to black people when they complain of police treatment! They speak from experience. At the same time, remind them of the irony that Rodney King probably suffered more or less accidentally from techniques that were developed for use against Joan Andrews. She is a more serious threat to the regime.

In the late 1980s, various incidents (Hartford, Los Angeles, etc) with torture holds and broken bones showed that indeed, the authorities had learned from the mistakes of Bull Connor, who proved to be a half-hearted softie compared with the new enforcers. The ugliest incident was at Pittsburgh.

Police who had removed their name plates (proving the incident was premeditated) reached for the female anti-abortion protesters as soon as they were brought to the jail.

Torture was not absent. A protestor with asthma was having an attack and asked for aid. In return, officers blew tobacco smoke in her face. As an asthmatic myself, I know personally what this is all about. A nurse stepped in *against orders* and gave her some oxygen before she died of suffocation.

But the sexual assault was worst. It was obvious that the "fun stuff" side of the law was presented as a reward for these officers' loyalty. It was not restricted to body searches. With lewd comments, the male officers would tear the women prisoners' clothes, or would handcuff a prisoner and cumm on various parts of her body.

Since these were fresh young sweethearts from the Baptist family picnic, or from nearby Catholic Franciscan University, it was more fun assaulting them than beating up some poor, worn out prostitutes. It was clear that the police had been instructed on the limits of rape by the then feminist mayor of Pittsburgh, who assigned them this mission. I grant them no escape clauses, however.

I call it rape, and if any policeman does that to a woman of my family I'll personally cut his balls off the first time I get him down. I hope this helps to make the issue clear. First point of honor: there are some things you cannot overlook just to protect your career.

So all these things have to be remembered. It was still possible that the law as a whole would repent of the excesses. Pittsburgh, the state and the United States each judicially discouraged this hope by displaying all-out advocacy of the rapist officers. Knowing full well that this kind of woman would not for any advantage lie. (Just the fact that they had joined this quixotic rescue effort showed that their whole devotion was to the truth, at whatever cost to themselves—and that they naively expected others to feel the same.)

The authorities used legal technicalities to prevent some women from testifying. They bought off others, and wore them all down with ten years of legal folderol. To the solemn approval of all the courts, they affirmed that no police could be held guilty of an assault as long as they removed their name tags before they attacked. Of course, the notion that a rapist should actually be *prosecuted,* as opposed to merely suffering a civil action, was totally rejected by everybody in power.

It should be clear why my family could not participate in protests like the one in Pittsburgh. As with all civil disobedience, they required "Men of Peace", an assurance we could no longer give. The authorities, of course, are too stupid and arrogant to ask how much the fall in popularity of *Operation Rescue* is due to people turning at heart to war, rather than capitulation.

So we hold up signs along arterials during the appointed demonstration days. As my twelve-year-old son was carrying an "Abortion Kills Children" sign, a San Diego Police cruiser drove alongside and the cop flipped the finger at him. This was Tom's first real civics lesson—and another point to remember. Policemen have repeatedly been quoted about how great legal abortion is in their personal lives, when a girlfriend needs to be cleaned out to protect the officer's career and bank account.

In 1993 dollars, the cost of bringing up a child was estimated to average $129,000 over 18 years. A later estimate, around 1996, was $145,000. This big money is weighed against the invisible, voiceless, friendless baby, and to the new breed of authorities the easy decision is made to squash the baby, by sucking out his brains if necessary. And the prize money can be split so many ways, once the job is done. There is no justice.

Little Sister never had a chance against the $145,000 per head bounty on babies. *But they could have treated her better.* Now that the decision is in—the gloating sanctification of that damned Pittsburgh rape—nothing remains but cowardice to bind to this legal authority. They lied, and they made a mockery of justice, and then they fucked those who reproved them with the truth. Their official words are sewer gas. Their legal parchments are toilet paper.

Good Use and Knights Errant

This turning of the law (the way a piece of meat turns) is not just something restricted to abortion. I picked that issue because it makes it absolutely clear (remember I am trained as a mathematician). But you can look at legal kidnapping, at drugging of schoolchildren, robbery and destruction of little businesses, whatever legal invasion beats up your peaceful neighbor: it is all part of a pattern. Heart rot.

Good news for young men and heads of families, who have been reduced to impotent junk by this suffocating monster. Does it mean you can stop paying taxes, or blow away the traffic cop who is pulling you over? Not quite! The answer is stranger than that, and you find it by looking back in history.

King Arthur of the Round Table was probably a historical figure, flourishing in the ruins of the Roman Empire in far Britain. He probably got his authority because he came from a family of old Roman governors. Never an Imperial decree for a hundred years or more—the Eternal City was ten times looted and full of deserted neighborhoods like the South Bronx. What did this leftover governor use? Rags and tatters of ancient legal scrolls?

Small animals (and small persons, like you or me) can shelter in parts of a great building even after it has fallen. Pieces of law remain valid even after their source has disgustingly rotted away. This should not be a surprise. While the big pigs are having their party, lots of old fashioned, responsible officials are doing their "boring duty" to the best of their ability, for instance with traffic laws—and *they* produce good stuff.

The legal doctrine of *Good Use* starts with the medieval saying, "A king is he who can hold his own." Like King Arthur, an official who can hold his own (no matter what the source of his authority) deserves attention as one who holds the fabric of society together. This is "use". If in addition his commands are "good"—serious and honest and rightful and adapted to the problem at hand—then they gain the force of law. This is a duty taught by Confucius. Perfection is not to be expected.

Here are some examples.

Even if you believe United States authorities derive legitimacy from the Constitution, the so-called "juvenile courts" can hardly share in this. Their authority derives from a hodgepodge of extra-legal usages that (as C.S. Lewis foresaw) add up to imposing unlimited punishment at will by changing its name from punishment to something else.

When my son went to court for his first traffic offense, my wife and I accompanied him to the office of the Juvenile Court judge. She imposed a very rational fine and punishment (involving writing an essay) and insisted on his considering the consequences of speeding. Her black gown was well-worn and her computers antiquated. She was obviously dealing daily with a flood of such cases, and was happy to find one showing a constructive attitude.

That is "good use". Neither we nor Tom saw obedience to her as any less than a *duty*. The weight of that duty would not change if the constitutional foundation of her authority were perfect—or totally nonexistent.

In Silicon Valley, there is a vicious legal and criminal dispute between two companies called "Cadence" and "Avant!". They compete in selling computer programs to design electronic chips. Avant! was founded by former employees of Cadence.

The story as told by Cadence is, "These people walked out of our offices with bulging briefcases, packed with our programs and stuff we paid for. Then they set up their own company, changed our stuff a little and started selling it under their own name." Avant! answers, "We were trying to do a good job but the Cadence management would not let us. We gave up in frustration, started our own company and did the programs right—and now they can't compete with us, so they whine to the law."

It is in the hands of the authorities, and rightly so. Our law does better with matters of money, and of business entities, than anyone else in the world or in history. (In many another country, it would be decided by who had the closest connections with the President, or the Generalissimo.) Like busy bees, prosecutors and county legal experts are going over the evidence in that case, in row after row of their document-heaped desks. They will do an honest job. Leave money matters to them. Give to Caesar what is Caesar's.

This is what I call "green eyeshade government," nameless and under-funded minor officials serious about their duty. My father was one of them. Confucius built his whole philosophy around them. The source of their authority hardly matters, as long as they use it well. They can be gang grandfathers or Nation of Islam project guards, and deserve every bit as much respect.

The other side of government is sleek, well-funded, and well-armed. They are always in touch with legislators, changing the law so that they can't be touched, no matter how horribly they mistreat people. The Child Protective Service, or whatever name the legal kidnappers go by in your state, is notorious for this. They like what they do; any who don't are quick to burn out and to quit.

Remember the ATF and the siege of Waco? They could have arrested Koresh any morning when he went out jogging. But they wanted their massacre. They got it in the end.

Nobody joins an outfit like the ATF unless he wants to pull that trigger. You could tell by their black commando suits. The whole Waco thing was set up so they could gratify their desires. And it was supposed to be a test case, that would open the door to more such actions whenever our masters wished. Luckily it didn't work out quite right.

They even had some *women* in those black suits: one of them acted as their spokesman to the slavish press. Women joining up as wannabe killers, armed to the teeth and slobbering for blood! This is a shameful perverted thing. If it had been my sister, I would take her gun away and kick her fat butt until she couldn't sit down for a week.

The other side of the coin is also illustrated from King Arthur. The legendary "Knight in Shining Armor" is specifically called the knight errant (or wandering knight). Noble and well-armed, he went from place to place, righting wrongs and defending the weak.

These stories sprang from the Dark Ages, after the fall of the Roman Empire. So did many of our traditional fairy tales. To understand their meaning, remember that the stories typically applied to the lives of ordinary people of those days, even though their main characters were disguised with grandeur.

The fairy tale *The Jolly King's Daughter,* for instance, applied to any humble family who fell victim to marauders or slavers, with the father laid out dead in front of the door of the hut. In the story the King dies and the Queen and Princess enter a long and vicious servitude. The ending offers hope of freedom, justice and a return to prosperity but only after long endurance.

In this light, consider the frequency of dragons and ogres. They have the habit of "devouring maidens"—there can hardly be any doubt what that means! And they always reign unscathed until the knight wanders in *from far away*, kills the ogre, and leaves.

People who assume the year 500 was simply lawless are assuming our ancestors were stupid indeed. In fact, all remaining scraps of Empire were treasured. There were bad scraps too, and bad governors or judges or army chiefs loved to enforce them. That ogre was not some romantic brigand, armed against the world: he'd hardly have lasted if he was, even in those days. The serious ogre took the trouble to cover his ass. He had official royal writs, and he did his dirty deeds with legal authority.

That was why the knight errant came from outside. And that was why he moved on after his deed was done. The only way to kill the dragon was to violate the law. And the ogre's higher ups were apt to take a dim view of the shining horseman who did in their official!

The knight errant is not unknown even here and now. Years ago, Jay Hoffman told me a story he heard on the news. All its actors and victims were black people from a battered inner city neighborhood.

A group of locals was relaxing in a tavern, when another man walked in. He began to tell the others about how he had just raped a 15-year-old girl. His gloating was precise and went into disgusting detail.

The next morning, his body was found hanging from a lamppost.

When police and reporters came to ask questions, everyone said: "We can't help you. None of us saw what happened. But he sure had it coming, didn't he?"

It does not often come to this. But that does not mean there is nothing that you can do. You, personally, can help the "good use" and frustrate the ogres. The younger you are and the less money you have, the more effective you can be. That is what is interesting about the tactics I am about to describe.

Tips for Scavengers

Always remember that it is a terrible thing that they have done to us, turning the law into a liar. A man of honor may never ignore this offense, or come to terms with it for cowardly reasons. That would be to sink back into the struggle to "get ahead", and to turn your own, your only life into just another piece of meaningless junk. Then you are indistinguishable from all the other suit and tie slaves.

On the other hand, you have a life to live. If like most of us you are a city dweller, part of the mainstream economy, you are inextricably wound up with the machinery controlled by our owners. Not so easy to break away and start anew—there is no America left for us Americans to emigrate to.

Up till now the only way to fight the evil (and not go equally bad like a McVeigh) has been political activism. Now it is 1997, and I announce what is clear to see: they have checkmated that approach. Laws require sponsors, and nobody honest has enough money or power to sponsor any change. Joining groups and signing petitions has had *over sixty years* to change our direction. With the single exception of homeschooling, it has absolutely failed even to slow the decay.

This means we have to abandon hope of an easy victory that comes from seizing the high ground (of centralized power). Instead we begin to pinch that power itself, while rebuilding the neglected ground of our own local place.

This has several encouraging results.

1. The ceaseless cycle of hope and defeat is broken. (We are currently trapped in this cycle because the people with money have rigged the game.) No longer does everything depend on some uncontrollable force, some campaigner or court or media empire. The new techniques center in your home and your life and neighborhood, where you have some power.

2. Because we repudiate the authority of the liars, we are no longer in a great rush. The essential wall is built for our families. Therefore

we can afford to take time. Time becomes our friend. Things can
be made to grow over many seasons. It is absolutely amazing what
you can accomplish, a little every day, when you have years at your
disposal. And you do.

3. We lighten ship so much by discarding the need for careers and re-
spectablilty. It's like striding out in shirtsleeves after you've trudged
under an eighty-pound pack all your life. And being loose and free
like that, we can focus on what is *really* worth having. Allies. Friends,
family. Ten men and women shoulder to shoulder are a mighty force
here or anywhere (had you forgotten that?) And at that point life
starts looking more like an adventure. Which is what it should be.

With all that in mind, I present my seven tips for scavengers, for small
human rats who live in the detritus of the fallen United States Constitution.
Much of the rest of the book will deal with these matters, but I will have
some introductory words here. The tips are:

1. Give to Caesar what is Caesar's.

2. Help the deserving.

3. The Sprizzo assertion.

4. The Feinstein response.

5. Rat on a rat.

6. Visualize subsistence farming.

7. Support your local lord.

Give to Caesar what is Caesar's

One area to abandon to our legal authorities is what they deal best with:
money. Pay your taxes. Submit money disputes to the courts. Keep good
accounts, and be honest in your business dealings. Follow the financial rules
set up by law.

There is a so-called "patriot" movement, chronicled in journals like the
Spotlight and the *New American*, which attempts to start with money matters in overturning the system. They have extremely legalistic ways of
avoiding taxes. Some claim they can even get a letter delivered for three
cents.

They are all doomed to failure, because they seek salvation in selfishness
and hoarded money, just like our owners. And our owners are better at that

game. We need to start by conceding the money high ground to the current authorities. It makes them feel less threatened, and it helps us concentrate on our strong points. Time and character.

Help the deserving

Each form of minor authority has its own character, some better than others. Border guards, for instance, are cool. I deal with them almost every day of my life, and I know. The laws they work under are mostly stupid, but the guards themselves by and large are nice young people, deserving of a salute and a wave.

Each petty authority, under "good use", rules his own little kingdom. It is our job to encourage the better of them. That has little to do with whether their commands are pleasant or inconvenient. Everything you do to make their job easier will help to keep them on that job. It will reward them for doing their Confucian duty, which is definitely what you want to do.

The Sprizzo assertion

Good officials spend as much time defending the people from the law, as they spend enforcing the law: a fact which is explained by the legal doctrine of good use, but not by any other legal doctrine that I know of. This will help *First Things* magazine understand the actions of Judge Sprizzo, who declared certain anti-abortion protesters innocent, even though they had prayed in a driveway, in clear violation of President Clinton's FACE law. His court stood between those protestors and the law. As was within his power, he ruled the prisoners innocent and therefore ruled the law guilty.

These official actions are going on all the time, whenever your child is protected from an unreasonable curfew, or an absurd building code regulation is left unenforced. (My friend once faced imprisonment of six months for each day that he stayed in a pre-1973 trailer. Five days of sheltering your family is a worse crime than rape! I have copies of the documents.) Those officials who endanger their position by asserting themselves like Judge Sprizzo are a great treasure. Exert yourself to protect and defend them.

The Feinstein response

Then there are the others. The following story was part of a political campaign and so should be taken with a grain of salt. Nonetheless it fits the kind of people Dianne Feinstein associates with, of whom I don't know what really pleases them more—mounds of corporate money or dumpsters filled with dead babies. So she gets a response named after her.

A man with a Chinese wife appealed to her office to help get his wife out of China. She was trapped there, and scheduled for a forced abortion. (This case was unusual, since it came to light *before* the event.) Senator Feinstein refused to help, saying that China was a valued trading partner. The abortion happened as scheduled.

If this is true, here is how you administer justice. The day you see Dianne getting it in a gutter, you do not jump in to help as you would a regular woman. You stand by with arms folded and never risk a bruise. If her army of police and lawyers is there to save her, well and good. Otherwise she is left to whimper and die alone.

The same goes for all the other vicious authorities: CPS legal kidnappers, Pittsburgh rapist police, ATF massacre troops. You do not need to lift a finger. And you (and all your friends) can wait. Sooner or later (and you may be surprised how often), they will need your help. Then leave them twisting in the wind, as they have so many of your friends and mine.

Rat on a rat

If there's a hotline, you can be pretty sure that the bad guys are in charge. Secret informers are a Soviet technique, and corrupt everyone. Your job is to bust up the secrecy. The first precept of Dimitri Panin's Prisoner's Code is: *Wipe out the stool pigeons.*

"Did you know it was my aunt that called the CPS on you, the day they took your kids away? She was tired of hearing them argue." Or: "You know that Ms Dorkina at the high school took your daughter in for an abortion last Thursday?" Then it is in the family's hands. They may cringe and pretend they did not hear it. Or the fur may fly.

Of course, the aunt or the daughter may not appreciate your role. Let them shriek. More seriously, Ms Dorkina and her abortionist friends may sue—if you have any money. What I am proposing is a big threat to their system. This is one time when having no money, and even being in trouble already, actually makes you *more* effective.

When the rat was justified, you also tell the person ratted on. "Jessie called the cops when she heard you beating up your girlfriend last night." The difference in this case is that you are standing shoulder to shoulder with Jessie—and with half a dozen other friends—when you give the word.

Visualize subsistence farming

You have seen those signs, "Visualize World Peace". Their idea is to promote a notion of peace. When I say "Visualize subsistence farming," I am promoting a notion of freedom. Yes, just like the woods hippies or the Amish, digging in the dirt with a sharp stick!

I will elaborate on the connection later in this book. Here let me say that there is no escape from it, and you are lucky indeed if you have relatives or friends that give you access to a farm. The clearest quote I have comes from an odd source, Christopher Stasheff's fantasy novel *Starstone*:

> "It is that, or starve—for in the cities there is no way to get food by your own effort."

Support your local lord

One of the greatest discoveries I have made is that here in modern Southern California—right among our neighbors—the ancient figure of the *lord* is returning to sight. I don't mean God or any mighty warrior, I mean the kind of minor lord that rubbed shoulders with the dirt farmers in medieval times. These people themselves have no idea of what they are; but I, who have access to the records of history, see one sign after another and they all fit. This, too, I will treat in more detail later.

A lord of your acquaintance can, I find, be recognized because he takes people under his wing. Transients, homeless, drunks, people down on their luck, bewildered young people. They throng under his roof. They work their way, they fix his things, they make music and have parties. If he has a family as generous as himself, these mingle with his other adherents.

I hope your neighborhood is lucky enough to have one (or more) of these; then you have little need to look farther. The hood is the place for you. Blow on this flame and make it grow. Your Confucian duty is focused right here, and any defending you can do will best serve if you defend this kind of man right in your own back yard. What a wealth of stories to tell, and little friends for your own children to grow up with!

Chapter 2

Honest Opinion

Here is an important objection to "good use". How can we avoid total disintegration of society, with everyone interpreting the rules in his own way and to his own advantage?

The answer to this is a great enlightenment—a mighty chance to turn a lemon into lemonade. It not only busts the liars' poisonous monopoly on law. It creates a foundation for self-respect that they cannot touch.

If you are bottom of the barrel "at risk" human junk, I'll show how you can be superior to the cream of society. Better than the rich and famous, higher than the great universities and professions with all their brains. *Just as you are*: no long drawn-out slogging through school to get a job and get rich first.

It was a few years ago. My family was passing out anti-abortion flyers near Euclid and Imperial, a San Diego street corner of evil repute. We already had enough experience by then to know that it was no use wasting our time in "better" neighborhoods.

There were little shabby row houses, and the sad poor women who responded to my knock often looked as if they were ready to apologize for taking up space in their own doorways. They probably thought I was some kind of surveyor for the Social Service authorities. There were young men hanging around the convenience store, and I asked them if they knew about the legal kidnappers. They did—but they were surprised that I did.

One drug dealer asked me if this wasn't really just women's business. I rather sharply delivered the standard answer—who put the women in that place, why dump it all on them? And he went into a hasty retreat, and changed the subject. I listened as he went on and on about his own personal notions and dreams, which I remember led to an odd hope that he and his friends would discover the secret for living forever.

It took a while to hit me. When it did, how I roared with glee. A drug dealer, flinching and troubled by words that touched his conscience. A drug dealer who was better than the American Bar Association, better than the American Medical Association, better than the Supreme Court and the United States Government! What a notion to turn the world upside down!

The Stringing Together of Words

Words are strung together as if they were opinions, but they are really not opinions. The power is not in the lie, but in the people who pretend to believe the lie. We are so used to it, we hardly notice it any more. An example is product endorsements.

There was a recent dispute in the sports pages about some kid, brilliant in a sport, who abandoned his education to go professional because he was already getting product endorsement contracts. People wrote in to condemn him because he was not making good with his life (no education). The sports columnist defended him: the American way is success, however it may be achieved, and we have no right to condemn him if he found a short-cut that works for him.

Well, I could argue with that, but what amazed me is that everyone ignored the main point. Product endorsement is a dishonest way of making a living! The sportsman isn't giving a real opinion. He is just spouting a string of words put in his mouth by whoever pays him the most money.

You can say this is harmless, it's only words, it's like found money. But consider it in more detail. *It must really work.* Do you suppose the company would pay the sportsman all that money, if they didn't get even more money in increased sales because of the endorsement? I think you can assume that they know their business.

Take Nike, the company that sells sneakers made by slave labor in Vietnam. When they pay millions to some basketball star to endorse them, is it out of pure generosity? I don't think so. They make ten times as much because kids listen to him. Mostly kids from poor neighborhoods.

I'm not even talking about the ones who kill each other for their expensive shoes. Just take a boy who demands his mom buy the $189 Nikes instead of the $18 generics that are just as good. Mom may work nights for peanuts as a waitress, but she gives in to keep peace in the family. That's a big hit on her tiny savings—maybe they can eat dog food for a week or two to make up the difference.

Would Mr Basketball Star really recommend that to some cousin he cared about? Of course not. The endorsement is a lie. And there is no weaseling out of the consequences. The only way Mr Basketball Star can get paid is if the lie works—and if the lie works, it does great harm to thousands and thousands of poor working families everywhere. Children are not responsible, and the sportsman uses his direct access via TV and his position of trust to manipulate them to empty their parents' wallets.

It is all perfectly legal, but when the star gets paid it is morally just the same as if he is getting his cut of the loot after a robbery that he helped carry out. The whole system works by *pretending* that he is expressing an honest opinion that just happens to coincide with the interests of whoever is making him rich.

American case law works the same way, by the stringing together of words that appear to make sense. That is the main thing lawyers do, and it is not always bad! Here is an example from our own lives.

We were selling our house, and the title search found a neglected lien still on the books. It was an oversight due to bad record keeping, but it gave someone a great chance to "hold us up" for big money or kill the sale. Naturally our buyer didn't want to proceed with this cloud on the title.

Our lawyer moved things forward by having us make a big deposit that would not be returned until the cloud was cleared. Then he talked to our title company (the one that made the mistake). They proposed to continue insuring the property for the new owner, since they were stuck with the liability anyway. Our lawyer declared the problem settled and the deal went through with no further ado!

This left our heads spinning a little, but we doffed our hats in respect and continued on our way. I guess the same title company can just go on insuring that piece of property forever. But this is the cleverness of lawyers, making their living tying together words in law and contracts.

Judgement is a declaration making grammatical sense and not self-evidently absurd as to content, which translates to action that settles a case. It is not hard to make grammatical sense and understand it, nor is there usually any honest error possible in what action is implied. The weak point is the valid content of the parts that are strung together to form the judgement.

That is why experts are so much used at law. The judge does not need to know everything in the world then. But it can only work if everyone is honest. So the current state of law (legal positivism) is subject to just exactly the same objection that I noted against "good use"!

Because the law is so willing to accept formulas that appear to make sense, collusion between groups of experts creates a new "right and wrong" whenever people in power need it. I will go through an example in detail.

It starts with the American Civil Liberties Union, a powerful lawyers' lobby. Stephanie Hopping, a Catholic journalist who is a friend of ours, once wandered into their San Diego offices and was stunned by the plush settings and the oak paneled luxury. Clearly these are the $300 an hour folks.

They have many judges on their secret membership list, so whenever they propose something in court, they can just turn around, put on their judge's hat, and pronounce "Excellently done, flawless!" *And they meddle in the schools.* They insist on atheism, since that allows them to fuck their secretaries. They prevent anything good from happening, like discipline, or the establishment of tough all-boys schools in the inner city. They are the ones who outlaw prayer and Christmas.

As a result, teachers are required to teach junk. History becomes what percentage of women were hookers. Real science, which is hard but actually *works*, is replaced by homosexual genes and loving animals. They take out Shakespeare and put in some half-literate feminist bully gloating about her abortion. Lots and lots of sex education, so the secretaries know to keep clean when they service their masters. Since God cannot be mentioned, there is no reaching for the stars, no adventure, no justice, no love.

So the schoolchildren get antsy and disruptive. After hours and hours of boring junk repeated in long meetings and sermons, a normal adult will behave exactly the same. If half a dozen teachers in each school would disobey orders and teach good stuff—including prayer and religion, even if different religions—the problem would go away. But that would risk their careers.

My youngest daughter, Alice, goes to a Tijuana primary school a mile south of the border fence. It looks like decayed project housing—upended cement blocks. The children march and dance and learn from tattered pulp textbooks, they address their teachers with formulas of respect, they sing childish patriotic songs with gusto. Teachers have no fear of mentioning God and religious symbols. When I walk Alice to school, I can feel the joy radiating from the place: her face lights up as she enters the gate.

Tijuana is not exempt from rotten influences. Just recently a new principal tried to get rid of old-fashioned teachers and replace their traditional formulas of respect and discipline with American models. The schoolchildren responded by naming him "snake-hair". With their parents they staged an angry revolt, mobbing his office and swearing to follow their favorite teachers to other schools. That was the end of that.

Such a cure is not allowed north of the border. In cowardly America, we crouch to obey the wreckers above. Any kick always has to be directed *downwards*. The schoolchildren must be blamed for the court-ordered junk they are fed. We therefore invent a new name for antsiness: Hyperactive Attention Deficit Disorder. Thus, the guilt for bad education is pinned exactly where it belongs—on a bunch of eight-year-olds.

The profession of Education now goes to the profession of Medicine and reports this strange new epidemic in the classroom. Like stock Oriental characters from Central Casting, they stand there bowing to each other. The teachers are expert in their field (so says Medicine), so we must accept their report of crazed pupils and prescribe a medicine to fix the problem. The doctors are expert in their field (so says Education), so we must accept their diagnosis and push their drug to shut up these kids.

So perfectly normal children are required to take dangerous psychoactive drugs such as Ritalin, which have nasty side effects like suicide. So much for those "Drug Free Zone" signs they mount on the street next to schools! As a parent, you are *forced* to drug your children, otherwise they are pushed into "Special Education", the school equivalent of Gulag. It is legally possible for them even to accuse you of child neglect, if you refuse to drug your healthy child.

And there is *nothing there*: it is all a pure lie, profiting both sides. The educators get peace in their classrooms without having to show enough courage to do their job. The doctors (and pharmacists and drug companies) get more business and more money.

And people accept this junk as though it were God's own word. I listened to a couple of harmless young women who were stocking shelves in a grocery store, and they were telling each other how they had both been "diagnosed" and drugged as school children. And journalists write op ed pieces that go on and on about this "issue" and many like it.

I've reached the conclusion that the journalists are honest in doing this: they are just overawed by the heavy expertise of their sources. Well, I am a PhD mathematician from Princeton University, and I am not overawed. And I am telling you: It is nothing! It is ad copy, promotional puffery, a marketing blitz! And it is filling our heads with nonsense, putting down our children, and doing physical and mental damage to them.

And that is only one example of the kind of thing I am talking about, of the dishonest pretense of expert opinion that dominates our country. Keeping a straight face allows you to do absolutely anything. Think about how often some "Official Requirement for the Oppression of the Poor" comes down from a distant power like the International Monetary Fund or the Environmental Protection Agency, to destroy someone's job or take his car. The local authorities fold their hands and plead "Oh please point that gun at me. Make me do it."

It is part of what I mean when I say that the lowest of the low— functionally illiterate underclass males from broken families, or whatever you want along that line—can easily be superior to our best and our brightest. Think over these cases in detail.

Your ugly gangbanger would be horrified if he walked into a room and found someone sucking the brains out of a live baby. I mean holding the baby down and cramming a vacuum pipe into its skull, so that the suction causes the baby's head to collapse. But to members of our proud Medical Profession—licensed doctors with MDs—this is legal and OK, all in a day's work.

I don't think our young punk will be too comfortable if he is walking past his neighbor's house and finds her crying and screaming, while a gang of kidnappers breaks into her house, dragging her children out from under beds and shoving them into a waiting van. Yet this is all in the day's work for a modern social worker or policewoman. If the punk's gang is decent it will expel or kill a fellow gang member who does something perverted like snatching a child from a school. But professional educators have no problem with handing over a child, no questions asked, to *legal* kidnappers—straight from the classroom, never to come home again. Teachers accept the official assurance that this does no harm and violates no rights.

I've never seen any of our local petty thieves stooping as low as to feed bleach or rat poison to a toddler. But as long as it was legal, many nearby American corporations were perfectly at peace dumping toxic waste into Tijuana gullies where it would poison the water of families who lived downstream. This was OK because nobody had yet thought to make it illegal. It became not OK when the Mexicans protested. If the companies can find other categories of little children that no one has yet though to protect, it will be OK to shift the poison to them.

When Nike got caught using slave labor in Vietnam, they protested (as do all these legalistic companies) that they "had not known". That meant they listened to their paid experts, who said everything was perfect, and took care *not* to listen to all the cries of protest from refugees, nor to ask themselves how these guys came up with labor costs of 18 cents an hour or whatever. Keep a straight face and everything is allowed.

Sacred Words and Dirty Mockeries

Why has the profession of law become a sour joke, looked down upon more than any other learned profession? The content of their work is the words of right and justice, the best efforts made throughout history to reach these high goals. Other professions like engineering and medicine just work with physical stuff, yet they get more respect. There is only one exception— the profession of politics—and interestingly enough politics too deals with those sacred words of right.

I will answer by examining an even more painful case: the religious profession, of priests and ministers and theologians. This gets hit less by common jokes, being so largely ignored. But to those in the know, the jokes are even more sour. *And all the bad attitudes are justified.*

The most corrupt experts are those dealing with the sacred words. Quote from the Bible (or even from a homemade pamphlet based on the Bible), and you can shock a drug dealer. In his life the sacred words are not used much, and when they are heard they have power.

When you read that the Catholic Diocese of Dallas just got hit with a $120 million judgement for protecting a priest who buggered altar boys, you have to wonder how they could fall so deep. Any ordinary businessman or junk dealer who never hears the Word of God in his life would be horrified at such a complaint. When the offending fucker started smirking and excusing himself, he'd be straight out into the paddy wagon.

Well? I'm a Catholic myself, a graduate of a Catholic university, and I know the reason. Others are awed by the law of God. These people spend years studying the Bible and the Fathers, the very words that are written down of the law of God. When you say a word over and over again (hamburger, hamburger, hamburger ...) it can become a meaningless noise. The only cure, the saints tell us, is prayer.

But these seminaries, where many of our priests and bishops studied, had TV and parties, not prayer. The sacred words become a dirty mockery. This carries them past the ordinary man's corruption, to which the Gospel can be an antidote. These people have heard all the Gospels and have heard them all explained away.

Once the expert has mocked the sacred words, everything becomes the same as everything else. The ordinary sinner, who might sneak a few CDs or check out Mabel's Whorehouse, will back off in horror from buttfucking the kids in the parish youth group. But the bad priest has expert opinions that neutralize every one of God's commandments.

For instance, a recent book by a Catholic priest scholar claims to prove that homosexual behavior is approved by God in the Bible and all other opinion is just prejudice. When the Old Testament says (Lv 20:13):

> If a man lies with a man as with a woman, both of them shall be put to death for their abominable deed; they have forfeited their lives.

—then it is *approving* male homosexuality. When St Paul says (Romans 1:26-27):

> Therefore God handed them over to degrading passions. Their females exchanged natural relations for unnatural, and the males likewise gave up natural relations with females and burned with lust for one another. Males did shameful things

with males and thus received in their own persons the due
penalty for their perversity.

—then, according to this priest, he is fighting for the rights of gay bath-
houses to stay open no matter what.

Nobody would dare so to insist "black is white" in enforcing any mun-
dane thing like a mortgage contract, but the Keepers of the Flame take
this stuff seriously when applied to the Word of God. The bishops, accepting these expert lies as worthy of respect, therefore protect the bugger
priests when they run into a little trouble with prejudiced parents and
old-fashioned laws.

Before condemning the whole lot of them, remember that scum rises.
The great majority of priests and ministers preserve enough prayer life
to come through the seminary sane (though usually cowardly). The liars
and sex geeks find it easy to rise in most dioceses and theology departments, however, while the scrupulous ones are hampered by a "glass ceiling". Therefore bishops, who are also trained in cowardice, are often surrounded by scum while patches of good faith continue in neglected parts of
the diocese.

All mainstream religious institutions, Protestant and Jewish and others,
are plagued by this corruption in their own way. All have their sacred
words, which (in the Protestant case for almost two hundred years) are at
the center of a well-funded manipulation and mockery. And all are sexually
corrupt, leading the way to legalize the most vicious abuses.

This digression into religion should explain the troubles of law. Professionals are expert in the sacred words, and they are paid for their opinions
by people who prefer opinions that give an OK to their corruption. Therefore they (or the ones among them who succeed) chain together words
to justify what their paymasters want. These word strings are not really
"opinions", they are commercial copy.

The ordinary person with knowledge of a subject is, by contrast, called
an "amateur". This word is very revealing. It means "lover"! Even the
drug dealer who is shaken by the words is acting (if only for a moment) as
a lover of the truth. He does not write and twist the words; he lets them
write on him, and leave a mark on his heart.

To be fair remember that many professionals are also "amateurs". Great
poets and writers like Tolkien are obviously in love with the words. As Jay
Hoffman points out, you can tell the difference by reading them. Tolkien
gave wings to his prose; liars like William O. Douglas create heavy, dull
words that crawl like slugs. Saints and scholars illuminated their holy
books with beautiful color; modern theologians turn the Word of God into
Mickey Mouse drudgery. Sometimes the difference is so great that the good

guys break through the glass ceiling into popularity. But they are never, never taken seriously *because the liars control the funding.*

Manipulative Speech

(This section is adapted from my article of the same name that was published in the Catholic magazine *Fidelity*, September, 1993.)

In revealing the connection between the so-called science of "communication" and Nazi authority's "psychological manipulation of the German citizenry" (*Fidelity*, June 1993), E. Michael Jones touched upon something huge. This is at the heart of the modern evil.

It is one of those things that are too big to be seen. Manipulative speech is to the American mind what the ocean is to a fish. In sheer volume, manipulative speech (advertising, journalistic and educational advocacy, political and funding campaigns) far outstrips all other speech put together. Look at your TV, your mailbag, your glossy magazines, the view along your streets.

This is the major distinguishing mark of modern American culture— the continuous roar of junk information being thrust into everyone's heads. When past ages had the will, they had not the means. Even Communism came nowhere near. I remember my cousins in Zabiedovo, Slovakia complaining about the daily harangue from the village loudspeaker. Now I think: how ineffectual and finally insignificant that was among the silent hills.

On the purely economic level, this speech leads to what stockbrokers call "churning". The steady rage of commercials has its effect, despite all sales resistance: meaningless motion, a frenetic rush of empty production and consumption. The financial tail wags the economic dog, and GNP skyrockets while real economic well-being actually declines. (Did your parents own a house? Do you?)

On the personal level, the human being erects an indiscriminate defense of insensitivity. This cure is as bad as the disease. Americans (uniquely among all the peoples of history) cannot be touched by the words and gestures of love: those receptors have been occupied by the machinery of Calvin Klein commercials and skin flicks, and the inner self has blocked them off in defense. Your wife's warm glance bounces off the same Teflon shield that blanked out the commercial wiggle of the beautiful model on the TV.

Thus, the American marriage dies of emotional starvation. Our society is not oversexed but disastrously undersexed: the lines of emotional communication have been seized by commercial interests. This is obvious to me because my life straddles the Mexican border and I have ample opportunity to contrast the two cultures. In Mexico, commercial promotion is in its infancy, and the male and female gestures of attraction are robust and effective. Commonly, a happily married Mexican couple will move to the United States and their marriage will shrivel and die. More surprisingly, we know of several cases of Americans whose marriages were on the rocks—until they moved to Mexico and their marriages healed!

Most evilly, manipulative speech is applied to children. Nobody has any right to speak to a child without love. The child's trust and docility are to be used only when the primary goal is the child's good. Yet we accept the commercials of "children's TV", alienated productions which use the child as a tool to pry open a wallet. We permit the education system called "political correctness", which foists on children what normal adults' critical faculties reject. Therefore, uniquely among the peoples of history, we have hard children: their defense mechanisms operate primarily against parents and teachers; wonder and enthusiasm are outmoded by age five.

In Disneyland, the American families present a picture of wretchedness pretending to be happy. Children whine and demand; parents endure with an obvious and impacted sense of duty. Mexican families by contrast are full of smiles and tugged along by wonder, even when the children's feet hurt. This is a microcosm of all family life, and is the real reason why American mothers seek career excuses to avoid their children's company.

In politics and religion, we have forgotten what the word "opinion" really means. It originally meant an honest perception of truth, meant to shine forth among our neighbors and make the world better. Among us, it has come to mean manipulation and verbal bullying without any attempt at honesty (as in pro-choice opinion). Again, the shield of insensitivity rises to block out the whisper of real perception and illumination as well as the shouts of the politically correct. Other nations riot at the least provocation; attempts to rouse Americans politically are dead before they start. We have accepted this too as normal without realizing it.

In the higher realms of communication "grantsmanship" is king. This is one-on-one manipulative speech, a smoothed combination of accuracy and subtle omissions intended to wheedle money out of a funding source. It is the new language of Catholic universities: you might call it Hesburgh-speak. To bishops and homilists it is now second nature. After a hundred seminars the possibility of anything else is forgotten. And the American Catholic Church crawls and pleads for worldly approval.

Thus the so-called diversity of views in America is now cold and dead as a stone. Only one thing is real: money, and the subservience to money. Chesterton foresaw it in 1908 in *Orthodoxy*:

But the man we see every day—the worker in Mr Gradgrind's factory, the little clerk in Mr Gradgrind's office—he is too mentally worried to believe in freedom. He is kept quiet with revolutionary literature. He is calmed and kept in his place by a constant succession of wild philosophies. He is a Marxian one day, a Nietzscheite the next day, a Superman (probably) the next day; and a slave every day. The only thing that remains after all the philosophies is the factory. The only man who gains by all the philosophies is Gradgrind.

The huckster or salesman has always been looked upon as a figure of fun. But modern techniques for the replication of images—print, photo, screen—have combined with an old, old pride to turn him into something deadly. That pride is akin to what made the great slaughters of our century, the hells of Nazism and Communism; the will to do and not to be done to. It had a form and specific content in those tyrannies; the brunt was to fall on specific groups, Jews or landowners. Our grinding of the weak is generic: smash the smallest regardless of their ancestry; the devil take the hindmost.

The wellspring and root of manipulative speech can be understood, and its hegemony challenged, by contrasting it to its opposite: Jesus Christ, the Word of God. In his deep article, "Self-Communication: The Essence Of Christianity" (*Wanderer*, July 16, 1993), George A. Kendall uses Sartre's art to illuminate the rebellion:

For Sartre, that is what life is about—hordes of people roaming around, each frantically trying to protect his own existence by refusing to love and safeguarding himself from the love of the others, and each doing his best to dominate and rob the others of their humanity.

Thus, a TV advertisement seeks to move the minds and actions of millions of viewers, while providing no return path for the viewers' desires to move the sponsor. He is not even present; a machine does the "communicating".

Genuine work is communication of the self to the other, whether through direct service to other human beings or by the creation of works of art. The modern world has rejected work in favor of careers. Where work is self- giving, a career is self-aggrandizement. We seek careers in order to dominate others and in order to avoid being dominated.

How well Kendall's words fit my old bosses at Boeing Airplane Company in the 1970s, filled with pride at having helped to make an airplane— and their contrast with modern feminist careerists, who in all their glossy articles never speak of anything of value that they produce, but only of how to manipulate the money and power (whose existence they take for granted) into their own hands.

This ugly and sterile hegemony presents us with a great present opportunity. Here and now, politically, economically, emotionally, the bitterness is coming home to America. The worm can turn, it can even turn against the money masters. I know brilliant young people, descendants of the hardened underclass, who are turning without any encouragement to the word of God (as to a thing found in an old book), wanting to know more. We need to reach out with firm words in the most unlikely places.

There is in such social change, such turning of the worm, a kind of gestation period of a decade or two, like a new orchard coming to bear fruit. The rejection of American money hegemony seeded in quietly during the 1970s, not just among *Fidelity's* founders but in many then-isolated circles. (This was a reason for the tremendous warm response to the Afghan resistance: it could not be reduced to a money motive.) Now we see fruit in powerful works which even as art bump aside the pallid "centrist" stuff that no one cares about. Get your hands on *Father Elijah*, or on a chronicle of the Afghan resistance.

The more the words and even the faces of the moneyed hegemony are drained of meaning, the more our little broadsheets will shine, like candles in a dark place. Mainstream politics is so thin and dead that just a few families freeing wives and mothers from the work force will create an engine of shocking power—as the homeschoolers have already done. The time has come to work Chesterton's and Mary Monica's "nine to five" enslavement in reverse, and create a wave of free, intelligent, politically powerful wives, who "just say no" to the money addiction. It's not that hard—my wife and I did it long ago—just cut back your useless "standard of living", let your wife quit her job, and rediscover leisure, love, art, thought—so many good things lost when you graduated, and forgotten in the years since. Do it *today*, and haul your TV to the dump while you're at it.

Our vocation here and now is to be firmly countercultural, to be Chestertonian with confidence. All evil cultures will pass, including the all-conquering American money culture. Just at the moment when there seems no hope for the world to become anything but a bare plain of well-financed cement, finance reveals its arid failure to bring human happiness. All its empty and cynical speech will not stand against the sweet passion of the trust in God. Even human desires are on our side. Give birth!

Never Vote your Pocketbook

Every piece of bad news has the seed of opportunity. "Yet seldom do they fail of their seed," says Tolkien of the race of Men. "And that will lie in the dust and rot to spring up again in times and places unlooked-for." It is our job to turn the rot into fertile ground for that seed. Time is not pressing.

Honest opinion does not grub for advantage. While the flood of rotten words streams meaninglessly by, we find shelter in this fact. It makes "good use" possible and frees us from paying attention to the yammering of the liars. It is a notion that any child (or teenager) can understand at once.

When the cop catches you at 40 in the school zone, you know very well that you are in the wrong. As judge of your own case, you'd say "Guilty"! With that simple resolution you establish your superiority over all our masters. There is to be no voting your pocketbook.

Anyone but the rulers of America can understand it. Could you ever justify voting your pocketbook if you were on a jury? If the guilty babyraper offered you a job, would that get you to set him free? There can be no more justice in doing that in a voting booth, or a panel of experts. You have to proceed as if you were the only one, the king, whose word decides everything for all the people.

One of the great deeds of the Afghan Resistance happened before the Soviets ever invaded. The Afghan Communists took over a year before then, and in their usual way set about buying the people's support. They seized big estates, and offered them piecemeal to the local land-poor.

It did not work. Bolstered by the words of their holy book, the Koran, these uneducated peasants refused the stolen land! What honesty—and what glorious political wisdom! For what the Communists gave, they could later take away, as they soon did in all the other unhappy lands they enslaved, starting with Russia. Here they withdrew in confusion, without legitimacy or popular gratitude.

What made this deed so historic is that *the peasants across Afghanistan were not in contact with one another.* Looking neither to the left nor to the right, each grim native did his honest deed against the powers around him. Only later did he find out that the whole land was with him. On this rock-solid foundation was built the will of the people that later became the Resistance that outlasted a World Power and has not yet submitted to any power on earth.

It is obvious that Afghan peasants do not need a Supreme Court to interpret the law for them. What is interesting is that America was founded on the same principle, by Protestants whose religious dogma was private interpretation of the Bible. This meant that the honest Christian could determine what the Word of God commanded. Applied to the political realm, it produced the Declaration of Independence and the Constitution without aid of kings or courts.

Here is the personal combination that makes it work. There is no grasping at control, no whining demand that the outcome be favorable. (This is beneath the dignity of a real man anyway.) Ruthless honesty is all that is needed most of the time (it can decide in your favor as well as against you). In the rare cases where you really don't know enough, you can deal like Éomer with the people advising you: "the Men of the Mark do not lie, and therefore they are not easily deceived."

Honest opinion gives you another huge advantage. You will have little trouble telling the difference between honest opposition on the one hand, and on the other hand the use of weasel words to manipulate you to advantage. Extend the civilities of debate to the first group, but enjoy the glorious freedom of simply dismissing the second!

An example: Anyone can understand the other side in a strike dispute, no matter if the disagreement is sharp, even violent. To a great extent it depends on the kind of people you know, who you feel you can trust. There are good and evil consequences to a victory by either side.

I listened to people discussing the UPS strike in my office and had a strange feeling of being on both sides of the dispute. My dad was a union man, I used to be an anti-union conservative and now my prejudices lean sharply the other way. But the union man and the company man can each be fighting for his family.

The same can be true, as odd as it may seem, about racial and welfare issues. It's a good thing to put on the other guy's moccasins when feeling too sure about these. Remember our owners love to say, "Let's you and him fight!" When the other guy is working as close to the edge as you are, just one odd moment of understanding can set you both a step forward—and push our masters two steps back.

On the other hand, there is nothing at all to say for feminism. I'm sorry about Germaine Greer, but she no longer owns the word, even if she got there first. The politically correct feminists who are paid to take charge of your child's mind and body will not be sweethearts like Germaine or Juli Loesch.

Feminism is a pretense of opinion by people who are interested in nothing but power. As anyone who has dealt with them in public discussion can attest. Feminism is founded on baby-killing (always remind them of this), so everything they do amounts to crushing the weak or sucking up to the strong. I used to give them credit for helping raped women, but no longer: they exploit raped women, keeping them mentally raped forever so they can profit from them.

Their employers, the billionaires, put them to the test in 1995. Choose between women and funding. They were required to crawl on hands and knees to the so-called *International Women's Conference* sponsored by the Rapist Government of Beijing, the tyrants famous for millions of forced abortions (so much for "choice") and baby girls killed at birth. That's *fifty million* dead baby girls (in excess of dead boys) so far, according to a U.N. report. They are selectively done in by abortions, by being drowned newborn in buckets, and by being dumped in "orphanages" where they are left to cry unattended until they die.

And the feminists never flinched. Hillary Clinton read a carefully toothless speech, obviously edited by China lovers, mouthing platitudes about women's rights without mentioning the offender by name, and definitely not proposing any pressure against them. The press flunkies cheered, the money flowed, and the slaughter of girl babies continued.

So never apologize for rap talk, and use the word *bitch* on whoever deserves it. The feminists are revealed quite simply as thugs for the people in power. It is the same as Soviet "worker" gangs and the Nazi SS: lying putdowns and punishment aimed at anyone who speaks out. Their behavior fits exactly; what misleads people is that they are women. Well, America is an especially wimpy culture. Americans are small and soft enough to be controlled by women bullies.

A Man's Home is his Castle

When you give away control, and with it the "security" of an imagined rich life, you gain the respect of your children. Your greatest fans are your children; they hang on your every word and deed. No one is more generous in valuing everything you do.

What then of the "generation gap"? It is final disillusionment; it is seeing you flinch too many times, worrying about that money and that career. You don't give up your job or your house. You don't forget your skills. You just mentally drop the absolute need to hang onto all those things—and recover that touch of warrior and knight errant that your young army is so hungry for.

There is another, lesser benefit. You can no longer be mentally rushed. Always, the flood of noise from the liars demands that you jump in response: whether it is laws, or commercials, or guilt campaigns. It is amazing how little of that stuff you really need. Being able to form your own mind, you can turn off one, then another of the command pipes from the masters into your home.

This brings me to a final digression, a strategy which has proved useful in the castle of my own family. For whoever is really fierce about offering his family a chance to be a seed, I will here outline *Heavenly Silence.*

The image presented by the media is far more real to us than real life. According to a recent scientific poll commissioned by the magazine *Catholic World Report* (March 1997), 68% of Catholic women dislike liturgical "inclusive language", but only 21% of Catholics *think* that most Catholic women dislike "inclusive language". It is this way with every agenda item of the Culture of Death.

We have a great number of lovers of life—many in the most unlikely places—but they cannot be a community. Each of them is an isolated individual, trapped in a pod with the shrieking TV and the spitting printed word between him and any possible allies. The multicolored flashing repetition is exactly that of brainwashing, and the only defense is a dull insensitivity that prevents comradeship as effectively as treason. Without realizing it, most of us have gradually been made unable to speak freely.

Begin with a pristine sense of your own personal dignity. What family would tolerate a houseguest who was in the habit of spewing muck and offal through the house? Not many loads of trash, and you would show him the door! Now do the same for your eyes, ears, and mind—more important than your house. It's the raw quantity of poison that wrecks us. We should not sit still for lies by the hour.

Killing your TV and burning *Playboy* are just the beginning. Go on to dump the major news magazines and (unless you are editorially lucky) the local newspaper, as well as tainted entertainment outlets like Disney. If faced with a standard sex-ed school system, either homeschool your child, or run a parallel teaching effort that debunks much of what his school is teaching him.

Don't cringe or apologize: be more touchy than a Frisco feminist, and wield the hatchet with holy glee! Apply high standards. Make those millionfold faces justify themselves or die. You can live without them. The objective is to kill off the great mass of the media, kick them out of your house, because they have failed to help you uphold the good.

After the massacre, your eyes will drift in amazement around the unfamiliar territory of your own life and people. Your ears will be stunned by the heavenly silence.

Let me relate here a true anecdote, presented to me by my son Tom. Please feel free to cackle and rub your hands with glee.

Debbie Reynolds' daughter started her acting career as the lead in the movie *Carrie*. The masters insisted she prove her willingness to fit in by playing some nude scenes. When she refused, she had to swap parts with Sissy Spacek who was playing female lead in an experimental sci-fi film.

As a result, Debbie Reynolds is now in the habit of introducing herself to audiences as "Princess Leia's mother"!

The overwhelming popularity of *Star Wars* (which has advocates of "serious" movies hissing with hate in magazines like *Newsweek*) is a tribute to human resiliency. After decades of high pressure conditioning, people still prefer the cup that is not poisoned. All the well-funded output of the Culture of Death is so much excrement, from which people will turn away with a gasp if only a puff of clean air happens by.

The first effect of Heavenly Silence is a shaky emptiness, a kind of detox. It will last for weeks, while the poisons of the moneyed media slowly drain away. My family went through this years ago. Have good books handy, and be prepared to spend lots of energy getting acquainted with your family. You will be exercising flaccid mental muscles, long atrophied by passivity.

Now pick up the tools of creativity. Whether with oven, piano, saw or keyboard, you will need to make something during your new hours of freedom. Being unharried and unhustled by pushing machines will leave you with an odd feeling of endless days. It will affect your children too: they will become more active and need more playmates and more attention.

Freed from the desensitizing power of the commercial media, everyone, especially children, will develop more pristine emotional reactions. There are small prices to pay, like the embarrassment of having your nine-year-old daughter freak out during a movie preview of LA being wiped out by a volcano. Seeing people being fried by a lava flow—or live babies having their brains sucked out—really ought to upset a normal human being. This is a return to sanity, just the first of many.

Children (and adults) will have no trouble being sexually normal—and normally shy. The feverish precocity of modern teenagers is wholly a product of moneyed pressure, as you will find when free of it. That doesn't mean you can let your guard down (in 1997, any more than in 997): but the chivalrous and affectionate instincts of normal adolescents will help you navigate these shoals.

Like a spring that is allowed to bounce back, you and your children will feel proper horror at those faces of the culture that are horrible. From homosex to cloning, the works of Satan will now beat upon you as an alien assault. The adventure of life takes the shape of a quest, instead of a crawl for money. Romantic love becomes possible again (how cowardly we have been, to let them steal that hope from our children!) while the jerking, barking motions of the crowds of ambitious slaves finally appear as absurd as they really are.

Of all societies in the history of the world, America must be the one where community is deadest. Everything is mediated by money: child care and elder care, food, clothing, and shelter, politics and art and rejoicing. Super Bowl watchers have taken to ignoring the game in order to discern the best advertisement.

Heavenly Silence leaves in its wake a gaping hole that has to be filled by real community. Unguided by national advertisement, you will have to choose products by word of mouth. It's fun to take a chance: visit some auto shop or restaurant in the scary part of town; find out what your children and your neighbors can fix.

You'll be happy to know you're starving your economic masters, while giving work to your job-starved neighbors. This is not a chimera. If Heavenly Silence becomes widespread in the *Culture of Life* (20% or more of the whole population) it will have a devastating effect on the so-called "growth" economy of our owners.

You'll find the clean radio stations, and replace your foul news magazines with small Culture of Life startups. These will inform you of things that you always have missed, through media censorship or arrogance. Your use of the expelled media, when needed, will become a social occasion, looking it up at the library, or watching the game at the tavern. The presence (and shouting) of your real life neighbors will puncture the compulsive power of the millionfold face.

By destroying the machine that pumps thousands of words and gestures into your brain, you make a space for the gestures and words of human beings near you. They could never outshout a machine, but now they can reach you. They turn out to be our brothers in prayer, the ones Peter Kreeft told us about. The sponsored camera never points toward them, the thousands of sponsored news articles miss them entirely, but you will meet them everywhere. You'll find "enemies", from rappers to terrorist communities, that turn out to be libeled friends. The same Enemy is oppressing us all.

After that we speak to each other, and join together. But that is another story, one that we won't know until we live it.

Valedictory

Honest opinion is the first and simplest requirement of honor. It has its effect in a crisis, but during ordinary life it merely requires that you *mentally* let go your life and possessions.

The reward is equally simple. You can look straight at people, including yourself in a mirror. You can value yourself as an Afghan hero values hinself, and know that lightness on your feet that only comes from not being tied down to lies.

You are superior to the wealthy and the powerful who rule America. You are superior to the Supreme Court. You are superior to the great universities. You are superior to the great professional organizations, and you do not need to apologize to anyone, even if you need a dictionary on your knee to read these words.

You can coolly and ruthlessly shut down the junk words of our owners and their mind bullies. Better yet: you can think and speak at last. I do not care where you start from. You will find you are more of a poet and a scholar and a speaker than you ever thought possible.

Learn where the libraries are in your town. Your real education starts here.

Chapter 3

Spend It All

An even more fundamental objection to "good use" is: Why not just vote the rascals out? Can't we save this America?

I grew up in the great days of purpose, the Cold War and the race to the moon. I got the full education and joined the professional class. I've lived this hope and can speak with authority.

It's a different crowd from the underclass of last chapter. It's the America that foreigners believe in: big suburban houses; careers of commuting on crowded freeways to tall wealthy offices; young men and women crisscrossing the green lawns of college campuses. It is affluent America, probably the home of most of you.

You can waste *years of your life* before you realize that this America has been ruined too. Trillion dollar GNP, a world power so overwhelming that you may not trust your feeling of unease. For thirty years I did not.

Here, in America, you do not see lines of wailing people waiting to be forced into cattle cars. You do not commonly pass shattered buildings and corpses on your daily rounds: that is at the distance of Bosnia coverage and war history footage. No crowds of bony refugees clutch bowls at international relief stations. *And yet we are not dancing in the streets*: America is a great but joyless place, except when the local sports team wins a major victory.

We used to live in downtown La Jolla, rubbing shoulders with the seaside wealth culture and the topnotch University of California at San Diego in a well-kept walking village. Now we live in working class Tijuana, windows wide open on the hot nights hearing the nearby families celebrating their *fiestas.* There is no comparison. Tijuana is the place where our kids enjoy life. Why?

There ought to be a life for the next generation. When judged on that

47

need, America offers much less than meets the eye. The singular lack of joy
has good reason.

Ruled by Fear

The theory behind modern America is the pursuit of self-interest. Each
driving careerist pursues his own profit, and money itself takes care of
community. This is called "the Invisible Hand" in economic theory, and we
extend it to other parts of life, like marriage and education.

In America, money stands taller than the highest skyscraper as the
absolute ruling force. There was an old American saying: "If you invent a
better mousetrap, the world will beat a path to your door." The reality,
and I speak here from professional experience, is: if you have money, the
inventors will beat a path to your door.

This is a stranger matter than it seems. We really all need just food,
clothing and shelter, but that accounts for only a small fraction of the bustle
on the freeways. And those who make life's necessities (farmers and roofers
and seamstresses for instance) are likely to be on the *bottom* of the pecking
order of money.

More: real riches exist in unmatched quantity in America. We could
feed the whole world unaided, for instance. And yet the economic order
seems best defined by its ability to *punish*. By continually scrambling, you
can stay on a level. Let one thing go wrong, one sickness or accident or
poor business decision, and a kind of trap door opens under you; a kind of
gravity pulls you down to poverty.

If you have worked with computers, you have heard the word "default".
It is the setting you get if you leave things alone, like a dial tone on a phone
or sea level on a tide table. The default for an American is unemployment
and economic uselessness.

You can pour out statistics all you like, about the increase of jobs and
opportunity. Try that line on someone who just got laid off, and see if you
can make his dead eyes light up. Any *specific* contribution to the economy
(like steel or shoes) seems always to face obsolescence. The growth is in
service or financial sectors, activities whose purpose is ever more vague.

I started aiming at rocket science, which went into decline around 1970.
Then came computers, rising in the 1970s, glory days in the 1980s, now
captive to marketeers and billionaire monopolists and welded shut against
small business. The California real estate boom (what can I say, at least real
estate is *real!*) flared and faded; there was biotech; there are now several
variations on the telephone (cellular, the net, etc). Each has more flash
and is less needed than the last. Even hospitals, nurses and the medical

profession have felt the cold breath of income failure recently.

Here's a mental exercise. Don't think about the stock market or about Vegas or other quick money. Shut off your TV, thrust aside your catalogs, don't visit the malls: stop all forms of window shopping among brightly lit goods. Just focus on one thing, a job. Drop yourself in a strange place, hit the streets and get that paycheck coming before you run short. *Now*, with no preparation. How friendly is our great economy now?

If standard economic theory were true, it would be as easy to enter a strange town and get a good job (exchanging services/goods for money) as it is to enter a strange town and find a good restaurant (exchanging money for services/goods). The real balance is wildly skewed toward money.

You can force the career confidence grin onto your face, but you know you are dangling from a string. No matter how valuable your skill, the man with money can dump and replace you. On the other hand, if you cannot find paid employment, *you* are junk. You can be talented, you can be entrepreneurial, you can be a renowned inventor: none of that matters. If the moody gods of finance frown on you, just get in line with all the other welfare cases.

There are paradoxes here (I will come back to that later) but they do not concern us now. The point is that this is the world that you and I and our children take for granted. We are like the City Mouse in the fairy tale. This incredible wealth is salted with fear, it is not really ours, it can be taken from us senselessly, with the snap of a finger.

Nobody acts out the Johnny Paycheck song, *Take This Job and Shove It!* (Not even the man in the song—listen closely.) On the contrary. An American sweats over his resume, and clings trembling to his job. He wastes decades of life doing what seems needed to advance his "career". Like an origami artist, he shapes every word and deed with dreadful care to keep weaving the mysterious money thread.

This is the eerie truth: in our rich country, far from famines and slave camps, *the adult American career person is ruled by fear.* It never ends until retirement, and usually not even then, especially since pensions good enough to live on are more and more a thing of the past. But the interesting thing is to trace the effect on young people.

The affluent American child has no money worries. His parents take care to lift him free, even if they are sunk mouth deep in the sucking bog. The little kid, oblivious to all this, reaches for expensive amusements and sports. He darts among his activities with youthful energy, in frenetic motion away from he knows not what.

I've read how superior Americans feel to the Eastern countries with *purdah*, where the free-running little girl is placed behind veil and wall at puberty. Well, we are the same. We offer our children our own version of the big move down. Short dresses, fast cars and computers are nothing but a cover-up. The freedom drains away, the income producing yoke is strapped on, and after all the party debris is cleared out, nothing is left but the long, dragging adjustment to economic fear and servility.

I've known people who got hit with this too rudely. Not long ago, a young woman from a rich family found herself with two children, dwindling possessions and a future different from the TV ideal. She blew away her children and killed herself. This trend is not yet well established. Usually it has been less dramatic: dead marriages, beaten families, alcohol and drugs and other manufactured stupors.

Ask yourself this: if the American individual's economic life is so great, how come one baby can sink it? A pretty flimsy boat, sent to the bottom by that tiny weight! Expensive sports cars and computers don't sink it, but a baby does. The baby departs from the model of *absolute selfishness* that is the straight and narrow of American success, and from the related commandment that all toys be hard and useless. To be quite precise, the baby, like all love, creates infinite liability.

The tremedous energy of young people was once a valued economic asset. Read Shakespeare. They burst from apprenticeship or tutoring (high school to us) into travel, war, responsibility, love and marriage. It was as if they were allowed to swing their arms when marching. They were allowed to do real things.

Higher education has to be viewed in this light. In back of our La Jolla rental was a tiny "honeymoon cottage" that housed its sequence of undergrad pairs. Not honeymooners; their economic impotence allowed no marrying, nor any children either. (University districts are prime locations for abortion clinics.) The sad disputes in that cottage were audible to my wife. Circle of parties, circle of studies, circle of waiting to have a life.

Higher education mainly has value as a center of knowledge, like a library. The op ed pieces say it trains the young to function in a more complex world, but any professional will tell you the new guy picks up his skills in the first few weeks on the job. Even in fields like medicine—the nurses do most of the real work, and they pick up their skills by doing.

The truth is that this is like dogs jumping for a piece of meat. If the dogs jump higher, the trainer raises the meat higher. If you want a job, you have to get a degree, and it better be a higher degree, and it better be from a more prestigious university, and so on, and on. Thus higher education serves a twofold purpose: (1) it screens out those without enough money, influence or persistence to graduate and obtain the diploma; and (2) it is a holding tank to reduce the number of employables in the market.

Recently, other darker purposes have become important. The ruling economic fear means that higher education is not an option. It is a necessity, and whoever controls the gates of graduation is master of the affluent young. Like a terrible natural suction, this draws the worst manipulators into positions of power.

To stay on the right side of those in control of your diploma, you have to write essays praising the achievements of sexual deviates and feminists. I just spotted some of their junk in my son's calculus text, borrowed from a local community college. Evil Christians burning virgins—in a math text! I kid you not.

Direct your moral enthusiasm toward animal rights or the environment: on other more sensitive subjects learn to zip your lip, especially if you want to get into medical school. Freedom of speech is not what it used to be; if your campus paper steps on the wrong toes, you are blacklisted for "hate speech". Science is not what it used to be either. If for instance you are supporting homosexual genes, no proof is necessary, while if you are opposing them, no proof will be enough to get you published.

Economic conservatives (people who believe that money is everything) assure us that this "political correctness" is distasteful but unimportant. The truth is that it is supremely important—witness the fact that economic conservatives cannot protect their own children from it! This is false art, false science, false culture and real physical and mental disease. It is years long training not only in subservience, but in subservience to money, and subservience to the lie.

Last chapter I mentioned a fat list of inferior people. Those corporate officials who poison children, those doctors who suck out babies' brains, those lawyers and judges and politicians who are nothing but corrupt— they are all products of this education. (It ruled the "best" universities long before it got its name and reached the lowbrow state colleges.) As a result, they form a community of shared subservience, to money, and to the lie.

The Best you can Expect

Wait, wait! (I can hear them shouting)—that was an unfairly gloomy picture you just drew. The 1997 job market has tightened up. Employers are beginning to struggle and beg for people. Some workers are in such demand that they can change jobs voluntarily. The Teamsters even won a strike!

Sorry, folks. That was just the beginning. I'm writing about people who play by the rules, and it is true that playing by the rules you can win. Just consider what it means to win. As I write this, I have just moved from years of slow economic decline to jobs among technology movers and shakers in La Jolla or Mira Mesa. So I am among winners and, for a wonder, most of them are good people too.

Just what is the winning life? It creates headaches (you have to wear a tie). Each day starts with driving through traffic jams (winning areas have the worst traffic jams) to work: desk, coffee, pretty secretaries, fancy restaurants in steel and concrete block buildings. There are getaways—in my case, to university libraries. The day ends with another traffic jam, dinner, relaxation, sleep. Saturdays are for catching up on errands. Sundays are a family day.

Here's what should make you uneasy: the ultimate victory, the ideal career, is to live the above paragraph without interruption from age 21 to age 65. Move up to bigger house, bigger office, taller title, longer lunches with richer people, but you know there really is no change. The thing is to avoid something bad happening: sickness, divorce, job loss, legal trouble. Success is defined as zero, everything else is a negative number.

Absolute selfishness, the definer of success in our society, translates quickly into absolute safety. This, for an ordinary citizen, is the highest American aspiration. We have done it to ourselves (we never had any business setting up selfishness as a virtue!) If there is anything left over, we can invest it, and then convert it into extra safety later, if needed.

For an extraordinary (independently wealthy) citizen, who has bought all the safety available, the rule of absolute selfishness creates a different highest aspiration. That is to make a computerized number spin around as fast as possible, like an automobile odometer gone mad. This number is total net worth. Bill Gates, for instance, is somewhere up around $20 billion and his number is just blurring along.

Suppose you actually want to *do* something. What is there?

No more shooting for the moon. They shut that down years ago, though they had success with Stone Age equipment by today's standards. Actually, there is a little left, but if you want a job at the Jet Propulsion Laboratories, you will have to stand in a long line.

There are no crusades deserving of the name. Now the U.S.A. is on balance a bully and a source of international corruption. You can fight in absurd little wars—I know one young man who sought his roots in Croatia that way. The experience quickly goes bad, and is not recommended.

There are clearer, more peaceful crusades, like the *Habitat* or *Corazón* people who help build houses in Mexico near where I live. My wife tells how strong and joyful they are, seen crossing back into America in their van. This one is indeed recommended! Notice, however, that it depends on poor neighbors across a border. It would be against code (safety again) to build *our own* houses.

Nearer to the family home, there is the prospect of love. Is there even one of you who did not flinch with sarcastic thoughts, when you read that?

Can that word be spoken any more without a snarl? In the name of honor there will be much more to be said about it later. Just now, look at it cold, from the unreconstructed view of the selfishness culture, and reflect on how dead, dead it is.

As for having a family, everyone assumes that is a kind of social and economic suicide. That is to throw your safety away, to paint a big red target on yourself for those who like to tear hunks out of people. Americans, including rich Americans, live in terror of their children: there is no insurance policy that will protect you from them.

Fame has its hot charge, but everyone knows how it sucks people down into degradation, from Elvis to Diana. If you are mentally strong enough, you will draw the inevitable conclusion that there is some poison where the famous people walk. Pass it by. At least take the attitude that Trish Burnison reports from among the Seattle punk rock culture: anyone who gets a big record contract has sold out. Stay with the people, or be lost.

Clean sports is really near the best of the lot. Your city is on the right track when it celebrates its AFL championship or National League West title. This is the only real meet-your-neighbor rejoicing that America knows any more. My children have good instincts, being free of TV, and I took note when Elizabeth began to cheer our baseball club, the Padres—a local sports team with a generous and decent attitude.

That's pretty pitiful for the richest and most powerful country in the history of the world. We are offering the shopping mall as the dull end of history, and if that does not satisfy you, then you can go, well, nowhere. Pretty much the whole world has been bought up, or is waiting in line. The few remaining corners will soon be razed and paved.

This paltry fraud against the young creates an odd kind of mental servitude. It is so obvious that big money is a perfect winner that people no longer admit, even to themselves, that a better, wilder, more varied and colorful life would be possible. From *Star Wars* to game rooms, from Middle-Earth to Brother Cadfael, all the tremendously popular fantasies of strange lands shout this lesson, but we are scared to apply our own perceptions to reality. The only exception was Afghanistan, and there the Afghans provided the fearlessness; we only needed to go along for the ride!

Whoever opposes a winner defines himself as a loser. Being a loser is the ultimate disaster. Therefore, even in our hopes and dreams, we voluntarily remake ourselves in the shape of the ruling concrete blocks, and box ourselves each into his own tiny cell.

Activism and the LICO Equalities

Any escape from this trap must be a form of generosity. A life that shrinks to fit, like the Ring fit Gollum—this follows inevitably from the deification of selfishness. That fact alone is enough to condemn the success culture.

It is also enough to begin to show the way out. Peel your fingers off the handle of lifelong security; be ready to fling yourself wholeheartedly into something. In your open hand God will place great treasures—time and strength are among the first. But there are false paths to beware.

My false path was conservative political activism. To those who protest that this is unjust, I point to results. Millions of good and effective activists through two generations have accomplished: nothing. When you throw snake eyes a hundred times in a row, you have the *duty* to conclude the dice are loaded.

Some may wonder why I waste space discussing conservatives. Aren't these the people who want Eisenhower back? (But in Eisenhower's time they wanted Hoover back.) Whatever wave is sweeping through people's lives, they aren't on it. They always predict the wreckage, and take credit for predicting it, but neglect the little detail of stopping it.

It's the same reason I've discussed the Catholic Church's internal affairs. Even if you are a Variag of Khand, it matters to you, it matters terribly, when the walls of Gondor are left unmanned.

Conservatives set great store by a quality called "civility", which is a kind of good manners requirement among the powerful. Think of twenty plantation owners sipping mint juleps under the magnolias. Nineteen of them treat their slaves decently, but the twentieth goes in for rape and torture. There are mutterings of protest.

Civility dictates that all the owners close ranks to protect the brute and silence the cries of the oppressed, because otherwise there may be upset. They may also pass quiet hints to the torturer that he should clean up his act. The thug will go on ignoring these hints forever, because he is in the catbird seat, and he knows it.

After working on behalf of a local pro-life activist who sought political office by a "stealth" campaign (a tactic that works only once), Jeanne and I went to an election night non-victory party at a supporter's home. Since all the campaigners were really conservative pro-lifers, we took the opportunity to pass around copies of a letter pleading for help for the anti-abortion protesters who were raped in the "Pittsburgh Nightmare".

The lady of the house, an important pro-life leader, tried to have us thrown out. She said the women in the letter were lawbreakers! Her husband, an old military man, refused to eject us. Sometimes there is much to be said for the military cast of mind.

As we went about our incendiary rounds, I suddenly realized the source of the problem. *It was the lady's beautiful house.* People who step over certain lines drawn in the sand by our owners can have their possessions seized. It is all right to talk about certain outrages, but not too loudly or effectively—because salvation is not in political victory, nor in justice. Salvation flows from secure possessions.

You will hear words of justice and outrage (this is what misled me for so many decades), but there will be no effect. To be precise, there will be effect proportional to distance. Conservatives (and liberals) were effective for Afghanistan, ten thousand miles away. When it comes to their home ground, they give everything away even when they win elections. They are perfectly willing to hand over their children to the authorities whose outrages they were just denouncing, rather than give up the campaign they trust to bring right and justice into their own lives. And the name of that campaign is acquisition of personal wealth.

Well, there is an obvious way to handle people like these, and you can see it written all over the corpses of your school Christmas pageants. I summarize it in a pair of equations, the LICO equalities. They may not hold with mathematical exactitude; but they serve as a good rule of thumb. And the farther up the food chain you go, the more accurate they are.

$$\text{Liberal} \quad = \quad \text{Liar}$$
$$\text{Conservative} \quad = \quad \text{Coward}$$

May this simple set of equalities give you strength when the direct mail starts pouring in!

Of course I am being sharply unjust to individuals, like the liberal Nat Hentoff and the conservative Father Paul Marx. But I am trying to instruct and warn the young. Before jumping in a river, judge the main current, not the exceptional eddy.

As you can see, the LICO system works perfectly for both sides in concert. One side gets the juicy tidbits it slobbers after, while the other can hug its wealth with a certain sense of moral superiority. Politics is by nature a very admirable occupation—trying to make right and justice real among the people. The collusion I speak of has turned it into a synonym for smell.

The LICO system protects those in positions of power and influence. It betrays outsiders, and most especially the younger generation, who are locked out, led wrong, corrupted and defrauded. Whereupon both sides, secure in their gated neighborhoods, put down the younger generation as graffiti-spraying trash (the liberals use their social worker talk to pretend to sympathize). And most young people accept this putdown as the natural and obvious truth.

The owners of this system think they have it all sewed up. But they have forgotten a few things.

Swing your Life like a Sword

At the moment when I am writing this, Tijuana and the world are still reverberating with the echoes of Mother Teresa's wake. God sometimes makes His points in rather a thunderous manner. With Mother Teresa dying a week after Princess Diana, it became quite clear, quite quickly, who was the real force and who was the lightweight.

A block away from our Tijuana home, on our residential street, is a long square building with a flat roof. It is a novitiate and old folks home of the Missionaries of Charity, Mother Teresa's order. We look straight from our south windows across a gully to see the nuns hanging their clothes out to dry on the roof every morning.

It is a bustling place, with a crowded little chapel where my wife sometimes attends morning Mass, and a long line of poor people coming for the weekly food distribution. Little groups of nuns are seen frequently, walking in the neighborhood in their distinctive habits. There is a Mexican revolutionary law that says that nuns and priests are not allowed to go in public wearing religious dress. Whether that law has been repealed I don't know, but it is long dead.

North of the border, there are much richer convents with long histories and parish schools, hospitals and girls' high schools attached to them. These are usually desolate places, with one or two ancient nuns sometimes in residence, or an aging careerist of ex-religious status. Their charitable works have turned into businesses, but as executives they are hardly in the fast lane. And there are no young nuns.

Mother Teresa's order is strict and old fashioned. They live in real poverty, have prayer instead of TV, and do daily hard work on the bedpan level and worse. They attract plenty of young nuns (and priests and brothers too), and they attract them from all over the world, including the United States.

It is this simple. To have a real life, you have to spend it all, to swing it like a sword; to lose it, in the sense of Jesus Christ. It is not what you can get, but what you can give. What you get is just to keep up your strength for the next step along the way.

The open hand, not clutching power and security, can and does both give and receive. The light foot, not weighted by the need to keep its wealth, and not defined by (and chained to) a position, strides across hills and valleys of an adventurous life. See what is needed, and say what is needed. Something will turn up. It is not as though there is no point in being here.

There is need for skills and everything of value; whatever position is useful ought to be filled. But there is no need for security. In fact, security is impossible. To be precise I must say there is no need for *the illusion of security*.

My wife was riding the bus home from downtown Tijuana one day, when suddenly everyone on the bus started crying and praying. A little boy on a bicycle had popped out in front of a car and been run down. Now the ambulance was pulling away, at a speed that indicated that there was no reason to hurry any more. Blood and pieces of the bicycle were still visible on the street.

What if you are the driver of that car? There is nothing open to you except to be crushed. No insurance policy or driving skill can protect you. The only thing that can be said is that it doesn't happen very often. There is no safety.

Americans have a peculiar reaction in that respect. We drive the streets and freeways, in considerable danger of life and limb (especially if you add up all the time we spend at risk). It doesn't bother us that a runaway truck may mangle us at any moment. But we grow terrified if we discover that we are running *without insurance*, in danger of being ruined by a lawsuit.

Being fried or crippled is worse than being poor, it really is! But the American gut reaction is exactly the opposite. The desperate demand for security, coupled with the fact that we can't have it, creates such an oddly blinkered response. Actually Americans get crushed by the disasters of life about as often as people from poor countries without insurance, like Mexicans. What we gain in coverage we lose in incidents of crime, family malice, nervous breakdowns and the like.

By definition, there is no need for something that cannot be supplied. Once you give up the spurious need for safety, you can swing your life like a sword. That is what those days and months of time are for! What strength is in your arm, what fine stories you will have to tell!

The first thing you get back is time. The safe American life, as I said above, has no length scale of time between a day (or a week, if you count weekends as different) and a career of 44 years. The life of a real man or woman has all the seasons God made for us, months, years, the coming of age of a fruit tree or a child.

This is such a tremendous gift. *There is no rush*, no "hurry up and wait". The demand for maximum safety creates such a terrible drive for consistency, for control, for identical unvarying pressure to advantage. It is a narrow way which is unlike Christ's. Its yoke is difficult, and its burden heavy.

The unarmored attitude toward work does the job without demanding control. Now we are just moving through, just keeping our end up. If the door is open tomorrow, good, we give our best. If not, we move on. The word for this is freedom of spirit.

You will find worthy tasks that stretch for a month, a year, ten years. You will turn aside to see them through. Everything of that sort was denied to you under the careerist system; you probably could not even see it! So much of God's good world of purpose!

And with time you get strength. And almost without effort. You can build tremendous things over years, with just a little bit each day.

That is the way they build houses in Tijuana, where the people get no loans. We call it "house seeds," to distinguish it from "house fungus," Jeanne's name for the orange-roofed stuff that instantly covers hills north of the border.

It works like this: The parachutistas crisscross a hill with chalk lines, and the people erect their plywood or sheet metal shacks. Water trucks come in to do business; electrical pirate wires tap onto nearby power. Slowly, houses grow foundations and walls; water and sewer are pieced in, and the electricity, after a while, is made legal. Roads are paved by subscription and often are a patchwork for a while. Around the time the kids are growing up, the area has become a stable, modest working people's neighborhood, like the one where I am living now with my family.

What you build during your quiet and peaceful years may well be huge by the time you use it. But you have to be ready to use it, spend it when it is ripe. When that time is, you do not know. But you should look forward to it, not fear it.

Someone else should fear it. With that time and strength you get space, mastery. You hold your place and possessions with a light hand, as if ready to toss them at any moment. The moment may never come, but there will be trouble if it does. It is as if you are lying in wait. Like a coiled spring ready to fly loose.

You may own and love your car, but you would (I hope) blow it all away in a moment to prevent a murder. A flick of the wheel, and crunch. Apply this attitude to every position and every thing. And keep your eyes peeled. You won't want to miss the moment when their latest offense against dignity or justice comes down in your area.

The call comes from outside, if it ever comes. You do not make it happen or choose its time—otherwise you are just another liar and terrorist. Control is evil but readiness is virtue. There is no hurry, no schedule, and no impatience. But your children do not need to be ashamed of you.

And here is another great boon laid in your open hand. *You do not need to be afraid of your own family.*

To a standard affluent American, his family is his greatest potential enemy. There is no insurance against them. His wife can ruin him with a divorce action. His son can perpetrate some enormity with the family car, and drag the whole family down into shame and debt. From arrests to pregnancies, the sour deeds of the children set their fathers' teeth on edge.

Watch the culture of selfishness squirming to solve this one. There are prenuptial contracts. There is contraceptive sex training for little girls who haven't even gone on their first date. There are the flinching petty restrictions on the young man: you feel at once that they are not to lead the son right, but to protect his parents from bother and cost. A suspicious shuffle, like people in a gloomy mystery turning and eyeing one another, wondering where the knife will come from. Soon we will have death with dignity for the aging, the sick, and the asleep. This is one problem that gets worse with wealth.

Well? We cure all that with one stroke. As a family, *we crash and burn together.* If a knife goes into my back, then down I go. Et tu, Brute. The notion of keeping your assets safe from your family goes in the trash compactor with all the other illusions of security. What a concept! You can look your own wife and kids in the eye!

And when you do that, what do you discover? A little army on your side. Of all the people in the world, the ones least likely to want to do you down. The ones most eager to share in your adventures and back you up in hard times. Oh, the treasons do happen (particularly in marriage), but even then, most often all the others will turn on the traitor. Give your little army a chance.

And it does not stop there. There are people around you, cousins and friends, who are more impressed with you than you will ever know. Give them something to hang their devotion on. Remember, no control—the occasion must present *itself*—but when it does, take a chance on them. Don't even flinch. If you crash, you burn. Whether you crash or you soar, you will make your move with style and strength, like a real man or a real woman.

The Calm before the Storm

The calm before the storm is a false calm. Nevertheless, it has many of the advantages of peace. There is quiet. You can go about your business at a normal pace; you can plan well ahead; you can use the tools of peace and culture, like libraries and public meetings.

To be in school or in what the world calls a career is to live in that false calm. There is no point in wasting the tools. There are inner-city inverse snobs who ostracize a child for doing well in school, and they are inner-city fools. Knowledge and books never did the dirty to your people. Hidden in them may be the escape rope that the people need.

Knowledge is a wonderful thing in itself. Libraries are sacred places! A teacher is to be revered, when he is doing his rightful work of teaching, and not acting out the demands of powerful bullies. Knowledge is like bread, and has to be remade fresh all the time. Otherwise arts can be lost, even science can be lost, and beauty can die of disuse, leaving only ugliness. All of these things happen frequently, because money prefers ugliness to beauty, and ignorance and helplessness create a favorable climate for marketing junk.

As you pass through college or apprenticeship, you gain knowledge and skills. This is good even if you are growing up in Soviet Russia or Nazi Germany. The White Rose would never have come together if they had not gone to a Nazi college. Still, be warned that it is a false peace.

Without being noticed, the poisons seep through the skin of your mind and turn you slowly into something less. Stood side by side across the years it is easy to see. *Something* happens to turn the heartfelt teenage debater into the cold, grasping junior executive.

On this, the light flashed brilliantly for me when I read some words of Mary Pride. She is a Christian author for the homeschoolers, and she was discussing some words referring to slaves in the Bible. Just in passing she said

> ... a slave, or in modern terms an employee...

Of course! People concentrate on the whips and the hangings, but these cannot ever have been very common. Otherwise the economy would halt, the slaves would revolt, bring blood and destruction—even in ancient times. Then it was just a workaday world like our own, with people who know what side their bread is buttered on.

You learn to trim your words (because you have to make the right impression.) Soon you learn to trim your thoughts (otherwise you will not feel comfortable with the right people, will you?) Join in laughing at the suckers who take things to heart. Join in shielding the Packwoods and Goldwaters when they go a little too far for comfort.

The push to conform goes beyond that low essay grade that will reward any honest opinions. Sooner or later the pinch will get more definite than that. All through history, the people in power have demanded loyalty oaths and open collaboration from their underlings. They are rarely so polite as to offer the option of neutrality. Do you suppose you're exempt? Try this mental exercise.

You are a newly graduated young German in the 1940s, accepting a job as a schoolteacher—the only job for which you are qualified—and you receive a form to sign. In it, among other imposed duties, you find the following paragraph:

> Bayerisches Landesgesetz, Article 2.5 of the Penal Code, provides reporting requirements for subversive and Jewish activities... Diocesan personnel must comply with those legal requirements.

And at the end you find:

> Policy Acknowledgement
> (to be completed by current personnel, compensated or volunteer)
> I,   , acknowledge that I have received a copy of the Policy on Patriotic Misconduct of the Diocese of Nuremberg, and that I have read the policy, understand its meaning, and agree to conduct myself in accordance with the policy.
> Signed   Date

Now what do you do? I take for granted that you don't turn in any Jews; that is not the question. This is the job you can do. And you need the job, and certainly none of this rat-on-Jews shit amounts to any real reason why you should be excluded from it. Do you sign the form?

It is better if you can evade it. But I can find no fault with you if you do sign. Whether or not they add "penalties of perjury." As one in need of a job, you are a slave being coerced by your master, and no one can expect more from you than just those words the master wants to hear.

This case is real; I have just changed a few words. This form is presented to my wife, a catechist for the Diocese of San Diego, and the reporting is to the "child abuse" authorities under California law. So far she has in each case pocketed the form, saying she needs her husband's approval (and her husband's approval is slow in coming). But she doesn't need the job either.

(An aside: if you think my analogy is exaggerated, you ought to meet some of the young mothers worked over by these creeps. On our own front room couch I've witnessed women telling about being interrogated for "child abuse", and I've witnessed women telling about being raped. The dull tone of voice, the downturned mouth, the sweaty face and clammy hands: there is no difference visible between the two. The experiences are equal.)

There is no clean way for a powerless person to evade this kind of thing. In the Soviet Union, brilliant people like Alexander Solzhenitsyn would select fields like mathematics (or chess), because it is hard for the correctness goons to corrupt something so definite. That may have influenced me too.

The trouble is there, even in engineering and hard science. Except for academics (who face their own mental corruption), people in these fields are always running dry and desperately scrambling for money. And dirty work always pays best. Tyrants want anti-personnel weapons and law enforcement (torture) instruments. Government agencies and employers want monitoring devices to keep track of their slaves. Drug and medical supply companies want better ways to kill babies. Even in "clean" fields there will come a time to turn something down. And it will be an inconvenient time.

But what if you are a naturally talented teacher or doctor? Wouldn't opting out be like abandoning your post? I have a wild thought: being unwilling to suck the brains out of a live baby may even make you a *better* doctor. If you can sneak into medical school somehow.

Here is the key moral principle. You can always accept authority as the default. You can always echo the words of the teacher without lying (much). When you do these things, you must not then conclude that you are tainted beyond recall. That is a trap set by the bad guys to suck you into their dirty system. Keep the tension alive—stay uncomfortable—keep on picking and choosing, taking what is good and heaving the other stuff out of your heart. It's a hand-operated bilge pump in a sewer boat, and you will be tired to death of it, but keep cranking.

In my own youth, I missed one practical point. Have a backup position. Gain skill in at least two fields, independent of one another. Get your plumbing apprenticeship alongside medical school, or your truck driving certification next to your teacher training. If your family has fertile land, that's good too—always a last resort.

Because your room for maneuver is limited. You cannot act out the evil. When they hand you a scalpel to cut up your first baby, then you *have* to declare yourself. Those years and dollars invested in medical school—all held lightly in the hand. All ready to toss away.

But even here, aim your move at victory. Even if it is dead against their rules, stand eyeball to eyeball with them and act as if you own the place. They have something invested in you too. They need you (sometimes you might be surprised how much), and they are afraid of you and what you can do.

Remember Judge Sprizzo! Don't make it easy for them, by being too shy even to get started, or by backing out voluntarily at the first whiff of impasse. Be in their system, as thoroughly tangled up in it as possible, and make *them* do all the work of throwing you out.

Take a lesson from the poor, despised underclass. Use your God-given arms and lungs, and *make a fuss.* According to Dimitri Panin, even hardened concentration camp guards are sometimes driven into retreat by—embarrassment! It can go on for days and days, and be quite fun (for you), some shaggy hooting and banner-thrusting, right in front of everyone, following them home. Especially if they've just turfed you out, and you have nothing to lose.

If I've got you actually hoping that such a crisis will happen, then I've done what I wanted. The disappointing truth is that you will probably have smooth sailing to your diploma. They just don't have the manpower to enforce all their loyalty oaths.

But you can be poised and ready for it, even if it never does come. That way, your spirit will be in training when you walk out their gates. You won't be the crouching little slave that they intended. Instead you will be something rather dangerous.

Afterlives

Boys love fantasies of adventure, and books and movies that tell heroic stories. The money worshippers claim these are a waste of time, that they are impractical (that is, unprofitable). They do not add to total lifetime income.

Actually they are more practical than all the business courses, which just lead you from the same thing to more of the same thing only richer. This is training for the mind, as valid as a preseason in sports. When the moment comes, it is a combination of external events and a mind that has been preparing for years. Without the preparation, you won't even recognize the external event when it comes.

The towering medical hero, Dr Robert Simon, had spent his years as a professor of emergency medicine at UCLA. But according to his notions, long held, Medicine was a high and generous vocation and centered around healing people, not just coining change. He was unsatisfied with "population control" as the daily bread of medicine: he wanted a place where he could roll up his sleeves and make a difference by *saving lives.*

Then came the news. I'm sure he heard it more than once, before he made the connection, the compelling connection. Word filtered out of Afghanistan that the Soviets, as an aid to their genocide, had stripped the countryside of doctors, so that people were dying of minor wounds and measles.

How many times did the wild idea go back and forth in his mind, at war with his "practical" side? But practical is meaningless if you never do anything real. What's the point of practical, if it's just preserving a piece of slowly decaying meat? Step by step, with careful preparation, Dr Simon forged his real-life flaming sword.

He sold his house, found guides, and against the advice of the State Department made his illegal medical tour of Afghanistan. This was in 1984, a bad time. The Soviets had actually *killed* the rural doctors. In the forbidden zone, Dr Simon set himself up and treated people for a while, knowing full well that any arrangement with guides (not to mention hundreds of patients) is doubtful, and betrayal could come at any time.

One time he was crossing a river on a raft made of inflated goat skins. While they were exposed on the water, a Soviet helicopter flew toward them. The guides paddled faster! If it wasn't for the bureaucratic nature of the Soviet army, this story might have ended suddenly. But the helicopter flew away, to report and get authorization, or so we assume.

Dr Simon received payment for his work. One man brought his son, far gone from a wound. Dr Simon did his best but could not save him. Afterward, the man inquired the fee, and the doctor only asked for some cucumbers and fresh fruit. The man disappeared. What Dr Simon did not then realize was that the war had wiped out all the local fresh fruits and vegetables (one reason why people were getting very sick from malnutrition).

The man reappeared several weeks later with a satchel of fresh fruit. He had crossed the 20,000 foot Hindu Kush mountain range on foot, 130 miles each way, to reach a market in Pakistan.

After this kind of experience, Dr Simon returned a changed man. When you give it everything you've got, you can take it for granted you die. Waking up and finding yourself still there is waking up to an afterlife. You may be amazed how often this happens, and how important it is.

When Dr Simon came back, it seemed that suddenly he spoke with a voice of thunder. In many cities around the United States (including San Diego), doctors and nurses set themselves in motion; volunteers appeared, liberals and conservatives, rich and poor. It is surprising how much good rich people can do, if some hero gives them the leadership they need.

They built an anarchic medical association, the International Medical Corps, out of all these professionals who were willing to risk their lives. They sent more doctors across that border, and started permanent clinics. They published papers in respected medical journals: I saw one on how to design a cave clinic to protect against the blast from attacking bombers! There were still not enough medics, so in the end they found ways to train— in nine months—semi-literate farm boys to be emergency surgeons. (Many came back later to gain their medical degrees.)

In the end Dr Simon became the associate of powerful congressmen and of President Reagan. His knowledge of the inwardness of the Afghan resistance, passed to these political figures, helped make possible the diplomatically absurd decision to give high-tech Stinger missiles to the camelback warriors.

The Afghans proved to be good shots. They soon took back their land and drove the helicopters from the skies. The Soviets had to withdraw from Afghanistan. The unbroken winning record of Communism was ruined. Not long afterward, other satellite nations began breaking away, starting with Poland. Then the Soviet Union itself fell, the Other Superpower, the Empire of Scientific History, the Tower of Victorious Genocide.

Swing your life with follow-through. It adds power to your stroke.

The heroic stories of your boyhood prepare you for the moment when *you must make the difference* for the people that are brought to your attention. This sounds like a cliche, until you think what it means to *you*.

You have been quietly teaching in the city high school for years, while things go from bad to worse, and real casualties multiply. Then one day you walk in on a lead thug doing his filthy work on someone in the hallway. Eye to eye, all of you, knowing that this is the moment and there will be no other.

The thug will immediately start spouting legalities (this kind of person always knows his rights). If you do your job, he will become quieter a few moments later, because your boot is smashing his teeth loose. Your job is to beat him within an inch of his life. But it will end your career.

In mathematics, there is an entity called a "delta function", though it is not really a function but a limiting condition. This is how you make one: Start with a straight line, stretching out at zero level in both directions, except for a wide, flat bump in the middle. Make the bump narrower and taller, keeping the area under the bump the same. As the bump becomes infinitely narrow and infinitely tall, it approaches the delta function.

The incident I described above is a delta function of education. Though it passes off in an instant, it accomplishes as much in that instant as the wide, flat years of a normal career. But it can also lead to an afterlife. As you flip burgers in your new probation-approved job, a parent approaches you, wants you to take a hand in tutoring her rough-edged son. Then another, and we have an academy of desperation starting here...

I based this tale on a much lesser event in my own life. During the 1969 vacation from the Princeton graduate school, I had a two month job teaching *maths* at Thomas Bennett School in Crawley, a large council-house (public housing) suburb in Sussex, England. This highly disorganized high school had a headmaster who, according to rumor, had gone insane from heatstroke suffered in the Australian desert. That was why they were hiring teachers for two months. Some of my classes were a little rowdy.

One day the toughest of them went over the edge into riot. As the others racketed from desk to desk, one girl, the worst of the lot, jumped up on my desk and started shouting at me. I slapped her across the face, and she fell off. Also my voice changed, which only happens when you turn white with anger. The class quieted down a little. Her large, hefty boyfriend advanced on me, his eyes on a level with mine. I stared back at him. He walked away.

I hustled the girl down to the vice principal, where she was disciplined. According to law (they told me later) no teacher must ever strike a student; but we stuck together and bluffed them down. Later, as I took my customary walks in the evening at a nearby pond, I found some pupils at that school would approach me to talk over the fundamental things of life. Among them, oddly enough, were some of the worst rowdies from that bad class.

Of course this is not a fair comparison. As a maths teacher I was a foreign hobbyist, and would not have cared if I lost that job. I made the right move more from instinct than from heroism. But it works.

Heroic adventure stories rarely fail to sweep in the theme of love—as an outgrowth of the heroism. It will not do to think of love or family as a kind of career (a form of money). In this way too, *Star Wars* and Sir Walter Scott are more practical than the most practical sex classes.

Alexander Solzhenitsyn, in *The Gulag Archipelago*, describes the plight of the Lithuanians who, for the crime of having recently been free, were deported *en masse*, men and women, to the labor camps. There, like other prisoners, they had a life expectancy of months as they were worked to death on an insufficient diet.

It happened that a men's and women's camp were separated (at Kengir) only by a wall. Surviving Lithuanian men and women started passing notes to one another like cloistered schoolchildren. What followed filled Solzhenitsyn with awe:

> In that very same Kengir, Lithuanian women were *married* across the wall to Lithuanian men whom they had never seen or met; and the Lithuanian Roman Catholic priest (also, of course, a prisoner in the standard pea jacket) would provide written documentation that so-and-so and so-and-so had been joined for eternity in holy matrimony in the eyes of God. In this marriage with an unknown prisoner on the other side of a wall—and for Roman Catholic women such a marriage was irreversible and sacred—I hear a choir of angels.

So they prepared to die with the dignity of wedded couples, family members, a people. They never expected to *see* each other.

Is it true that there are deeds and vows so magnificent that they can make God Himself back down? Or is it His dearest wish that the people will rise to such a level of spirit and courage that armies cannot stand against them and stone walls crumble away? Such stories seem to cluster around the Lithuanians.

It was at Kengir that the thieves' revolt happened. It was there and only there that a complicated alliance was made between enemies, and complicated miscues slowed the authorities, and an unprecedented attitude brought slaves to reach for a moment of mastery. A long chain of improbable circumstances arranged themselves for forty days *and brought that wall down.*

> Eight thousand men, from being slaves, had suddenly become free, and now was their chance to... live! Faces usually grim softened into kind smiles. Women looked at men, and men took them by the hand. Some who had corresponded by ingenious secret ways, without even seeing each other, met at last! Lithuanian girls whose weddings had been solemnized by priests on the other side of the wall now saw their lawful wedded husbands for the first time—the Lord had sent down to earth the marriages made in heaven!

Was it followed by a bitter end? Or by an afterlife? I don't know; cases probably differed; perhaps every love has to come to a bitter end, if only by natural death. But I do not think that really matters. There is a fine old Spanish bridal song, to be sung by a woman—*Write on me.* The wall fell down, the marriage happened—he wrote on her! Let later events take care of themselves.

They had each other, a fearsomely high blessing beyond the hopes of a lovesick loner or prisoner. For forty days, does that not multiply the bounty? We who are given years to be with wife and children flatten out this blessing, and set to zero what any teenage virgin knows to be almost unbearably good. But one thing breaks this dullness. Loss, or the fear of loss. Just sitting at home when she is unaccountably not there, wondering whether something has happened to her—that drives feelingly home to you the truth of how high in love you are, how far you have to fall.

When I was a child, we often visited the Kraňaks, an old Slovak immigrant couple who were friends of my grandmother from the old country. They had a little farm in Kirkland, an area near Seattle that even then was being swallowed up in suburbia. Mr Kraňak had an incredibly sharp scythe, and could teach the skill of making the grass fall like a dying army as you walked by. Mrs Kraňak was an accomplished cook and filled us up with *koláče.*

Their house, like many pious old-country homes, was studded with small Catholic shrines. They had been married since youth, one of those fine peasant marriages built simply of sex and loyalty and long alliance. They seemed, to us children, unchanging.

Then one day Mrs Kraňak died. I never saw Mr Kraňak again. They said he was changed totally in appearance, his cheeks sunken, his face suddenly aged. He died two months later. He died of her not being there.

In Jere Van Dyk's excellent heartfelt book about the Afghan resistance, *In Afghanistan*, he writes of traveling to Kandahar and meeting Khoudaidad Shahazai, a legendary hero of the resistance.

> His beard was black; he had a thick handlebar mustache; he was lean, and he had eyes—that's what really got me—that were on fire.

This was not a man who was rising in the world. On the contrary. He was a man who had once had a life, but who had been shot through the heart.

> He told us his story: "Before the Russians came, I was a shopkeeper in Mazar-i-Sharif in the north. I sold rope and twine. [I tried to imagine this wild man peacefully selling two yards of twine in a dusty bazaar shop six feet square.] I was married, with two sons. God had been good to me. I was a happy man. Then... the Russians came. My wife was raped and killed. I made my two sons go to a refugee camp in Pakistan, and then I went up into the mountains to think. My wife had been violated and killed. It was my duty as a man to avenge her death. It was *badal*, blood revenge."
>
> He clenched his fist in the air, and his eyes burned...
>
> "I have two bullets in my stomach and pieces of metal in my leg. That is why I take hashish.
>
> "I fight alone. I belong to no man. I have God, I have my gun, and with them, I will drive the Communists from Afghanistan."

A harsh afterlife indeed, but with purpose! This hero did not care whether he lived or died, but he could take some enemy down with him. And so what happened? *He could not get killed.*

> Ismail smiled and told us a story: "Last month, the Russians began to build up their forces in Kandahar to combat our successes. There were more helicopters, more troops. Our morale

was low. We needed a success. Shahazai, in the middle of the
day, sneaked up to the airport, past the mine fields, the dogs,
the guards, cut through the fence, and with his old British rifle,
shot out the tires of a big Soviet airplane while it was being
unloaded. And then he escaped. Everyone knows about this
exploit. Shahazai's wife is dead, and he is in pain, but he is not
afraid of anything." Shahazai was quiet, embarrassed by the
praise and sad at the mention of his wife.

Enough of this and the ball gets rolling—fame and success!

Everyone knew him. Two old ladies, unveiled—they no
longer cared—carrying bundles of branches on their backs, recognized him, called him over, and chatted with him, imploring
that he fight on. He spoke gently with them, as a grown man
would to his mother...

Heaven's sense of humor can shade toward irony, and is known to be
rough at times. Jay Hoffman says God is like a seven-foot red-haired giant
that you meet in a bar. A friendly fellow: He slaps you on the back, and
the false teeth blow right out of your mouth and go skidding down the bar.
But it is all in good humor, and you'll be glad He's at your side when the
trouble begins.

Chapter 4

The New Creation

Is money more real than people?

Logically this is an odd question, because of course without people there would be no money. If there were gold coins remaining after everyone on Earth was exterminated, they would have no meaning. If like the Master of Lake-Town you are lost in a desert where nobody can be found, then your bag of money does you no good. This can be true even late at night in a city, after the buses stop running.

Yet the practical reality of American life is just the opposite. Attached to the name of an old and feeble financier is a huge number representing his investment portfolio. He dies, and that bank account goes on unchanged, right down to the last decimal place. Everything follows that number: the freedom to live in expensive places, to buy cars and businesses, to influence laws and purchase daily necessities. The human beings attached to the number are insignificant and interchangeable. Nobody remembers them once the will is probated.

Carrying this paradox farther, money creates persons that are more real than anyone born of woman. These are "legal persons"—corporations—whose stock prices are the main news item anymore after the end of cold war history. Compared to these mighty towers—which outdo Bill Gates in that their only purpose ever is to make the big accounting numbers spin—the two-legged stockholders and employees are itty bitty antlike figures. When you look out the broad windows of top-floor corporate offices, all human beings are reduced to the size of insects.

I need to deal with this paradox, which eats up most of the lives of most people. I cannot be deterred by lack of resources, since this work is necessary to instruct my children. This is the dismal science, economics, and at times I must rely on statistics, but more often on anecdotes. These

71

include several more paradoxes of the "too big to see" variety.

The common theme is arrogance. The ultimate breathtaking vision is dismal indeed: a "new creation" in which money, acting as God, remakes living human beings in its own image.

The Artificial Famine

There are schools of thought, which have taken over fields like education and serious journalism, that say that economic efficiency is the foundation of all human life. Their fountainhead is the *Wall Street Journal*, and you can recognize them by their repeated use of the word "market" (as in "free market" or "market forces"). They all take for granted that what they are talking about—"enterprise" is their favorite word for it—is the most important thing in the world. This notion, called "economic determinism", was shared by Karl Marx, the founder of Communism.

And yet even the term "market" needs to be examined. The poetic critique is as follows: Real markets (like the colorful block-wide covered markets that we have here in Tijuana on certain days of the week) are rapidly being obsoleted by shopping malls. This happens worldwide thanks to the capital flows that the "free market" theorists support! Actual markets are replaced by abstract dealmaking in glass and steel offices. Money is more real than the market itself.

So there are two levels of paradox. The first expresses itself in a thought exercise. Suppose you are the winner of a big tax-free prize. How would you rather have it: as cash, or as usable stuff, like bags of grain? Is there anyone who wouldn't say "Keep the prize, give me the money please!" I know I would.

On a bigger scale, whole countries think this way, Japan for instance. Whenever people talk about balance of trade, they assume money coming in (and stuff going out) is the better alternative. Political candidates like Pat Buchanan take for granted that whoever sucks up money (the immigrant worker, for instance) is hurting our country, even when he provides necessary services and goods.

And yet it is obvious that what we really need is the stuff. The only reason money is any good is that it buys our necessities when we want them. The great economist, Adam Smith (author of *The Wealth of Nations*) founded the science of economics on this fact. He debunked the money-only approach to economics (which is called "mercantilism"). The paradox, which I will explain in a later section, is that mercantilism is still alive and well as a gut reaction.

Essential to that explanation is the second and far worse paradox, the employment dilemma. This one strikes at the very foundations of life as we know it. It starts with the old cliche about life's necessities: "food, clothing, and shelter." These parts of the economy have not stayed the same but have changed radically because of technical progress.

In my son Tom's economics text (*Economics, Free Enterprise in Action* by David E. O'Connor) is a graph showing the percent of people employed in agriculture over the years. In 1820 in the United States it was over 70%, and this fits all previous eras of history. In 1980 it is down to 2.7%. Most of this is due to technology, which makes an individual farmer much more efficient, so he can produce food for more people.

The paradox is that this applies to all the other necessities too. If you crudely equate clothing and shelter with food, add a fourth category of "other" for necessities we have missed (like hospitals), and allow a fifth of manufacture of needed tools and a sixth of distribution, you get a figure of 16.2%. That percentage of the people can produce everything that is needed by everyone. Five sixths of us are economically unnecessary!

You may object that by my logic, we would have needed 420% of the population to provide necessities in 1820, and everyone would have died. But that actually strengthens my point. By that logic, $\frac{100}{70} \times 2.7\%$ or less than 4% of us could support everyone, and only one in twenty-five of us is economically needed. In my six-category approach I am making a big concession to the modern fact of specialization. Old-fashioned farmers made their own clothes, built their own houses and so forth. If you want to push it, you can say *at least* five sixths of us are economically unnecessary.

Put it another way. We have six times as much economic efficiency as we need. This knocks the *Wall Street Journal* people into a cocked hat. Economic efficiency turns out to be a very unimportant thing. Technological efficiency makes economic efficiency obsolete. It's like collecting rain in Seattle, or providing ice at the North Pole—any old system will do.

There are areas where we have a real need. For instance, our marriages don't work, and America is crying out for some way to reduce the 50% divorce rate. But an efficient economy is our last priority! We could all be registered slaves of the Egyptian Pharaoh, with crowds of clerks trailing after each work crew, scraping their quill pens across rolls of papyrus. We could troop around in circles, burning incense daily at sunrise and sunset to the Great God Hermes, Patron of Motion. We'd still have all of what we need, even with a 500% waste rate.

That is not the last paradox, though. According to the above, we should all be kicking back, working about one day a week for everything we need. What has happened is the opposite. It used to be (even back in those bad old medieval farming days) that a man could support his family. This is rarely true any more. Since the 1960s, more and more wives and mothers have *had to* go to work just to help their families stay even.

Here I have some real science to offer, called the "weariness index". The idea is to figure out how hard people have to work for the basic needs of life. In order to do it right, I start by clearing away some bad foundations. They have to do with average earnings figures.

First of all, "family earnings" conceal what we want to find out. If more people in the family are working, family earnings can rise even though they are being paid less per amount worked. We look only at individual earnings.

To explain the other problem, consider this scenario. One third of all earners are poor working stiffs, earning \$5.00/hour. One third are skilled or lucky, and get \$20.00/hour. One third are doctors, lawyers and other key people and get \$80.00/hour. (These figures are chosen for easy calculation, not to fit times, statistics, minimum wages etc.) A doctor bill costs \$140.00. What is the average hours of work needed to pay the doctor bill?

If you take the mean (average) of earnings, that is $\dfrac{\$5 + \$20 + \$80}{3}$ or \$35 per hour. That gives four hours as the average. If you take the median (middle of the list) of earnings, that is \$20/hour, which gives seven hours. But the \$5/hour person must work 28 hours to pay the bill. The \$20/hour person must work 7 hours, and the \$80/hour person 1.75 hours, yielding 12.25 hours as the true average.

Both mean and median underestimate the effort. The true figure comes from taking the average *hours per dollar* among the workers. This is the mean of the inverses (MOI), and in our case it is $\dfrac{0.2 + 0.05 + 0.0125}{3}$ or 0.0875 hour/\$. If you want a figure in dollars per hour, you invert it to get the harmonic mean. This is \$11.43/hour, which is a whole lot different from the \$20.00 or the \$35.00 from the standard statistics.

The explanation is as follows. The MOI assigns equal importance to everyone's hours, whether they are rich or poor. The standard mean gives more "votes" to the rich person's hours in forming the average. The median is (as usual in statistics) a compromise, only half wrong. It usually comes out at about the geometric mean of the other two figures; so it still amounts to giving more votes to the rich person's hours, but by a lesser factor.

As a side benefit, this approach gives a solid measure of the gap between rich and poor. To get it just multiply the MOI by the mean earnings, or divide the mean by the harmonic mean. This is a pure number, the spread, and in our case it equals

$$\text{Spread} = 35.00 \times 0.0875 = \frac{35.00}{11.43} = 3.06$$

Of course this is an absurdly high value and real spreads are just above

1. But it is a very sensitive statistic and just a few percentage points shows a rapid concentration of wealth.

Finally, I get the weariness index by multiplying the cost of living by the MOI, or dividing it by the harmonic mean income. I form this into an index starting at 100. Thus,

$$\text{Weariness}(\text{Year}) = 100 \times \frac{\text{HCost}(\text{Year})}{\text{HCost}(\text{Baseyear})}$$

where

$$\text{HCost}(\text{Year}) = \frac{\text{CPI}(\text{Year})}{\text{HarmonicMean}(\text{Year})} = \text{CPI}(\text{Year}) \times \text{MOI}(\text{Year})$$

The index requires an honest cost of living index, which the standard consumer price index, or CPI, has thus far provided. Note that there have been recent proposals (the Boskin commission) to corrupt the CPI for the sake of making the inflation figures look better.

My calculations are based on a set of published and unpublished data provided by the courtesy of Bruce Klein of the Bureau of Labor Statistics, Washington, D.C. Details are in my unpublished paper *The "Weariness Index" and the Mean of the Inverses, Preliminary Report*, October 22, 1988. Modeling is required because the data is a short histogram table. The model is crude but demonstrates a trend.

Uncorrected

Hourly

Year	Arith	Harmonic	Spread	Weariness
1973	100.0	100.0	1.210	100.0
1974	107.3	107.2	1.211	103.6
1975	115.5	115.7	1.208	104.7
1976	122.4	125.0	1.185	102.5
1977	131.2	133.4	1.190	102.2
1978	140.4	143.0	1.188	102.7
1979	157.1	154.3	1.232	105.8
1980	173.0	171.8	1.218	107.9
1981	187.4	184.1	1.232	111.2
1982	200.0	191.8	1.262	113.3
1983	203.2	197.1	1.248	113.8
1984	209.8	202.8	1.252	115.3
1985	219.7	209.2	1.271	115.7
1986	227.4	215.0	1.279	114.7
1987	234.4	221.3	1.281	115.5

Salaried

Year	Arith	Harmonic	Spread	Weariness
1967	100.0	100.0	1.139	100.0
1969	109.8	108.4	1.154	101.3
1970	115.9	113.9	1.159	102.1
1971	122.3	119.1	1.169	101.8
1972	135.3	125.1	1.232	100.2
1973	147.2	136.1	1.232	97.8
1974	156.9	144.8	1.234	102.0
1975	169.6	154.8	1.248	104.1
1976	178.8	163.5	1.245	104.3
1977	191.6	174.0	1.254	104.3
1978	204.6	185.7	1.255	105.2
1979	227.7	201.5	1.287	107.9
1980	246.8	218.1	1.289	113.2
1981	267.5	235.3	1.295	115.8
1983	300.9	259.3	1.322	115.1
1984	315.2	270.3	1.328	115.1
1985	328.7	280.3	1.336	114.9
1986	341.8	290.2	1.342	113.2
1987	355.0	300.7	1.345	113.2

Corrected

		Hourly		
Year	Arith	Harmonic	Spread	Weariness
1973	100.0	100.0	1.210	100.0
1974	107.3	107.2	1.211	103.6
1975	115.5	115.7	1.208	104.7
1976	122.4	125.0	1.185	102.5
1977	131.2	133.4	1.190	102.2
1978	140.4	143.0	1.188	102.7
1979	152.8	156.6	1.180	104.3
1980	168.2	174.4	1.166	106.3
1981	182.2	186.8	1.180	109.5
1982	194.4	194.6	1.208	111.6
1983	202.2	200.2	1.222	112.0
1984	208.7	206.0	1.226	113.5
1985	218.6	212.5	1.245	113.9
1986	226.2	218.4	1.253	113.0
1987	233.2	224.8	1.255	113.7

		Salaried		
Year	Arith	Harmonic	Spread	Weariness
1967	100.0	100.0	1.139	100.0
1969	109.8	108.4	1.154	101.3
1970	115.9	113.9	1.159	102.1
1971	122.3	119.1	1.169	101.8
1972	129.4	125.6	1.173	99.8
1973	140.7	136.7	1.173	97.4
1974	150.1	145.5	1.175	101.5
1975	162.2	155.5	1.188	103.7
1976	171.0	164.2	1.186	103.8
1977	183.2	174.7	1.194	103.9
1978	195.7	186.5	1.196	104.8
1979	211.1	200.8	1.197	108.2
1980	228.8	217.4	1.199	113.5
1981	247.9	234.5	1.204	116.2
1983	274.8	258.0	1.213	115.7
1984	287.8	268.8	1.219	115.7
1985	300.1	278.8	1.226	115.5
1986	312.1	288.6	1.232	113.8
1987	324.2	299.1	1.235	113.8

In the above tables, Spread is exact (*not* an index). Corrected values include a model fix for change in the data categories between certain years.

This is a heavy confirmation of what everyone felt: a rapid worsening of the cost economy, especially around the "inflation" year 1980. A 13% increase in the index is huge, and accounts for almost all the driving force pushing mothers into the workforce. I have no later figures, but my guess is that they got worse again in the early 1990s with the "downsizing" craze.

All of this makes no sense from an economic point of view (considering the technology and efficiency increase shown by the farmers). The poetic way of understanding it is to think of the money persons (corporations) gradually pushing the real persons into a corner, where they have to thrash harder and harder just to stand still.

What does it mean for an ordinary set of families? Downsizing means a lot of people are falling off the edge of the economy. Suppose one out of four. To get a 13% increase in the weariness index when (shall we say) efficiency has improved 20% over the period for those who stayed on the lifeboat, you have to have the following:

Family 1 through 3: index decreases 20%. Not really, of course, because my index is too optimistic. It does not count the rise in taxes and "infinite obligations" like hospital bills and legal liability that hang over everybody. When my mom had me (1947) her hospital bill was seven dollars a day.

Family 4: index increases 112%, or more than doubles. They have to work more than twice as hard just to stand still. I don't think mommy is going to stay home with the kids any longer.

When mothers have to go to work, they usually call the reason "economic necessity". But following Adam Smith we see that is a subtle error: economic necessity bites less now than ever before; there is plenty. It is actually *money necessity*. All the plenty does her no good if she has no money to buy it.

To get the true image of what is going on, go back to the "Lifeboat Exercise", taught in many school ethics classes to get the children to accept abortion and other forms of the crushing of the weak by the powerful. Here the student is to imagine himself stranded on a lifeboat with a few other people and food running out. The question is who will be killed and eaten (or at least killed) so that the others may live. The answer (in real life) is whoever is weakest and most friendless.

There are several false assumptions in this exercise. The one that concerns us here is that food is running out. As we have seen, food is in abundance. It is *being withheld*, not running out.

The true image has a high fence running down the middle. On one side is the economic abundance: roasts and fresh bread and strawberry shortcakes covered with cream, every kind of good thing flowing from the horns of plenty onto the long banquet tables. On the other side are the starvelings, begging and hustling for a chance to get some of the goods. Guards stand at the gates through the fence, admitting only those who have certain chits or slips of paper.

On the one side, food ages and is shoveled off the tables and discarded. On the other side, mothers, who don't have enough push to make it, withdraw to the edge of the crowd, where they quietly cut their children's throats, rather than see them starve. Central in the midst of guards are those heavy, business-suited figures who have rolls of chits to distribute. They are surrounded by crawling, slavish figures begging in the mud.

This is the inevitable conclusion and end result of my three paradoxes. It is an artificial famine. Do you think this is too extreme? Then you have not really felt it bite in your own life.

A comparison with literal famines is instructive. According to Panin (p 65),

> mass cannibalism ... occurred during the famine in the Volga region—especially in 1923—or during the government-planned starvation of the peasants that was part of the collectivization process in the Ukraine and other areas. In those days it was not uncommon for a mother, driven to desperation, to devour her own child behind the closed shutters of her hut.

In these days it is not uncommon for a mother, driven to desperation, to devour her own child behind the closed shutters of an abortion clinic. This exact parallel extends to the shutters (called "the right of privacy" by *our* owners). The shameful deed is easier to do if no one is watching. When the Ukrainian mother devoured her child, it provided physical nourishment for her starving body. Devouring an American child provides $145,000 of financial nourishment to the bank account of its mother.

The Assault on Heaven

In the pretty downtown walking village of La Jolla is a Catholic parish, with a little whitewashed Spanish-style church that has a real bell tower. My children went to their school and Jeanne and I have long sung in their classical chancel choir. As the years have passed, that church has taken to trimming away from the word of God those parts that would offend the wealthy and powerful. Just recently (on Sunday the 28th of September) they omitted the following reading, which I therefore reproduce in full (Jas 5:1-6):

You rich, weep and wail over your impending miseries. Your wealth has rotted, your fine wardrobe has grown moth-eaten, your gold and silver have corroded, and their corrosion shall be a testimony against you; it will devour your flesh like a fire. See what you have stored up for yourselves against the last days. Here, crying aloud, are the wages you withheld from the farmhands who harvested your fields. The shouts of the harvesters have reached the ears of the Lord of hosts. You lived in wanton luxury on the earth; you fattened yourselves for the day of slaughter. You condemned, even killed the just man; he does not resist you.

This is not the first incident of this kind. Previous lectors have trimmed Ephesians 5:21-24, the famous "Wives, obey your husbands" passage which is too much for modern American ears. Socially acceptable clerics, with little zeal for the Word of God, do know which side their bread is buttered on. Financial and volunteer support for churches comes from upper class women activists who refuse to listen to Scripture of this kind.

From well-financed Catholic universities and institutes of theology, the envoys of money (armed with vague chancery authority) arrive at parish rectories to tell the priests what is allowed to be heard in church. And the priests crouch down and do as they are told. This is an instance of what conservatives call "civility".

It is also an example of the overweening arrogance of money. Money is perfectly sure of its right to rework the word of God. If you expect then that money will also insist on reworking the *work* of God, His living creation, natural and human—if you expect that, you expect rightly. The human being, created in the image of God, will be remade in the image of money.

Free market theorists like George Gilder applaud this process. They claim that everything is for the best when the money markets are left free to do what they wish. These are led by "the best and the brightest" of the human race, anointed by success, and it is *morally* wrong for anyone who is less successful (that is, less wealthy) to criticize their actions.

So, start by examining the quality of these our masters. Let me begin with a matter of my personal expertise. I am a mathematician. In this field there is an immense range of skills, from a store clerk to great theorists like Gauss and Einstein, who prove theorems that must openly pass the test of pure logic applied by critics worldwide.

The money people, who rule hundreds of billions of dollars, are just above the clerk on this ladder of skills. Their skill is equivalent to an advanced high school senior: they do logarithms and exponential functions in their interest calculations. Any engineering student goes beyond this (to Bessel functions and the like) while he is still an undergraduate.

The money leadership can do nothing constructive for itself, and always relies on the skills and creations of others. These skills and creations are often academic, traditional or family based. When you listen to rich people talking among themselves, you will often hear one of them telling the others about "a little place" she has found. A Peruvian restaurant, or some artistic shop where homewoven clothes are sold. Whatever was good was there before the money people came on the scene. They merely appropriated it.

Real science and technology spring most often from academic, military or bureaucratic circles that are protected from marketing pressures. The recent market-driven technology spews thousands of product announcements, but is actually biased toward wrecking items of value. Two examples are personal computers and architecture.

The best and the brightest money people cannot even do their own job right. Every time the economy makes any downward motion, hundreds of banks fail. It is well known that the economy periodically slows, but it catches them by surprise every time. These multibillion dollar entrepreneurs then have to be guided back off the rocks by the much-scorned *career bureaucrats* of the Government banking regulatory agencies. The poor, slogging taxpayer has to put up money to rescue them. (By contrast, the less exalted career money managers who handle the money market funds rarely if ever fail, unless owned by stockbrokers who run in the fast lane.)

Everybody in a standard occupation succeeds by performing his trade. Doctors heal; truckers roll; plumbers fix toilets. Only investors gain stature by *refusing to* invest, by withholding their money from feasible projects until reams of documentation are supplied proving that they will get it back ten times over in a couple of years risk-free. Such "business plans" are, of course, tongue-in-cheek nonsense, which handicaps honest people tremendously. So when the money is tickled loose at last, it often falls into the hands of a scam artist, which is the story behind most of these huge bank failures.

These money leaders, by their own standards, fail dismally to bring prosperity to Americans. Their ideal is "enterprise" or "entrepreneurship"; well, a rough gauge of making it entrepreneurially is going public with a successful stock offering. Make a reasonable guess that about ten people get rich as big founders on each offering, then count the number of successful offerings—around a thousand yearly—and compare it with the number of people who die each year—over a million. Under the vaunted entrepreneurial system, more than 99% of Americans die failures.

Well then, why do these flops rule the roost? Go back to the lottery paradox: why is the cash prize better than real goods? It is because we are suspended in midair. We are helpless to provide for ourselves, and we depend utterly on the cooperation of others to supply our needfuls, starting with food. Money has become the only way to organize this cooperation. Therefore money is god.

There are other forms of cooperation: volunteer society, family, charity. They are all dying on the vine. Money is a jealous god, and will not suffer rivals. Each other form of cooperation is seen to have negative money value. Volunteers are replaced by paid workers, charity by government funding. Families break in pieces and the pieces flee to careers.

There was a joke, circulating a couple of years back, about Bill Gates buying the Vatican. It is not really a joke. The Culture of Wealth hates the Vatican with a passion, because they have not succeeded in buying it. (They have dragged their feet on clearing the land mines in Afghanistan for the same reason.) The United Nations, a creature of the billionaires, campaigns intensively to wreck the Church in poor countries worldwide, even going as far as corrupting little children. This is the same approach that Microsoft shows in its microcosm, the personal computer world: wreck whatever you do not control.

The revolution worked by money is far more effective than anything the Nazis or Communists did. Those tyrants even acted as a chrysalis, sheltering national cultures from the fast-working corrosion of upward mobility. Our wealthy friends, vacationing, found sturdy native culture still vibrant in —*Outer Mongolia.* But for how long?

Selfishness is the essence of the new creation: the cringing selfishness of safety, whose salvation is the limitation of liability. The world and the human being shall be recreated in the image of the corporation.

Think about the poor chicken. Instead of scrabbling in the dirt, pecking seeds and laying the occasional egg, the new chicken is a *vegetable*, tethered to one spot until death, laying on schedule. Hormones maximize production. The chicken has been recreated in the image of a corporate department, and exists for one thing: to spin the numbers to the maximum.

The child, like the chicken, no longer scratches around in the dirt of vacant lots. The child is remade in the corporate image, scheduled, productive. Score is kept. A ranking is made. Those who fail are discarded. That is, they are humanely placed in special classes where even they can lead a productive life in their limited way.

The human being is a function of his bank account. Speech is marketing (as with sports stars giving endorsements). Activity is value, as long as a money number can be attached to it. Net worth is the essence of the human being. In all this, the human being is reformed as a tiny image of the corporation.

The frenetic pace of the stock market floor is copied inhumanly onto the real world. TV entertainment images flash discontinuously more than once a second. Instead of being erected like a building, laws, changing on demand, are projected instantly as if on a movie screen. Pure will creates immediate results in a way far beyond the dreams of Nietzsche.

And what is to be said of love? Is love productive? Does the cash register frequently ka-ching, and the numbers spin, gaining the approval of those who rank and keep score on love?

Love is a shaggy alien in the world of limited liability. The self prospers by reducing its attachments to uncontrolled others who can pull it down. Love does the opposite, makes one vulnerable to the beloved. Therefore, love is for suckers.

But wait—the pleasure! We still have a place for love in the corporate image. The orgasm is the ka-ching of the cash register. Each orgasm can count as a kind of coin. By saving the orgasm while eliminating the attachments, we define corporate love.

Homosexuality is corporate love. That is what explains its phenomenal political success, far beyond the tiny numbers of its practitioners.

The god of money seems to smile on homosexuals. It is common knowledge in Catholic circles that homosexual priests, whatever other troubles attach to them, typically excel in fund-raising. Corporate support of gay rights is as universal as corporate support of Chinese and Vietnamese slave labor. The entertainment industry promotes gay causes industriously: nearly every TV sitcom now has its compulsory homosexual character, always favorably treated.

The Cunanan debacle did not harm the gay cause, any more than did other gruesome indicators like the Dahmer cannibalism. The more fashionable the circle, the more receptive it is for gay demands. For instance, William Weld, the Massachusetts governor, was enthusiastic about giving gays access to public school children. For this he got massive support from the Boston elite and the local and national media in his recent ambassadorship debacle. Making a Cunanan/Dahmer/access-to-schoolchildren connection is *verboten.*

I've seen this kind of thing too often not to recognize it. For Soviet supporters, abortionists, pornographers, feminists—the favorable press, the lack of money problems, the channel to schoolchildren, the ostracism of opponents who harp on real atrocities. It's the open door to the Culture of Wealth. The thing to do is to ask why.

Both males and females have rough edges that do not fit smoothly into the corporate mold. He pushes for high wages, security and benefits to support his family. She raises inconvenient questions of maternity leave and keeps wanting to schedule her work around her children's needs. They can't be moved around freely. He and she form an attachment that, even in modern America, lasts for years and causes explosive problems if either is treated as interchangeable. Even the childless, contracepted couple is like a live grenade, ready to burst into a spasm of selfless, fertile love just because of some accident of romantic mood.

All this amounts to old-line human stuff butting into the machine, like a chicken wanting to scratch in the dirt. How much smoother is the homosexual model! Children do not appear. Permanent partners are rare. The ideal homosexual is the perfect corporate functionary (commercial counters only—toys and clothes). And from the point of view of orgasm coinage, there is nothing in the straight world that even comes close to the gay bathhouse. When you bring that into the picture, not even sterilized heterosexuals can compete.

Real people, including homosexuals, are better than this model. More on that in a moment. But perception is everything: the new creation scents a success in this corporate love, and everything that money can buy is pushing for it.

Can there be peace between old-line humans (a phrase of R. A. Lafferty) and the new corporate man? In a word, no. This should be clear from the ruins of the mom and pop grocery store and the small software company. The economics commentators always sneer that they had to go because they can't compete. But by this set of rules, there is no hope for anyone at all to compete once high finance has decided (to use the nasty phrase now current) to eat his lunch.

What is deceptive is the face of the harmless old geezers who abound in the world of finance. More than anything they seem befuddled by life: how can they be at the center of a great evil? The answer is not in what they do, but in what they exclude. They are dominated by fear (of losing their money). So most of what is good and generous in the world will never be allowed even to speak with them. This opens the door only to avarice and malice.

As the anti-Microsoft sweatshirt proclaims: "Resistance is Futile. You Will Be Assimilated." No part of the old-line human space will be left in peace. As for faraway lands, tell me one where the American dollar has not penetrated! You can neither run nor hide. So you better think about what kind of world will be left after they have *eaten your lunch.*

Each gift of love receives its gesture of hatred in return. If your mother has prepared you a birthday dinner, and you answer by going out to a restaurant, you are expressing hatred very effectively. The corporate takeover spurns each human gift in detail.

There is only one reason why feminists push for women in combat: old-line human males give their lives in defense of their hearth. This gift, a cause of desperate love in all old war stories, rouses the feminists to fury. In the same way they reject the *Promise Keepers* whose attitude is a great boon to any human woman.

Gay adoption similarly seeks to strip the childrearing mantle from generous parents. Few gays will ever really adopt a child—that would deprive them of all their political advantage (they'd be paying for and attending their little girl's dancing lessons: no time or money left for activism!) But by declaring for it they can avoid concessions to the real lovers who must nurture their future sexual fodder.

In the same way, the money people will never leave the Catholic Church that they hate, but will cling to position and influence there. All the boring rituals and tiresome sweet-talk at catechist's conventions are a small price to pay. To leave a healthy opponent in peace is a figment of old-fashioned sportsmanship. The real winner eats an opponent alive from the inside, like a wasp larva or a hagfish; so there is no truce even within the sanctuary.

There is no hope of peace. But we can turn the fight to our advantage. We need not restrict ourselves like conservatives to preventing their vile future. We can raise our sights, and take back much of what we already thought has been lost forever.

Crosscurrents

The ethic of total selfishness solves the employment dilemma in the way that leads to the tightening vise of our experience. As the economic surplus increases, the players devote themselves to maneuvering for ownership of the surplus. You improve your position by reducing the number of people you must pay to maintain your property. Others, lacking in clout, are locked out and scramble for whatever scraps of economic usefulness are left them. This is called "downsizing" (or "rightsizing", as the money worshippers would have it). It explains how wealth can increase at the same time as ordinary families experience ever increasing hardship.

The Weariness Index does not usually increase within a job. It increases from job to job. After the small store owner is bankrupted, or the worker is laid off, they must pick up the pieces of their economic lives in a new position under drastically less favorable terms. Their children too are pushed down; in their case it is disguised as ever increasing requirements for education, and for percentile standing within their class. The change is gradual and is accepted over the years. Grandpa and Grandma had house, store, large family. Grandkids live in ratty little apartments and need welfare to help with their children.

The domination of selfishness gets more and more blatant. Here's an

example. Years ago, it was accepted that medical insurance for employee
and family came with a decent job. Gradually this has been nibbled away,
except under welfare. Just this week, I received a job offer to work full
time at half salary. It declares that medical insurance, if any, will be *for
me, the employee, only*. This is no McJob—it is chief scientist in a major
engineering development! What we have here has become standard operating procedure. A healthy employee is of direct value to the employer. His
family is worthless to the employer, so they can go die.

This pulling apart of the family goes the other direction too. After
World War II, when cigarettes were the only money in wide stretches of
new wasteland, the westward roads of Europe were clogged with millions
of ragged refugee families. A private group called *Aid for the Church in
Need*, led by Father Werenfried von Straaten, raised billions of dollars to
resettle these families—that was when a billion dollars was real money! In
each case they found place for the whole family, and even arranged reunions
when possible.

This saving of whole families is an instance of what is called "the bowels
of compassion", and these have shrivelled or calcified in the new end-of-
century human. For efficiency's sake, aid agencies now tear the needy child
away from mother and father and place the child in a foster home. The
child is lightweight, hopeful and easy to save (so goes the logic) while the
parents can be left to rot. Of course, the child, being a sane old-line human,
does not see it this way at all! In the September 21 *San Diego Union*, the
reporter described how the social workers separated a little girl from her
mother: the girl made the San Diego baby jail echo for hours with her cries
for mommy. The only regret the social workers had was that the mother
had not been eliminated earlier.

Another example: the environment. Can a public-spirited antipollution
drive be called harm to the powerless? Yes, easily—when it is enforced.
They take away a working mother's car, so she can't pick up her daughter.
Then that little girl has to wait at a darkened bus stop, and she is caught
and raped. That is the price we pay.

Let me shed light on it by describing "the Sweet Breezes of Tijuana."
As a sensitive asthmatic, I have noticed the air is much less polluted here
than in San Diego where we used to live. As you drive south across the border, you see the lights sparkling crystal clear on the long ridge of Tijuana.
Looking north from Mexico, you often see a pall of pollution starting at the
border.

The Mexicans drive their smoke-belching 1967 klunkers while the California smog laws are unmatched in severity, yet Tijuana air is cleaner. How
can this be? Simply: Tijuana is a compact city, more like an East Coast
metropolis than like the sprawl of Southern California. Fewer people drive

cars, they drive them fewer miles, and the cars carry more people each.

You will never hear it mentioned, but this gives another way to combat auto pollution. Stop commuting! But that would impact the rich, who live in San Clemente or Santa Paula and drive several hours each day to and from Los Angeles, and who have far more cars per family member than ordinary working people. The laws deliberately ignore both these factors, and concentrate only on pollution per car mile, so that they can place the entire burden of environmentalism on the poor.

All this has a good side. You are relieved of all moral obligation toward the environment. Just say, "I'll start fighting pollution as soon as the executives all move back into the inner cities and stop their long commutes." You have been trained to lay a guilt trip on yourself (if you are too poor to afford the best and the cleanest). Now you can shuck it off like a dirty blanket.

This is an example of crosscurrents. The ethic of selfishness creates a backlash against itself. I am able to turn that half-price job offer down, because I now have a job from a tycoon who, according to the ethic of selfishness which is presented as the laws of economics, simply should not exist. He could enforce far worse terms on his workers in today's market, but as a personal idiosyncrasy he prefers to do well by his associates. Such generous reality seems to come from nowhere, like flowers breaking through the concrete.

When my wife, confused after the birth of our youngest, wandered off with the children, I found them—all together—in a room in an East County police station. This was the social workers' best chance at tearing apart our family and they missed it! Some night duty officer had very carefully *not* called the next link in the chain of command. Thus our family stands unviolated to this day. Flowers breaking through the concrete, indeed.

Here is the paradox: we are taught in each case that it is a *moral imperative* for us to cooperate in our own oppression. If you are an economic loser, you should accept family sickness as the price of not being able to compete. If needy, your gratitude to the welfare agency should keep you from making a fuss when they take away your children. You owe it to the environment to leave your little girl at the dark bus stop. If something happens to her, she is just more "people pollution" anyway, and the world is probably better off without the burden of her presence.

At the same time, an undercurrent gathers to oppose the degradation, if we only have the courage to hold out for it. This apparent contradiction is easily explained—the new creation and the ethic of selfishness are inhuman and unworkable. Still, every time it happens it is a surprise to us, steeped as we are in the propaganda of inevitable defeat.

For twenty years I was in the middle of the computer industry, which has now shrivelled because of the ethic of selfishness. In the 1970s and 1980s it was a creative blast—little business startups blossomed, every good thing was rewarded. That has come to a screeching halt in the 1990s, with the rise of a monopoly that actually prospers by harming its customers.

Suppose car manufacturers could transmit an electronic signal that would make your fuel lines plug up, or cause your steering to unravel. That would sure get you back buying more parts and cars. But would they do it? There is some pride in making a car that works, in selling the customer a good thing. It is a special triumph of the "laws of economics" that the dominant figure in the new computing is willing, as a standard business practice, to prosper by wrecking (creating incompatibility).

Interestingly, even Microsoft can be thought of as a defense against an older application of the ethic of selfishness. Like all engineering, writing software only needs to be done once. Your program works perfectly! We congratulate you for a job well done. Now we won't be needing you any more. You can take this last payment, clear your stuff out of the office and go starve.

Computing, of course, is not really that important economically. The daily sight of some poor little secretary staring dully at her bollixed office machine is no economic disaster: the 500% surplus absorbs it easily. Studied discourtesy profits billions because the flow of wealth is not essentially economic, but essentially manipulative.

I have also recently seen the crosscurrent. Microsoft's policy is to destroy whatever it cannot control, by churning standards. Let a hundred flowers *not* bloom. Snuff them, every one! Small handheld computers, the size of calculators, have recently developed into a modest market with lots of independent software sources. This market's total size is tiny compared with Microsoft's core business. Still, it existed and was independent. So Microsoft took the trouble to create a crippled version of Windows, in order to destroy it.

The resulting new product (as detailed in a deadpan review in *The HP Palmtop Paper*) is bulky, expensive, wasteful of batteries, and lacking in ability: it does not even have a decent calculator attached. So all the old DOS palmtops were *pulled from store shelves* to make way for it. (If the market is deprived of a superior product for long, customers will forget it ever existed.) Result: a sharp backlash, which generated enough demand to bring the superior product back. The little Palmtop software community has created enough value to rouse their little user community; and generous people with an attitude, working for outfits like *The HP Palmtop Paper*, have come up with schemes to keep the independents alive. All contrary to the laws of economics of course (it is funny to watch them apologizing for this).

Of course the most wholesale violations of the laws of economics occur in the realm of the family. Despite all the heavy penalties, the average American still acts out of love of husband, wife and children. The heaviest legal oppression and money parasitism centers right here, where the prey are most numerous and juicy. It starts right at the hospital where the baby is born. Despite the huge hospital bill you are paying, they won't give you a safety car seat for your baby. But they will legally kidnap your newborn if you don't buy one.

As we've seen, corporate love—homosexuality—offers a way to get the cash of orgasms without the drag of dependents. It is the greatest triumph of the new creation to date: a new class of fuckers, free of all the drawbacks, gaining educational and custodial authority over the offspring of the shabby old-fashioned slaves, while leaving all the burdens to the suckers. Can it be that even here, *even here* there will be flowers breaking through the well-designed concrete?

Bill Lullo, the old organist of our classical chancel choir, is an accomplished composer. When we sang his *Requiem* in a large nearby church, our children sat in the church "crying room", a one-directionally soundproofed space often found in churches to prevent disturbance at Mass. But they were not the only ones there.

Elizabeth slipped up to her mother afterwards and quietly asked, "Why was that man crying?" He had been stretched out on the first pew of the crying room for the whole concert. He frequently moaned, because he was dying of AIDS. The concert was a benefit for the AIDS Foundation, a charity dedicated not to making political hay from AIDS patients, but to finding them homes and care in their last days.

Such behavior loses the blessing of the god of Money which gays typically enjoy: the AIDS Foundation recently went bankrupt. But that is no matter: they had already done it. The ethic of total selfishness failed even its sexual standard bearers. They turned to fruitful love in the end! Even if in their case the "child" was in a kind of dreadful time-reversal, returning to inarticulate physical helplessness at the end rather than the beginning— still it is valid. It is the key of salvation, and surrounded by the echoes of that thunderous *Dies Irae*, they will ascend.

Hospitality: the End of Economic Determinism

The blessing, of having many times as much economic power as is needed, turns into a curse because of the ethic of selfishness. It turns into a job shortage which makes most people poorer instead of richer. The better things get, the worse they get: a paradox indeed.

The standard categories of economic thought, which are based on scarcity, have to be stood on their heads. Here is a thought exercise: Suppose not only Mexico, but the whole of Latin America came to our southern border and had to be fed by us. Disaster? No! Full employment, and a boom of unheard of proportions!

We could probably feed them all without even putting new land into service, so much of our farmland is held inactive now to support prices. But there really would be need of increased production. More jobs, more people into the countryside, which would be revitalized. Rural skills would pass to new people. Printed money, to cover the new food, would cause no inflation—it would be chasing *more* goods.

"Feeding All the South" is just one of several possible ways to cure the employment dilemma. (A real and surprising instance like this did happen, not long ago, and was decisive for world history; I will detail it below.) The common point is that as soon as selfishness is dethroned, the problem solves itself. George Soros quotes Francis Bacon, the medieval philosopher and economist, as saying that money is like dung—it does no good until it is spread around.

Makework is one technique common throughout history. Never laugh at Egyptian pharaohs for building pyramids: they were doing great good for their nations, even then. By arranging for work gangs from all the settlements to be hauling big stones from one place to another, they saw to it that everyone got a meal ticket. No coincidence this—they were solving a problem that could arise even in ancient times.

And they in their wisdom were doing it harmlessly! The point of makework is that you build to no use. You can do harm (weapons of war; cars and pollution). It is better if you are like the Pharaoh, with a harmless project. Best is a great work of art or exploration: cathedrals, Columbus, a space program.

Makework may be fueled through taxation. This raises the hackles of the economic conservatives. Following their star of selfishness, they object to paying taxes even though after all are paid they still have far more wealth than they personally need. According to them, taxation is a kind of extortion: a Government gun points with a message, pay or worse will happen to you.

There is much to say for this model of taxation, especially as applied in a legalistic culture. But it is not the only model. A better one is sharing the cost of a pizza. Courtesy demands you chip in for your share, and each reveler is normally proud to contribute even to excess. If anyone is caught short, nobody minds (except possibly the guy who is short, and insists on making it up later).

In an economy suffering from the employment dilemma, even very high rates of taxation do no harm, as long as they are applied to channels of surplus money flow. (This is not true of regulation.) The spirit of cooperation can create a "Kennedy era" attitude that quickly blossoms into a golden age. It is, after all, a form of public generosity. At times, in stratified societies (where generous people did not have to worry about their competitors taking advantage), such great works have even been subscribed voluntarily, without need for taxation.

There is a simple mathematical exercise showing how little harm it does to give generously, in a culture where others are doing the same. The formula is

$$1 - x + x^2 - x^3 + \cdots = \frac{1}{1 + x}$$

Here x is a number smaller than 1, but it can be very close. The x is what you give away in taxes, donations etc.; the square term is what you get back of what you give away; the cube is what you give away of that, and so forth. Even if the x is a Mother-Teresa-like 99%, you still end up with more than half of what you started with[1]! In an economy with 500% surplus capacity, you (as wealthy man) are still far, far ahead, while the poor man suddenly has no wolf at his door.

In the toughest, meanest environments of the world, the custom of hospitality has made travel and wide experience possible. It is the true safety net, blessed by the real God. It saved Afghanistan.

Vincent Martin told me this story, which happened in the early 1960s, before hippies went worldwide, and long before the resistance struggle. A young man wanted to travel through Afghanistan and was warned that he would be robbed and killed for even meager possessions. So he stripped himself down to ragged clothes, carried no weapon, did not even carry money in his shoe. Then he set out. When the tribesmen discovered he really did have nothing, they turned to their ethic of hospitality, invited him into their homes and shared food and stories. He completed a trip of many months, and not a hair on his head was harmed!

I had much the same experience when visiting Pakistan to set up an aid channel. I was invited off the street to visit a Pak family in Peshawar. And I was *not* lacking in possessions. Yes they were tempted—I saw them fingering their knives—but the great ethic held. I ended up photographing them and later sent them several family pictures.

Unconquerable—the Afghan resistance who held to the ethic of hospitality. Jan Goodwin, the editor of the Ladies Home Journal, traveling there

---

[1] Because $\frac{1}{1+.99} \approx \frac{1}{2}$

during the war, was entertained in a bombed out village by the one family that remained. This wealthy family saw it as their duty to stay in the free fire zone, to see that those passing through would not lack the hospitality the village owed them.

On her return trip, Jan Goodwin found the house bombed, the family killed. But they and thousands like them had done their great deed. Like a superfluid, the people and the warriors could pass around the country through these generous homes and never be trapped or exterminated.

The warriors of the Panjshir (Five Lions) Valley resisted repeated full-scale Soviet invasions many times. Once they were occupied at last. Refusing to submit their families and children to the officials and social workers who came to "re-educate" them, they handed their fates over to Almighty God, moved up to nearby mountain caves (one donkey load of supplies each) and sent appeals to the West through Pakistan, pleading for help before they starved.

No response came from the West. But people in a nearby valley, who were close to famine themselves, sent supplies in time. Soon after that, they were able to return to their valley. The Soviet soldiers had retreated. The stones of that valley must have burned their feet.

Not far away was the deed of hospitality that, in sheer size, dwarfs all the others.

When I made my trip to Pakistan in 1984, it was to newly huge Peshawar that I came. The streams of traffic, flowing through each other without aid of stoplights. The complex and nameless streets. The wildly decorated buses that looked like stained glass windows of reflective metal. It was the cockpit of *five million* refugees who had descended suddenly on a poor country that hardly had enough to feed itself.

Instructed by Islam and their noble traditions, the Paks welcomed one third of all Afghanistan, and trusted in God. When they turned their eyes on the United States, on Saudi Arabia and the international aid agencies, they were eyes that did not flinch—because *they* had already committed themselves. And this country, where a sheet of paper cost fifty cents (a goodly fraction of a day's wages), succeeded magnificently. The border disturbances that international observers awaited—they never happened. Peshawar's economy was actually stimulated by the enterprising newcomers.

Soviet agents finally killed President Zia of Pakistan, but it was too late for them. The deed was done: the Pakistani safe haven had made it possible for the Afghans to win. And then—awesome sight to anyone trained in the ways of welfare, but no surprise to those who know the ethic of hospitality—the camps emptied. The guests returned to their old homes, now devastated and mined and more strange than the alien but blessed existence they had led under the neighbor's roof. The deed of that faraway and shabby country is finished, but it ought not to be forgotten. Do we have one to match it, we who cannot even find house room for our own "unwanted children"?

Hospitality creates wealth, but it is a wealth unlike what we have come to know. Have you ever considered the fact that, measured by the sheer size of what she controlled, Mother Teresa was a millionaire and a world power? Generous to her full strength, like a mother. Unflinching in the expectation that she will be taken care of when need arrives. Ready to help the process along, when necessary, with a sharp tongue—the sharp tongue that goes with the generous keeper of an old fashioned, welcoming home.

The lordly virtue of hospitality is the king which, by right, rules its natural slave, the realm of economics. Once you admit this rule, all the good business practices return in their proper place. The tycoon cannot let himself be cheated out of his wealth, otherwise he will not be able to do his job when the time comes. You may be sure that Mother Teresa used every good management and accounting technique to organize her immense charitable enterprise.

So looked at from the outside, the rule of hospitality does not immediately differ from that of economic determinism. (And so it was in prewar Afghanistan.) But in the state of mind there is all the difference. Instead of the disposable slave waiting for the axe to fall, there is the hidden prince awaiting the moment when he will have a surplus to share with the objects of his generosity. And this works on every scale, from the largest to the smallest, from Ferdinand and Isabella exploring the world, to the least little mother feeding her baby.

Immanuel Kant and Economic Action

It is easy to be discouraged by the massive edifice of finance, which clearly dwarfs anything one worker can accomplish. Nevertheless it is true that the shining stream of money is less real than what it points to—the skilled man in the pickup truck, who is capable of fixing a toilet. Economic action must find a way to span this gap, if it is to be of any use.

As in politics and law, I proceed from the small. It is true that the Culture of Selfishness controls everything from the top down. The United Nations, for instance, is totally manipulated and tyrannical, deliberately insulated from all the popular pressure that can affect a democracy or even a dictatorship. We may neither collaborate with this corruption, like the liberals do; nor waste our effort trying to turn it from its nature, like the conservatives do; nor may we give up. For us the only possible way is from the bottom up, from our families and neighborhoods out.

The philosopher Immanuel Kant noted this basic law of morality: that we are to judge a proposed action, by asking how things would be if everyone did this same thing. The Kantian law of economic behavior is the same. Proceed as if millions are at your shoulder, like an immense chorus line, doing just the same thing as you. Not only justice, but economic power! And you would be surprised how literally true it can be at times.

And I set my sights high! "Have it all," indeed—why not spaceships plying the interplanetary lanes? And the Inn at Bree? And great art and song in all the cultures and languages of Earth? Lost arts reborn! Every city neighborhood and every rural village blossoming with quiet unheard-of work, so that beyond each hill there is really a new world. Welsh song in the backwoods of the Okanogan! Skyhooks! Housewives who are world-class scholars; monasteries and cathedrals; the Watts Towers gleaming in intricate enamel just a few blocks down crooked city streets.

They tell us all these things are economically impossible. Well, I have put down the notion of economic impossibility. That 500% surplus can bear fruit. Here is my list of rules:

1. No debt slave

2. Judging castles

3. The sacred purse

4. See to your family

5. The Jay Hoffman List

6. Support your village

7. Frustrate Chief Justice Marshall

8. Starve a rat

9. Free women!

10. There is time

11. Poetry and adventure shall rule

No debt slave

The financial manipulators "create needs" by advertising and promotion. Your life becomes an ever-hastening sequence of meaningless motions (earning and spending) so their numbers can spin faster. Your arms, legs, mouth, gonads twitch to serve them, and you are fed whatever tasteless gruel you choose. As Chesterton wisely pointed out, what the world calls "pleasure" is typically just expensive tedium.

Your duty is to be free, and that means free of debt. (The one case where that is almost impossible, they have us so neatly one step behind, is buying a house—so submit, and consider it rent. Do you know that Israeli families typically give their children a paid-up house as a wedding gift; and then the children use the money they would have spent on interest to get *their* children's houses?) You will find this debt freedom surprisingly easy to maintain. Real human needs are quiet and undemanding compared to the hype, and our economy is very strong, even in the current poor state of distribution.

Judging castles

There is no *automatic* guilt in being part of the modern economy and taking advantage of this odd state of affairs to amass some personal wealth. Accepting the boss's judgement on what is worth doing is right and honorable when you are accepting his nickel. The customary purchases of the rising American, though seriously flawed, still have their potential for good—if used right.

Here is an example. Medieval lords, like modern executives, had gates and guards to keep *hoi polloi* out of their upper class space. By their standards you can judge them all: When trouble came, according to the feudal rule, the gates did not swing closed. They swung open, and all the poor huddled peasants poured *into* the castle. The lord put all his power into defending them, and shared their fate.

Can our "gated neighborhoods" say as much? Too often their purpose is quite the opposite: to stay above the battle while the underclass goes to its fate alone. Your gate must swing open, when the crisis comes. Otherwise your lock and your heart are under the shrivelling curse.

The sacred purse

The Mexicans have not forgotten what all the peoples of Christendom once knew. The way to good fortune is to give to the poor. Tijuana street beggars dispense a blessing for each coin. They still throng the intersections and the borders, though the Tijuana city government, falling under the influence of American social workers, keeps trying to drive them into a social service ghetto.

America has gone wrong in this. Our streets should be more thronged with beggars than anywhere else, what with our massive superfluous wealth on the one hand, and our tremendous family breakdown and drug problems on the other. But our Calvinist policies have most effectively separated the crippled from the strong (that is the real purpose of welfare and social work), and so the curse has bitten deep into our shrunken hearts and stiffened families.

Have a change purse in a likely place, perhaps in your car. It is sacred to the poor, not to be plundered by your children for instance. It makes ready cash available for the real cripples as well as the enterprising car-wipers and the like. Don't leave your judgement at home—*food* instead of cash might help the liver of the "Will Work for Food" signbearer plying your intersection. But be there for whoever has hit a bad streak of luck, and watch what icebergs begin to break up in your own home.

See to your family

You are to help your family prosper *even if they betray you*. The dirty tricks that go on in custody disputes does not make you an ex-father or ex-mother. Do not let your generosity dry up because of the fear of being played for a sucker, or of having the "winning" traitor gloat over your position of disadvantage, or exploit you, or lie about you. You only get one of each of these children, and one lifetime in which to do your best for them.

The more firmly you are separated from your children, the more intent they are on every clue from you. Lies are a desperate defense against this, and children are surprisingly astute about them. The seed can fall in just a few moments, to outweigh the traitor's years of possession—if you do not fail to prepare the ground in what may seem an endless winter.

And for those with *happy* families—have I succeeded in convincing you of your blessing? Is it perhaps the fear of waste, of future disappointment, that is choking up your generosity? Then try for a pleasure that is not expensive tedium: watching your young grow in confidence and skill. Admire their sewing, their car and computer repair, their live translation, their artwork. Evade the youth-hating regulations that forbid them to work or drive. Entrust them with more and more of your family needs, and enjoy the long talks you have with them, as they fix what would have baffled you.

The Jay Hoffman List

The first precepts have taken an economic life for granted. Not so the next few. You can spread economic strength by your very existence. You, and those millions at your shoulder.

My friend Jay Hoffman has, during the dry years, found how to make his way with almost no income. He searches his network of family, friends and acquaintances to form his list. You must remember people with needed skills, especially creative and repair skills. You meet them on occasion in a long lifetime, and each such clue is a valuable piece of knowledge, in a world of deafening hype and mistrust.

The value of reliable information increases as language is cheapened. What persons are true to their word, even in such "small" matters as keeping an appointment? They are increasingly hard to find, when most people have conditioned themselves to say whatever brings a moment's advantage. If you don't know them, you can be left hanging in a moment of real need.

The list is not a private matter. People owe each other favors. Exchanging this seemingly humble information with other persons (met on other occasions in a long lifetime!) creates the foundation of a real economy. It does not take much to create a customer base. More years pass; times change; opportunity can knock (it can take no more than announcing the expertise to a receptive ear). In the meantime, Jay's list can make it possible to keep things in motion (cars are a good example) at twenty or thirty percent of standard expense.

Support your village

The other side of this is your exercise of economic power. You will have noticed that "Immanuel Kant" works a lot like voting. In a way it is better: your importance is more than proportional to your size, because you nourish what was marked for starvation by the Culture of Wealth. A loaf of bread is much more important to a hungry man than to an overfed gourmet.

I'm not talking about Hillary's slave village ruled by career social workers. Your village consists of people near you and people you know. They are not perfect. When Vickie proves enterprising enough to start "Vickie's Hot Meals Service" for shut-ins, you support her all the more because you know her past history. When you want some designer clothes, where better to get them than from the designer who lives down the street—the lady with a sewing machine, who has been making her little bits of artwork for years?

Think of how much money you spend on impulse purchases, on interest, on cheering yourself up when feeling empty. Channel just part of this toward the people near you who are trying to struggle up from slavery. The difference in price is tiny compared with the difference you (and your chorus line of millions) make toward these, your brothers and sisters in need. You will end up spending *less*—because their cleverness and skill is now on your side, finding ways to solve your problems that you never thought of.

J.R.R. Tolkien anticipated my message years ago: "Families for the most part managed their own affairs. Growing food and eating it occupied most of their time. In other matters they were, as a rule, generous and not greedy, but contented and moderate, so that estates, farms, workshops, and small trades tended to remain unchanged for generations." Ponder the connection between generosity and the little trades—it hardly fits WalMart! Where did we ever get the notion that cutthroat competition and bankruptcy for the small is better than this kindly state of affairs?

It is not often remembered that happy families can spring from broken ones, as well as the other way around. Many badly hurt persons are capable of protecting their children and building a better life for them—if given a little opportunity and aid. You have to work around the idiosyncrasies of the wrecked mother or father: the children will supply the affection. We once met a beautiful young college girl wiping cars in the Tijuana border wait. She told us she was filling in for her father who was sick that day. Did he rear and educate her on the proceeds of his cleaning rag? Then more power to him!

Frustrate Chief Justice Marshall

Chief Justice Marshall, in the early days of our country, said, "The power to tax is the power to destroy." (This is even more true of the power to regulate.) That has to be the point of view from the top. Under "good use", it is our job, and that of minor officials, to trip up Chief Justice Marshall. This is an exception to my principle of leaving the money matters to standard law. When law gets in the way of someone's need to make a reasonably honest living, it is everyone's duty to undo the law.

Safety, the environment, and various labor regulations are all to be winked at—when the endangered enterprise is small. This is a common occurrence in everyone's working life, even in America. The duty becomes more serious as the struggling little guys are pushed down harder.

In dealing (for instance) with cash contractors or illegal immigrants, the promoters of legalism, with their networks of informers, manipulate groups of low-income people with "Let's you and him fight" propaganda. There's always a reason why some other poor Joe, of another race or culture, is the enemy. Don't fall for it! Our job is to remember that "there, but for the grace of God, go I." Whoever rats on a harmless worker who is trying to feed his family is not a patriot but a traitor, and ought to be reprimanded and ostracized.

Starve a rat

More freedom for your conscience! Are you a little leery of applying the Feinstein response to a real human being, however deserving? Then do it to a *thing*—a corporation, massive and arrogant, that is guilty of an offense. Like Manville, which died for the offense of concealing the poisonous facts about its asbestos, a corporation can be killed without a qualm. No real human being goes down, not even any real wealth or skill is lost, it only gets moved around a little.

As a child, I was aware that all promoters and most of their "youth culture" meant to use me as a tool against my parents, to mock them and bleed them. I preferred my parents, who would come to my aid at 12:30 at night, to those rich dorks, who cared for nothing but my money and servility. On *that* one I was so right! When the corporations try to milk your family through you, turn it right around—be, with your family, a knife that cuts a hunk out of the corporations.

Boycott at the drop of a hat, even for offensive marketing—and boycott like a pit bull, with a death grip that never lets go. These are the people that campaign in Congress for slave labor, that wreck small businesses, that take amusement park money from the very families they mock and undermine, that poison little gully children when they can get away with it. The corporate culture is now so malignant that starving selected rats should be one of your main shopping activities.

This is the opposite side of supporting the village. Spread the word, get everyone involved. Be like an old fashioned citizen warrior. At peace till the moment comes for war, but when that moment comes—wreak merry slaughter, shout for joy, take pleasure in the wreckage! Their moneyed heights are a flimsy speculative scaffolding, and it does not take much of an earnings hit to bring them down in crashing ruin. It can be done—you will be surprised how easily. Look forward to the moonlight dance on the rubble.

Free women!

Once freed from the slavery to marketing, the family finds it needs to work fewer hours for money. Pulling an adult human out of the labor market starves a rat in another way. It creates a labor shortage, drives Greenspan nuts, forces up wage rates, sets even more slaves free. Not to mention clearing the freeways, making a home for the children, exercising family political power during working hours, and any number of other boons.

The freed wife (she had better shoot the TV and lose the shopping mall too, so she doesn't become a slave of another sort) is a mighty creative power who cannot be fenced in. I know this, because my mother was one, and my wife is another. Among all the little businesses and theaters and charitable works, just think of a single example: *real higher education*, liberal education, with no money motive, can be revived by freed women taking learned degrees. What a rebirth of knowledge and scholarship! What a subversive effect from new authorities who are not tied to anyone's purse strings.

This effect will snowball. The freed wife, gaining skill and transmitting it to her children, will soon have her man out from behind the eight ball. Before you know it, *he* will be starting his own business or studying or adventuring a new life. The old notion of retirement (the military model, closer to age forty than sixty) can come alive again once we break the stranglehold of compulsive consumerism.

There is time

I'll get back to this heading, and the next, in more detail at the end of the book.

Have you ever seen images of pre-industrial women behind spinning wheels, slowly making the thread which will clothe them? Did you imagine an intense frustration? Think: They had as many hours to pass (or to "kill," as we ominously say) as you or I. We stomp pedals or stare at a screen or huff and puff around a track. They spoke to their neighbors or sang to their children while, slowly but surely, a good and useful thing emerged from under their flying fingers. Just how is our way superior?

Making good things *that take time* is quite beyond the power of the "market economy". They have got to have it today—the stock market will stand nothing else. What takes time? Dreams, digestion, fruit trees, children, art, language, the Inn at Bree, good wine and good neighbor-hoods and skilled trades and learning—just about everything but compul-sive twitching—all of it belongs to our side. The word *cul*-ture refers both to civilization and to farming (agri*cola* = Latin for farmer), carrying with it the assumption that anything worth doing takes at least a year.

There is a more subtle advantage of time. This is the slowness that makes the world big again. That simple fellow, who doesn't stir outside his town but once a year—we need him, so that there really will be *different* towns, and not just a global village with most of us superfluous. Let the mystery of our neighbor, that really is always true, be made manifest. We can have a small horizon, and spend long years on our own project, and lack even superficial knowledge of his project, until the time is ripe.

It is so forgiving to realize that you have years, that you do not have to compete in speed. You can add just a little each day and within months you will have so much. Let the slaves twitch, twitch, as their TV screens flash from one demanding image to the next every second. And your poor little children should never have to race to excel like hapless Japanese suicide-track pupils. The Iowa wheat fields are pushing sunlight into bread grains for you. They are doing it *for* you!

Poetry and adventure shall rule

The "free market" system fails every test of the human spirit. Stephen Smith reminded me of the 1969 enthusiasm when we walked on the moon. He was sure that we would be having commercial tours there by now— and he should have been right. Instead we get telephones, video games, and self-worshipping new billionaires on Pressure Cooker Earth. What a triumph!

Even though its skyscrapers are still rising, this system is obviously junk. So bide your time in confidence. You are like a tiny wedge of ice in the stone. Your very existence, your resolute presence dooms the new creation *because it is inherently unstable.* Its exhausting compulsive activity, its lack of real pleasure, and its ruthless malice make it essentially inhuman and repellent.

Have the confidence of beauty, and always make poetry superior to economic efficiency. Small example: the English system of weights and measures must remain—because it is poetically better. (Did anyone ever sing about "a smile sixteen kilometers wide"?) In the same way, supposedly useless old crafts must remain alive. Many languages must flourish. Adventure on every level is needed for the poetry of life, and we will pitch in and make it happen.

Then, freed from the idiot selfishness, how mighty we will be. The space program, when it flourished, created $7.00 in value for every $1.00 that was spent. Just let us start doing that *everywhere*: every nation upon earth (and some that we thought had gone to Heaven), spending that 500% surplus on rockets or songs or inns or cathedrals. The glory is in the lack of efficiency, which is the generous freedom, which means the great world comedy is playing, and you have a part in the play.

Chapter 5

Sex

This is the harshest one of all. Any modern young man or woman is bristling with tough talk on the subject. Underneath is always the question: how do I find one? How do I find a real lover, not a cheat and a mockery? Where is real hope (not self-deception) for this basic foundation of most people's life all through the ages?

Revel for a moment in the irony. Health and freedom and untold wealth, rocket science and depth psychology, access to the entire world in a few hours, phones and lights and glittering cities. And yet the meanest slave, the poorest dirt peasant or windblown fisherman in some war zone or plague zone of the past, could take for granted what slips from our clutching fingers. Plain love and solid marriage, simple family permanence and watching the kids grow up. May you see your children's children, as the Bible says. Without a court order!

The terrifying part is that it totally depends on someone other than yourself. There is no hope that some form of training or strength or teeth-gritting determination, alone, will see you through to the happy ending. And such an approach obviously does not fit anyway. Harsh tools of conquest ought to apply to anything but love.

Yet they can be pointed somewhere else, to prepare the ground. Immigrant ancestors of ours often took upon themselves a bitter doomed life, so that their children could have a better one. They walked open-eyed into the poisonous mines and factories, clearing a space for the younger generation among schools and clean plots of earth. It could be this way for you, or it could be better. It is not true that you are powerless.

It is definitely not true that there is no way out of the present mess. Understanding is possible, if not politically correct. In this chapter I have to go beyond the bounds. I will not only show how they have wrecked sex—I will even deal with race, and explain "the plan" as it applies to black people.

I will draw from sources as diverse as Biblical wisdom and the Song of Songs, and Tolkien's letters to his son, and dark tales from the Soviet expansion. Also of course from my own experience and my wife's. Some of the material to follow is originally found in *It Is Not Good For The Man To Be Alone*, a pamphlet I wrote ten years ago, as well as other unpublished writings of mine.

Los Reyes

Our move to Tijuana was dictated by necessity, but it gave us a unique view on childrearing. It is not pristine, not the Swiss Family Robinson—nearer the opposite in external circumstances, a grab bag full of everything—and yet its effect was in a way pristine. The standard American influences were chopped off at the root (or, to be more precise, available only at second hand). Our little ones were loose in a mishmash of a world with everything from jailbirds to pious grandmas, but nothing dominating—except a very strong cultural imperative to protect women and children.

Where is the generation gap? It is nowhere. It is fun to watch your kids gain strength, like sturdy weeds in a vacant lot. Bad companions? Pretty weak, more like a chance for your children to gain judgement. We know now where the evil influence comes from, and it is not from your children's little friends. Don't look at the small neighbor standing outside your door. Look *behind* you—at your own home space, harnessed by the culture, like a virus-ridden cell.

Where are the terrible "birds and bees"? Where is the fear that your children will randomly turn gay? These are things that rack parents-to-be and fill up the advice magazines. They are nothing (as long as you strangle the American culture first). Your sons and daughters, growing up like weeds, will be sons and daughters indeed, long before the age of five. They leap onto their sex roles. You couldn't beat them off with a stick.

Little boys are little heroes as soon as they can grasp a toy gun. Fireman, the occupation of choice—rescuing people! Fight the evil enemy, kill, crush and destroy. Be sure to gross everyone out with the details. Learn chemistry to understand the details of bomb-making, and learn computers to understand the details of virus-making. The faster and more dangerous and destructive anything is, the better. Insults and physical thumps are the theme song of comradeship. "Gay" is the universal putdown.

Little girls are playing house, doing each other's hair, building families of dolls and kittens and teddy bears before you can yell "Clean your room!"

Every shared detail of *TV novelas* (or of neighborhood real life) is grist for their mill of human understanding. No birds and bees needed. The ancient, shaggy wisdom of Mom is sought in hushed tones whenever things get too deep for the childish councils. You have grandchildren before your little girl is six: huge, floppy, jealously named ragdolls.

The essence of little children's sexual development, as anyone can see with half an eye, is generosity. Ditch the accounting, whether it's orgasm cash or economic cash. Take everything in reverse time order, just as your children do. Babies and families come first, childbirth and pregnancy next, and sexual intercourse last. The shyness and embarrassment are protection for the secret adult taking shape: tear the shell open, and you wreck the developing being inside! The homeschoolers are right. Be a junkyard dog if necessary, but keep the geeks' hands off your teenagers.

Children's instincts can be well balanced, if unpressured by the lie machine. My son chose an all boys high school. Let each side of the sexual divide get a chance to develop in full. But it had an interesting side effect. It brought out, in full color, the way that the childish generosity carries on without a break into adolescence.

Single-sex Catholic schools traditionally go in boy and girl pairs. Thus Tom's high school, Saints, has a "girlfriend", Our Lady of Peace. They share some classes in senior year. More importantly (yes, I mean that), the girls' school supplies the cheerleaders for the boys' sports programs.

Cheerleading is something the feminists must hate with a passion, but they dare not touch it, it is far too strong. They would get smashed flat, as they deserve. You know it as soon as you see the mothers of the cheerleaders at games in their own old cheerleading uniforms, and the little sisters of the cheerleaders in tiny cheerleading uniforms laboriously sewn by hand. This is like aging men reminiscing about their years of war service.

The separation of the schools sheds light on this system's generous nature. The jumping girls are shouting the name of the other high school, not their own—and joyfully indeed, as you see with a glance at their faces. They droop and cry at a defeat too; that is part of the package. They say "Fight, fight, fight" and that is what it is. The boys on the field are in a comedy war, defending their loved ones. Often enough the comedy becomes reality, and boys and girls from the two schools marry each other. These games echo down their memories their whole adult lives as great good times. That is the way you can tell there is something right about them.

The fact is that this cheering and game-fighting is real sex for boys and girls of this age. It is sex adapted to their strength and state of mind, and it is generous. The afternoon latchkey parties with the condoms and the booze and drugs—those are not real sex, even though fucking happens (look at the faces afterwards, all sunken and sapped of joy). The partying is a stale mockery, and the young folks really know it, even as they do it.

The right way to look at it is this: sex *always* remains a subheading of heroism and generosity. To "sweep a girl off her feet" you must have strength to spare, which you donate to carrying her. The bride is a "little mother" before she is a mother: she babysat, and helped her family, and shepherded little children visiting her high school. Any shared effort, bazaar or college stage production, is fine, but there is nothing like helping at a charity or soup kitchen. He and she are shoulder to shoulder, more generous to make more real sex, even falling in love. The bridal reality can be found like turning a page, just that quickly. That is the way they did it in the old days, with arranged marriages and no fears about compatibility. Good-hearted comrades are always compatible.

The mighty sex drive of a young man does not stand alone. It is part of an all-out, mighty whole. He is really himself only when he is swinging a battle-ax or steering a 100 MPH behemoth. When you rescue a girl (yes, such incidents really do happen occasionally, even to the most "ordinary" man) you may notice afterward, almost as an afterthought, that your body is crying with sexual frustration. You passed it off without a thought because, for once, *all the rest of you* was just as mighty. All together now, getting the job done, and a tip of the hat to the bewildered girl, who just now is beginning to think of her own reaction to this rescue! It is comedy not commerce, and she is not allowed to pay. Let the impasse be. If anything is meant to happen, another time will come.

Boys and young men are built for a thunderous and roaring life. Any adventure story or Shakespeare comedy can teach us that. The resulting risks, which are great, are still less than the self-destruction that comes from a "safe" suspension of activity at just this moment of life. Our stupid leadership hates young men as a disruptive element. They never can figure that the young men themselves, with a terrified sense of duty, are internalizing 90% of the destruction and tearing themselves to pieces inside. Then on top of that they are hobbled, curfewed and punished for the paltry 10% that leaks out.

And young women: how dreary to train them for easy sex when they are built for a strong and terrible loyalty. Untapped! G.K. Chesterton remarked once that it was bad to hire women employees because they do their job too well, and begin to demonstrate a "wolfish wifehood" on behalf of the "invisible head of the firm". There was a story in *The Book Of Knowledge*, a twenty-volume set printed circa 1914 that I cut my boyish teeth on, that described a medieval woman whose husband was condemned to death in error. She walked a thousand miles through the snow to appeal to the King of England and saved him.

In my opinion, the most awesome berserker in all of literature is the Tolkien hero Éowyn, a young woman. Years of pure loyalty and love push her over the edge. No longer just a pretty blonde, but white to the lips and armed. "Flinch" is not a word in the Éowyn vocabulary. Read and ponder that character sketch in depth and then think about women you have known. What idiots the critics were who said that Tolkien knew nothing about sex! As if it all reduced to the heavy breathing of a pornographic novel.

And can such a woman be loved? Can a young man be king enough to turn that ice-blue sword maiden into a cuddly sweetheart and future mommy? The answer in the story is yes. And once again wisely. Every man has ten times as much kingship in him as he gives himself credit for. (I wish I had known it when younger: one poor despairing girl might have been much better off.) We are made to thunder. We lift her terrible strength in our arms.

There's a character I meet now and again in these 1990s. The grim young woman from a broken home, determined to turn it right for her children. She will have no defeatism. This fierce bride will look you in the eye and carefully recount her very first instance of obeying her husband. Just try a putdown. You will feel the lash of her tongue.

It nags at me: I met her somewhere long ago in a good book. Of course, Kate—from *The Taming of the Shrew*. Once again the idiot critics can't see it, and cringe with embarrassment at her final speech on obedience. Well, what did you expect? Trapped among wimps and manipulators, despairing of ever finding a way out, and here comes this fine tough sailor aiming just for her. Of course she will be on his side, now and forever! The only thing that really shook her was the fear that he wouldn't show. But he did. The rest is downhill for one of her mettle. She finally has her seat on the bus of comedy. And she though she never would.

Spanish fairy tales, read to me by my youngest daughter, speak of *Los Reyes* which when translated literally means "the kings". But in context that means a wedded pair, and in English we have to say "the king and the queen". I think the Spanish phrase does better, capturing the shoulder-to-shoulder strength of that mighty alliance and deep comradeship. You simply have no idea of your own strength. If loved, seize what is yours.

Viewing the Rubble

R.A. Lafferty invented the term *pornocracy*, meaning rule by sluts. As E. Michael Jones has documented, it describes the deepest essence of the American regime, which now (through agencies like the World Bank) is becoming the world regime.

The ruling sluts are aging men, Packwoods, who have to use strong measures to tweak their feeble gonads into functioning. This is why the rivals (young men) are shunted aside, kept eternally in college, paid poorly, trapped in debt so they can't spread their wings. All the favors—educational quotas, careers, medical procedures—are extended to young women.

Of course, favors are expected in return. It is taken for granted that the fresh women are destined for an environment (office, school) where young men are throwaways and the wealth and domination are in the hands of aging power figures. Usually male: but in all cases, desiring sexual services from fresh women.

You can tell even from the compulsory dress code. The skin display is required by senile sex, which needs a strong push to get it going. The young man doesn't need that stimulus, and will stay cooler without it! Friendlier to *him* would be long, flowing dresses such as medieval ladies wore.

This kind of "favor" is extended to whole races. E. Michael Jones has uncovered and documented the plan for black people. Tillich and others wrote this script, and W.E.B. DuBois protested against it. It is just this: a few decades ago, blacks were reclassified from cotton pickin' slaves to sexual slaves. They are on call for services to the masters, both male and female. And their pay is mighty damn poor—just look around.

The difference between me and Jones is that he shows some bitterness toward the black people, because of the way in which they permitted themselves to be used, while I sympathize with them (old friends of my wife, for one thing) and am more angry at the self-destructive fleeing whites. Who of us has not had the experience of being led down the garden path? It is really not a racial issue. There but for the grace of God go I.

You don't really need Jones to prove this to you. Just think of the stock phrase, which (as William Buckley says) can be typed by striking a single key on a liberal typewriter: "racism, sexism, and homophobia". Who is it that piggybacks support for abortion and perversion onto the genuine historical grievances of blacks? If you are a black activist like Jesse Jackson, who wants to play in the big time, you are required to toe the complete, three-part line.

In *The Destructive Generation,* Peter Collier and David Horowitz describe a rich white civil rights activist—who was a real woman, but you can take her as a fictional archetype if you want. The book destroys her name so I will not repeat it here. She cannot defend herself, being dead, and I wouldn't want to take for granted that what they say is fact about an individual. The point is that it is true of a whole class of people.

This activist is the ultimate filthy bitch—cheats on her husband, kills his baby, plays lesbian games and all. She makes Mad Bomber Bernadine

Dohrn look like a corn-fed Kansas sweetheart by comparison. She and her rich friends make a hobby of sexually exploiting black prisoners. The ultimate status symbol in her upper class circle is the Ku Klux Klan's nigger superfuck. Can a flimsy little pigwoman really exploit a big, muscular male prisoner? You bet she can!—and drag both of them down to degradation and death, as the story tells. A stud is a variety of slave—never forget it.

Check the records of any city. Whenever a new sex or contraceptive program is started, the pilot program is always at a high school with mostly black students. My wife had a black friend in La Jolla, and whenever she sent me to pick her up somewhere, everyone assumed myself + black woman = john + hooker. That included a couple of black teenage girls, at a home where she was picking up some clothes she left with a friend. Those girls gave me dirty looks which I could not figure out for a long time—they thought I was checking them out, as Hookers #2 and #3. White man bitten by racial stereotype!

The owners also use black people as a human battering ram, to smash the object of their most intense hate: the Catholic Church, which dares to tell them that what they are doing is wrong. It is true that the human battering ram gets beat up even worse than the broken gate, but they don't care. Again, black people are expected to remain on call, for the next campaign against polacks or micks. Watch which black activists get funded.

You will understand our rulers best if you remember they always have their hand in their pants. When they have worked their way through the Catholic girl Virginia (in the Billy Joel song), and the black woman and the black man, they go on and on, through AIDS and beyond, to virtual reality and vibrators and glossy beaver shots and cumm-covered TV screens and 900 number moans. All of this forms a seamless whole, and our owners will defend any part of it like junkyard dogs. For this is where their heart is, pumping what pale drops of blood they have left in their dry money veins.

So much for sources. They've had forty years to work, and the poison has branched out a lot since then. Can I touch all the evils even briefly? It is worth trying. Clarity is a start toward hope.

I'll start by flicking aside one false concern. Sexual function (or dysfunction) issues don't even get on the scale. The virgin bride and bridegroom both wonder: Will it work? Will I make a fool of myself? The answers are Yes and Yes.

Now go on to a real issue: the fear of what can be done to you. I peel open parts of your mind that, perhaps, you did not want to understand clearly. There is a saving virtue to ignorance sometimes—a kind of veil over the eyes. Here are two stories to illustrate it.

One day in La Jolla, a girl was raped in broad daylight across the street from our house. Our neighbor to the south actually witnessed it but did not understand what he saw. He thought the man had helped the woman into a car. When he found out later, he was furious with himself. My wife went to Lincoln High School in Seattle, and she found that black men have a cultural thing about protecting women (good for them!). So this man had missed his big chance to break a blond rapist into pieces on the spot.

When the Child Protective Service grilled my wife in our home, I took it for a standard bureaucratic hassle. It was only later on understanding her response that I realized it was an official rape. You don't string up and cut open a mother that way. We left the country, if only to give ourselves time to cool off. Not. Looking back from seven years distance, I only pray that God preserve me from meeting such a social worker in action again, because if I do, I'll grind her face into the pavement.

Why then remove this protective veil? Because it is too late for peace. The masters had their chance to listen to people like Joan Andrews and the women in Pittsburgh, and look how they treated them. They are obdurate. No use protecting them from the consequences.

The main problem with sex these days, dear young man and woman, is that love is severely punished. This may be some comfort. It is enemy action.

What happens at the end of a marriage? Whoever is most vicious and unloving wins in court. For example, it is now standard operating procedure to use false accusations of sexual abuse as a tool in custody disputes. It is then legal to treat the "paper rapist" inhumanly.

This contrasts with real rapists, who know their rights and are treated with kid gloves. They are useful to the people in power. When the social workers force young parents to take "parenting classes" under threat of kidnapping their children, they may put one real babyraper in the class and have him gloat over his exploits while the normal parents are forced to listen. This is to train the normal parents that they are equivalent to the rapist. It is an axiom of legal kidnapping that everyone is as filthy as everyone else, except for the officials in charge, who have the right to trample the powerless as a winemaker crushes the grapes.

Parents who take those classes report that they come out feeling physically dirty. Many of you will know what that is a symptom of. I am glad that I refused (at some risk to our family) to let my wife take the class. There might have been violence done.

The child abuse system punishes only lovers, who are the only ones who are hurt when their families are broken up. (Real butchers and rapists can always pick up another kid somewhere, they are all the same to them.) The legal kidnapping system is everywhere corrupt and irredeemable for the same reason as torture: only insane people and perverts want such a career. Of those, the insane people (who take it for granted that all parents are abusers) are easier to deal with, because they may still be goodhearted deep down.

When spoken to in a firm voice, the insane social workers will usually wander off. The perverts are more tenacious, since it is actually their pleasure to ruin families. In the notorious Alicia W. case in San Diego, they spent a year brainwashing a girl until she falsely accused her father of rape (physical evidence proved him innocent). When this came out they were unrepentant and unshaken: the same brainwashers are still in office, and now have more powers and greater discretion.

The child abuse system protects and makes use of secret informants (which are unconstitutional, but nobody cares). In this respect it is only part of a greater whole. Children are trained to rat by their schools, by feuding camps of divorced parents, by TV ads braying about hotlines. In fact the essence of law, as it affects ordinary people, is to gain advantage by reporting on someone else. Honesty and courtesy lose.

A little relative, only ten years old, was staying with us one summer. For the first few days he would report on his mother as if by reflex. My wife would always reply, "I'm not Lexine, I don't care!" In the clean air of Tijuana, he finally got the American rat vapors out of his system—for a while. When he got home, he reported on us to his mother.

Do you know that the whole child abuse system, with its protected informants and hatred of intact families, started with the old pro-abortion slogan, "Every child should be wanted"? It all makes logical sense. Those who kill their children need to punish those who let their children live. You need to know what you are up against, and how powerful the real enemy is, and why she hates you.

They have a trap called "privacy" which eats teenagers alive. Recently we got a call from a teacher saying that our son was in danger of failing a required course. He had not turned in an assignment which (he thought) required him to interview a stranger on a personal matter. He had not even mentioned the problem to us. Such is the power of embarrassment over an adolescent.

High school counselors know how to lock a pregnant girl in the trap of her own embarrassment, isolating her from all aid, while they slowly induce despair in her and guide her toward an abortion. The counselors are professionally trained in closing off all options of hope in the girl's mind, as a murderer would seal every chink in a closet so as to suffocate someone inside. You may be sure that this has happened to many of the women you know. If you could see into their hearts you would see the gaping bomb craters, the hag-torn scar tissue and unwashable hands like Lady Macbeth. You have these counselors to thank for poisoning your generation.

If you think that the United States makes war only against teenage girls, you may get a rude surprise. The United States makes war against anyone who loves. One *San Diego Reader* cover showed a reproduction of a local tagger's under-the-bridge artwork, a large image of a baby picture that had been torn in half. They interviewed the artist and found that some time before, he had made his girlfriend pregnant. Despite his pleas, she had listened to advice and aborted his child. This artwork—which evoked anger and opposition from the advocates of personal freedom—was his way of working out his bitterness and grief.

Follow this reminiscence by Mary Ann Kuharski in a letter to *Fidelity* Magazine (October, 1987):

> ... In one circumstance, I talked a runaway couple back to Mom and Dad. In fact, I escorted them home and helped break the pregnancy news. Both the young girl and guy begged me not to—so set were they (after a classroom presentation on abortion) against abortion, and so sure were they that their parents would insist she have an abortion. My trust and naivete were crushed the following morning when the young father called and tearfully described the abortionist who came out to the girl's home and took her off to the clinic, after refuting my "distorted lies"...

This is enemy action, and it serves as quite an incentive to stay shut up inside your clamshell. Just so you know why you find yourself feeling that way. In the words of Procol Harum in their song *The King of Hearts* (from the album *Prodigal Stranger*, Chrysalis Songs), you become

> The King of Hearts no more
> But King of the Brokenhearted

Defense of the Hearth

It has always been known, even by the ancients, that a man has to be willing to die in defense of his hearth. Farmers fought for ancient Rome, medieval village boys met the Vikings at the gate, Yankee settlers responded to Paul Revere. The willingness to die has to come *before* love. In fact it has to stand before and behind and on all sides of love, because without it the love nest is merely food for the biggest predator.

This is real, as the preceding section ought to make clear. It is unlikely that you will have to kill a legal kidnapper to prove your love for your wife and child, but you should certainly be willing to do so. There is to be no flinching here, not by you. That is the only way you can look a good woman in the eye.

There is no guarantee either of victory or of happiness. As long as you sign yourself off as dead, right at the beginning, every better outcome can be counted a gain. To put it bluntly, a man is expendable, but there are things he does not have to tolerate.

Rape is one. The defense, in the Kurt Matthews murder case, said that he killed his girlfriend's mother because the mother was dyke-raping the girl. If true (and of course the mother was not there to speak in her own defense) then he should have got a medal. Instead he got the "poor man's life sentence"—death. I cannot judge the facts, but it was noteworthy that the prosecution claimed in response to the girl's complaint that the single mother was "lonely".

If that sort of thing is really being done to your lover, it should not matter much to you whether you get death. But use some wisdom anyway, to improve your chances—just to annoy them. Don't loot the place, as Matthews did: that makes the Sir Galahad motive hard for the jury to believe. You've got a message to deliver, not just a blow. Leave the rapist's stuff alone.

Don't romanticize a job like this. Rightness yes, victory maybe, but happiness very unlikely. Have you ever wondered about Sir Galahad himself, the Virgin Knight, pure, in shining armor? Never wanted a woman, but went around killing perverts and oppressors? I'll bet something pretty hideous happened in his childhood, to burn him out from day one.

There's another thing to watch out for: your friends and comrades, the men all around you, and your leaders. How about defending some stranger's hearth against all of them? It can happen in a flash. The fate of a woman can lie in the palm of your hand—a deadly test indeed.

I remember, in the last days of the Soviet Union, reading about the terrible self-destructive alcoholism epidemic there, so bad that life expectancy was actually declining. The explanation came to me suddenly, in words recalled from Solzhenitsyn's *The Gulag Archipelago* years before. He was describing World War II from the Soviet side. Among the rules of engagement (as we would call them) was one brutal detail: German girls could be raped and shot.

There you are, just an ordinary farm boy, free to do this thing, ready to join the gang, and with a captured girl in your hands. What a vicious trap! You better be man enough to protect her. Otherwise that dead girl will walk beside you for the rest of your life. And how are you going to get away from her?

It was in the 1970s that the wave of aging Soviet men was drinking themselves unconscious, drinking themselves to death, dragging the life expectancy into its negative curve. The very same men who saw action at the front thirty years before. And not long afterward, the Soviet Union itself choked on its own self-hatred and died.

So much for the easy cases. What happens when the Government declares genocidal war on your family? Mrs Kuharski's young man made his quixotic stand and was crushed. But look steadily even at his defeat.

In the ruins we discover certain essentials. He is the head of his family, even though his child is dead meat down the garbage disposal, and his child's mother is a traitor. That kingship he earned in battle and paid for with his heart's blood. In this he differs from the ones who gave up ahead of time and did not try to meddle. The ruined community is still a community, which is more than legal America can say for itself.

When America declares that young families can be raped and snuffed, it is not community, but the absence of community. The overburdened losers go to the wall! This is Hobbes' war of all against all, with the added insult that the wreckers have the color of legality on their side.

Law—no-fault divorce, legal abortion—is the tool used by the strong to peel off and dump the weak. The rights of the strong are like armor plate, while the rights of the weak are like eggshells: one crushes the other. Counselors stand ready (it is their bread and butter) to enable the powerful to dump the powerless: aging wives, unwanted children, jobless husbands.

Law is the tool to destroy burdensome community. As Mrs Kuharski found out, it is practiced swiftly and effectively. And yet in so doing, its practitioners destroy its foundation, in a very specific way: alienation. This is not some hippy dippy feeling. It has a precise meaning, expulsion from citizenship.

And having alienated the father and his family, the United States, in each case, makes treacherous and unjust war upon them. Just like Nazi Germany raping Polish girls. And every American who upholds the legitimacy of United States law is complicit in this unjust war. Just like the "good Germans" to whom we habitually feel so superior. As citizens of the oppressor, we have no right to complain, whatever that father does to us or to our country. Any more than a citizen of Nazi Germany could complain about being caught in the crossfire from an aggrieved Jew.

The heartbroken king, therefore, is a rightful outlaw and has freedom of action. What a price he has paid for it. There is not much that the rest of us can say to him. He may wish to remember Gandalf's words:

> Many that live deserve death. And some that die deserve life.
> Can you give it to them? Then do not be too eager to deal out
> death in judgement.

Or he may not.

I urge only one thing: no violence against the lover, even though she is a traitor. His job of protecting her remains. Maybe she was more done to than doing. Here are two stories from my wife's side.

When my sister-in-law was a student at Thompson Junior High School in north Seattle, she once heard a commotion in the parking lot. She found a classmate of hers struggling against her mother, crying out that she did not want the abortion. The mother shouted for help, and four young men that she had brought with her proceeded to hog-tie the girl and throw her in the back of a truck. My sister-in-law tried to interfere but was no match for them. Money was served; the girl came back shattered. Later, according to my wife, two of those young men were lost in suicide games that were popular among Seattle youth at that time.

According to some Australian researchers, three of eight (37%) of the women who have abortions try at the last moment to back out, and have to be tricked or forced to finish the operation (*National Right to Life News*, June 6, 1989). Visiting the rest room at Lincoln High School in Seattle when she was a student, my wife encountered the corpse of one such girl hanging from a ceiling pipe. This girl had asked for help a few days before, but had been forced to go through with her abortion. Such events are the everyday reality behind the wave of young suicides that belies the facade of American well-being.

The main thing is to pray to God, and to order your life, so that no such horror is ever likely to enter it. And with good fortune it can be so (it has been, thus far, for my family). That leaves only the smelly detritus of family problems that affect everyone in America: divorce, drugs, emotional collapse and insanity, juvenile delinquency and the like. Here we are dealing not with the malice of the law, but with its incompetence.

Family court judges are not always bad hearted. They are always overwhelmed. Because marital treason (divorce) is the standard and lies are rewarded, there is no justice even when the authorities try to do right. This is because there is no information to base justice on.

The reality, therefore, is a kind of nasty anarchy in which the law's actions are like random raids by a foreign occupying force. There is no use looking for betterment from that source. Have the mental strength to simply abandon hope for law to right family trouble. Fight the guilt twitch which responds to news of some disaster by making a new legal gesture.

In the affairs of your own family, you have tremendous power. Use it for justice—taking over the duties of the crippled vows and the crippled laws. Grandparents and others must insist on justice even against their own children. Always keep the door open for the "return to the nest", one of the best and most generous features of American family life in this sad chaos.

Grant goodwill as much as possible in family affairs. It is terrible how often this cooling step is neglected. For instance, when the authorities grab a child from his mother and give him to his father (or vice versa), people tend to treat it as a real snatch, worthy of blood feud. It is not! The kid is still with his parent(s), and no irreparable damage is done! Remembering such a simple point can save much unnecessary suffering.

Coldly discourage ratting, except for open declarations facing the accused. Have the mental strength to take the guilt hit for those few who would have been saved by cowardly informers. (They are fewer than you think: how often is it really that *no one* else knows of the trouble?) Ostracize informers, and blow their secrecy. This is like a great sewage cleanup, that will help us all when we act together to finish it.

There is only one real cure, and that is true loyalty by all family members. This goes on independently of marital happiness, which is quite overrated. Nobody has that pink cloud expectation of any other important task, at work or at war, for instance. But steady loyalty is needed everywhere.

For the young man who proposes to defend his hearth in the ancient fashion, that is the first thing to look for in a lover. And here, after all the wretchedness and misery of the past two sections, there is a glimmer of hope. Because women, given half a chance, are great at just this virtue. Wives and mothers of generations past, women of your own family tree— just look at their stories. Hope indeed!—but only after the other false hopes of our rotten law and culture are abandoned by you and by your bride.

Population Control

The previous sections were a kind of surgery or pruning, to cut away the false and poisonous growths which parasite off sex and love in our culture. I want to have the man and woman alone with their God-given powers. But there is one last chain attached to their very gonads, a thing that clamps onto his balls and her ovaries, without which they are both afraid to move.

A few years ago, I remember reading, a couple tried going back to nature to see if they could survive with nothing. This was not just a camping trip: campers typically take packs full of tools that were hardly available to cavemen. These people spent a year on a deserted island without any of the technological doodads that we think we need.

Except one. They had a supply of contraceptives.

Because of our separation from the land, the American human being is now a helpless potted plant instead of a hardy weed. It is simply inconceivable for most of us to approach a member of the opposite sex without the backing of the manufacturers and marketers of contraceptives. Sex is a private matter between a man, a woman, their doctor, their pharmacist, and their rubber seller. Most people do not realize the mind-bending power of this total dependency.

It used to be said that Ronald Reagan was "the Teflon president", because scandals and disputes that would have damaged another did not stick to him. Well, population control is the 100% Teflon political movement. Because of everyone's personal terror of being deprived of their product, they and everything they do is absolutely above criticism. We are not free until we break that taboo.

The scene is pretty ugly once you do that. Here are found the nastiest masters in corporate America, the ones who directly control the sexual slaves and are free to lie and poison people because their product is so needed. If you doubt me, talk to someone (especially one young and attractive) who has dealt personally with heavyweights of the news and entertainment industries, major supporters of population control. "The honeymoon comes first," one said to me, "the marriage later—maybe."

Years ago, a strange disorder was noted among some Puerto Rican girls: precocious maturity, like a five-year-old menstruating and looking like a tiny sex model. People waved their arms about the great genetic mystery, carefully refusing to notice the contraceptive manufacturers who were pouring huge amounts of sex hormone effluent into the local water supply. Even after someone called them on it, they simply shut down the investigation and went on doing it. Teflon.

Laws against child abuse, in states such as California, make an exception for contraceptive suppliers. When babyrapers bring their sex slaves in to be refitted, the suppliers are allowed and encouraged NOT to report the offense. Some cases of this have come to light after years of such a cozy relationship.

The counselors who enforce despair on pregnant teenagers are usually supplied by Planned Parenthood and similar agencies. A decade ago the movie *For Keeps* depicted a pregnant girl who rejected abortion and her selfish parents, recovered the baby's father and married him, and ended happy in her poor but proud household of three. This movie was merely a commercial venture playing to a certain market, but it breached the wall of despair, which must be impermeable to get the job done.

It was briefly popular, but was soon blackballed due to Planned Parenthood's nationwide campaign against it. They even forced the star, Molly Ringwald, to do public penance. I noticed long afterward that it was still popular as a video rental: the censorship against hope was not quite total.

The organization called *Catholics for a Free Choice* has nothing to do with Catholics, but is a corporate outreach, funded by the same people who sponsor Planned Parenthood. Its function is to control the gonads of the poor dark-skinned natives of foreign countries with a Catholic heritage. It does this by spewing filth on their popular pieties. A typical project was a pamphlet handed out to Brazilian girls, which said that in Luke 1:26-38, the Angel Gabriel was offering the Virgin Mary a chance to have an abortion.

The real Catholics (like the National Conference of Catholic Bishops and Father Paul Marx's *Human Life International*) keep tabs on these guys and continually expose them as frauds. Their efforts never catch up with the damage, because they cannot stay ahead of the avalanche of corporate money.

Pro-Familia (sic), the German affiliate of Planned Parenthood, mounted a hate campaign (1987) against Mother Teresa, calling her "nightmare of women" and "puppet of the devil". Their reason, openly stated, is that she fed the poor and clothed their nakedness, thus permitting them to stay on the population rolls.

The fact that nasty people run the population control movement will come as no real surprise. It may give some support to the pristine feeling of violation felt by the teenager who hates putting the dirty things onto her body. But it is not enough by itself to answer the points the controllers make. The rest of this section is devoted to that.

There is an inescapable mathematical logic to their position. Malthus, two centuries ago, claimed that population increases geometrically (or as an exponential function) but resources increase only linearly. His prediction has proved wrong since then, and he is put down as a doomsayer. But taking the long view reveals that he is an optimist.

There is nothing but technology to sustain that linear increase, and it must ultimately run up against shortage of raw material—no increase. But nothing stops an exponential function. Even if it is a slow one (like 5% per generation), it is easy to calculate the time when every square foot of Earth's surface will have one person, and nobody can take a breath. It is surprisingly short, something like 6000 years—no longer than the span of time from the beginning of written history until now.

The interesting thing is that the analysis does not stop here. Another 3500 years and 1000 people are standing on each others' shoulders on each square foot of land. As P.G. Wodehouse remarked in one of his novels, it then gets pretty squashy for the ones on the bottom. This situation is literally impossible—or if not it, then some later one, when all the carbon and hydrogen have run out.

In the language of logical proof, this is a *reductio ad absurdum*. It simply proves that exponential population growth cannot exist—and it proves it equally well if every family has ten children. In fact it goes beyond that, and proves that (in the long run) population growth itself cannot exist: it is asymptotically bounded above. There is a "roof" which it cannot pass.

Thus in propounding the Malthus theory, the population control people are actually cringing away from something even more scary, which is the nature of that roof. The advantage that 1990s people have over earlier generations is that we are no longer so terrified of these implications. Things have become pretty dry and dusty, and not many of us believe in the happy ending any more. A big disaster will not do much to *further* break our hearts.

So take a ruthless look at the possibilities. The first thing to notice is that the controllers' solution of zero population growth is completely unrealistic. Human beings are not like cement filling a mold. Each person is the subject of his own story, moving his world, going forward or back. There is no motive for a static one child per parent going on unchanging forever.

The population stasis birth rate (about 2.1) acts like an unstable equilibrium—an egg standing on its end. In real countries, the population is either increasing (Mexico, India) with a birth rate well above 2.1, or it is dying off (Germany, Japan) with a birth rate well below 2.1. In some countries like the United States this is disguised, because one subculture (immigrant) swings to the positive side while another subculture (affluent) swings to the negative side. The result looks like stasis but is really a massive shift.

When people feel purpose in their lives—feel that they are moving their world—they enjoy expanding this kingdom among many descendants. People suspended, however comfortably, in a purposeless vacuum have no need to pass this nothingness on to (expensive and troublesome) children. 2.0 is then better than 2.1, but 1.0 is better than 2.0 and 0.0 is better than 1.0. This is the tragedy of Europe, especially Germany and Russia, whose people feel that their history is behind them.

The demographic transition does not come from the end of resources. It is almost always accompanied by an *increase* in per capita wealth. It comes from loss of touch with the land, the end of frontier and colonization and enterprise for ordinary families, the closing in of the walls around a city life of meaningless motion and passive manipulation. People are no longer needed so, after a little delay, they die off.

What this means is that the roof is not 6000 or 9500 years away. It is quite close. A great flood tide is turning into a great ebb before our very eyes. There certainly is no need to *help* population control along—as if you were to help the sun set.

I will present three simple models that between them will sketch this sea change to the mind's eye. One is of ordered decline, one of continued increase and one of disordered decline. It makes no sense to consider any of them either more desirable or more likely than the others. We need to discipline ourselves and apply "desirable" and "likely" only to real individuals and families to whom we can reach out today—and let God handle the rest. Besides that, reality is likely to prove to be a combination of all three.

The first model I may call the Tasmanian model, after a race which was so impressed by the superiority of the invaders that they simply failed to have a next generation. If you complete the logic of what is happening in Europe this is what you get.

It is not quite true that a whole people can be without purpose. Even with a super-efficient economy and no external goal, there remains one thing: filial piety. The younger generation gains purpose from the needs of their retired and dying elders. This provides full employment for a generation of a certain size.

Imagine farming even more advanced than now, so that 2.4% of the population total can provide all the needs of the others. Imagine another 2.4% functioning as nurses for the aged (not unrealistic for rest home and hospice care), passing out mush and orange juice, emptying bedpans, listening to reminisces, burying the dead. This means there has to be one person of the active generation for each twenty persons of the retired generation.

If one couple out of ten has one child, the rest none, this system provides full employment and genuine purpose for all the active generation. The retirees have leisure to record their stories of the old days when there was something to do. A projection of the population of the active generation follows, if the whole world were to swing this way a couple of decades from now:

2025	8,000,000,000
2050	400,000,000
2075	20,000,000
2100	1,000,000

This restores Earth to the density of Eriador in just a few years.

The second model, of increase, must be combined with migration away from the cities or it does not work. A new frontier. If the skyhook is found, or even if not, why not reach for the stars? Then even for those left behind, there is more room—more room in the mind, because everyone can understand the broadening of possibilities.

A similar feeling of increase is possible if the Earth's countryside is rejuvenated. The Europeans are currently missing a huge opportunity, with the reopening of all the old Soviet lands—a bigger frontier than America ever knew. Generous participative art on the local level (inn, theater, cathedral over every hill) can bring the village back up to stature and crisscross the landscape with connections that employ everyone. This ends the claustrophobia without need of physical space.

We are not really crowded yet: we crowd ourselves. The countryside is everywhere being deserted, as people huddle in the cities. Only a few miles from daily traffic jams, there are freeway call-boxes so that motorists stranded in deserted areas can get help.

The things people make crowd us more than people do. A single affluent American generates more garbage, clutter, and carbon dioxide than any fifty traditional Asian farmers with their water buffaloes. Far better than world population as a measure of crowding is world real GNP. This goes hand in hand with migration to the city, and with the increase in communications which creates a "global village" that devalues all real villages.

Suppose you have a world whose population is doubling every 40 years. Add these other effects, making the world "shrink" every 40 years by a factor of 10, and accelerating. Then the crowding doubles every 9 years—and the crowding accelerates even if the population growth is tailing off. This more closely fits the common experience (at least of urban Californians) and explains the popularity of the notion of "population explosion". And that brings us—more quickly than we may expect—to the third model.

There is an old saying: "God forgives always, man sometimes, nature never." Looking at things from nature's point of view, we are like field mice or weevils that leave the hardscrabble existence on the land to converge on some silo or restaurant where the stuff is abundant. We proliferate but our life is increasingly artificial. We are all crawling on top of each other.

Nature, or the restaurateur or farmer, cheers this development because it makes his task so easy. Tenting solves the problem. Our large biomass means nothing to the exterminator, our closeness to one another is everything to him. Many generations of increasing prosperity come to an end in a single day.

It could be something as predictable and banal as those millions of Chinese surplus males using the technology we are giving them to launch an all out war. (Perhaps this is already secretly being threatened: extortion would explain our military giveaways and one-sided trade deals with that nation.) It could be as odd and peaceful as the vision of one science fiction author, of everyone hooked up to virtual reality machines—followed by a massive failure of the life support.

How about AIDS III (spread by sneezing)? Or a lot of suitcase nukes? Up until now terrorists have had an incredibly polite and constructive attitude, never using the full power of technology in the way that we expect computer virus writers to do. This could end any time. And you don't even need that much. Plain cheap riot and murder can do the job (our rioters have been incredibly polite too—take a look at Africa sometime). And nature hasn't had her innings for a long time—say, Spanish flu?

It will probably be something we haven't even thought of. The important point is, we are ripe. This is the real meaning of the drug crisis, and the deep down reason why the authorities are so panicked by it. A good, solid two-figure percentage of the population does not care whether they live or die. They are already dead at heart, and just have not stopped breathing yet. It makes our masters frantic because they cannot control it, even among their own families. It is destroying their whole world from the inside with the inevitability of termites.

As I told my children years ago, the extermination of the Canaanites by the Hebrews (or the extermination of the Carthaginians by the Romans) was not so painful an atrocity as it sounds. The doomed cities had been burning their children to Moloch for years. Their wealth was built on the cauterized hearts of hollow mothers. Filled with the ghosts of children's playmates, and the echoes of your little brother's screams as he slipped into the maw of the god. I guess they were actually relieved to be put to the sword.

Returning to my birthplace in Seattle a decade ago, I found my old Catholic school, Christ the King, still alive and active. But the public school, Broadview, which was nearer my home, was abandoned—a block wide wasteland of fences and weeds where once there were children playing. Were the ghosts of dead babies wandering there, looking for a teacher? Later they razed the place and replaced it with yuppie shops.

It reminds me of a Robert Frost poem about a heartbreak that every generation before our time had to suffer: the burial of their little children in the family plot. We alone have been freed from this, and where is our rejoicing? Our children are saved from death so we kill them. You cannot get more ominous than that. As the Spanish saying goes: "Take what you want, says God—and pay for it."

So much for models. They ought at least to relieve you of guilt about moving the world with *your* children, whether or not you are "unemployable" or "underclass". But reality is likely to be more complex.

I have a custom of meeting my wife for dinner on Thursdays before choir practice. She awaits me at the Santa Fe Depot, an active railway terminus. There she frequently sees Mennonites—in full homespun dress, speaking German—on the move from somewhere in the East toward some unspecified destination to the North. These are people who still have ten children in a family, and they seem to be filtering out of their accustomed lands. It creates an eerie feeling of silent motion in the dusk. The countryside is not being left all empty.

The wrong-way lemming gets no news coverage, but lives. Who knows how many of these little oddball migrations are going on? You have no idea how big the land is, and how far the back roads can go. The woods hippies for instance are alive and well, maybe in the millions. They simply moved away around 1970 and never came back.

The wrong-way lemming must both reject the culture and (at least with part of his family) return to the land. If he rejects the culture and the land both, he is still suspended economically among the meaningless machinery, and can hardly avoid sharing its fate. If he only returns to the land, like a rich exurbanite, his children will orient by his cultural compass and go back to the living center of his past.

If you are not part of the culture you do not have to associate your own childbearing and your own family with either the population growth or the population crash of the culture. You are of another world. (They have conveniently abandoned most of the land to your other world.) We have been readied for this too: the attraction of the "bright lights" to our children is pretty much cancelled. It is now mostly fear that keeps us here. To fear there is a simple answer, long known to the much-scorned Russians with their family garden and pig: autarky and subsistence.

The same year marks both your small seedbed and their churning cesspool. But it is as if you were later in history, looking back—King Arthur looking back at falling Rome. It is sucked down like Carthage to its noisy end, and you, like those durable Mennonites, follow another path.

It is an immense relief to be freed from population guilt (like environmental guilt). This turns out actually to be a greater burden than poverty. Without needing to apologize any longer, you can make shift like so many generations before you, and enjoy the years-long process of getting acquainted with your young army. To *little* children, an extended family in a rural setting provides an endlessly interesting life.

Hot and Cold

Now that, as I hope, I have the man and woman alone and stripped of their chains, we can deal with the fact that it is not all a cultural problem. No indeed! Not since Adam and Eve shared that apple. So the last two sections of this chapter will relate (mostly) to the man and to the woman, respectively.

The beauty of ditching the culture is that now you have all the cleaner cultures of the past to help you. People have been dealing with this problem for thousands of years and have fine, fine thoughts—from Confucius to Shakespeare, from *The Arabian Nights* to Dante—you can immerse yourself! Even quotes from the Bible can function as advice to the lovelorn. Perhaps it is a function that would embarrass St Paul or Solomon, but I'm going to stick them with it.

And what does Dickson have to add to all these? Not much, except maybe to make some connections. So let me do that. Here I focus on the young man as male, snorting with readiness, capable of cornering some unspeedy female and fathering an unscheduled heir.

War brides: they were a commonplace for returning American soldiers at the end of World War II. They may be in your family tree—your own grandmother. But look closely and you find no commonplace at all, not like the standard marriage we expect. Take a closer look at 1945.

A war bride is a hapless girl picked up among the ruins, lifted out of the fire, like the girl in Jules Verne's *Around The World In 80 Days*. She is in fact the better flip side of that Soviet rule of engagement I mentioned above. The magnanimous American soldier (unlike his leaders) covered himself with glory in that war, and blessed our country for a generation. The noble Marshall Plan was a slam-dunk for a nation with that fire, and elbowed aside the Morgenthau Plan that expressed our leaders' deadly spirit. And those war brides were one slice of Germany that did not wither. Their children still abound.

A war bride does not worry about whether she has rights, any more than a happy child does. She exults in being precious to this man who carried her away from the fire. Usefulness is no part of it—he has to teach her word by word a new language. Someday, at whatever homestead they end up in (better than seared rubble), she will be surrounded by children that look just like her. An improvement on the Soviet story—disfigured dead meat on a temporary barracks floor.

That is what you are made for: carrying a bride. Quickie sex does not satisfy, though the whole life of devotion can start quickly. Why then the wasteful and frustrated impulses? Did God make a lousy design? Remember you have been lied to—but the lies have a kernel of truth. Hookers exist everywhere, in all cultures.

Every man has a self-contradictory personality. Intensely prudish as well as intensely horny. The first impulse (denied in our culture) is very powerful and dangerous too. It is why a man often rejects the woman after sex. Sometimes after a rapist has done his thing, he will be filled with disgust and resentment at the woman he has just raped (how unjust can you get), and take it out on her. That is what lies behind those wrenching headlines like "Girl's body found."

I never understood this conflict until years later when I took Lamaze classes with my wife so I could be present and assist at the childbirth. It is true that all parts of sex and childbirth, though vastly different in shape, are made of the same cloth, like a business suit. Well, a woman having a baby struggles for hours beforehand with "contractions". They are painful, frustrated childbirth motions by her body, which do not push the baby out, but only stretch her womb into shape so that she can later do so.

The frustrated single man's impulses are the same. They even hit hard and later go away, just like contractions. Why two contradictory impulses? Because they are *meant* to be frustrated—he is still far too resentful of women to let one into his life. And what are they stretching into shape? His personality, of course—and hers.

"It is not good for the man to be alone," says God (Genesis 2:18). Every frustrating collision brought about by those 9 PM impulses of his leads to a new acquaintance, or new understanding of an old acquaintance. It all seems pretty dangerous—the consequences of a misstep!—but haven't we noticed before that contempt God has for danger? And it does force you to think about the well being of another human being. You can sure get her in a mess, can't you?

After a few years of this you may really want to carry away a bride (not just ride her one night and sneak away anonymously next morning). Then just do it—you wish! It is here that the enemy action comes in. They have sawn off your economic arms and legs; you can't raise a house; you can't seek your fortune like a younger son in a fairy tale; you have to go on and on for years doing some empty educational ritual before you get your entry level job and your fully adult level debts.

And the poor girl, who imagines she is welcoming you with her physical slimness, so easy to lift—she is like a half-ton anvil, mere male flesh cannot move her! Her $xxx,xxx expectations (or what you imagine to be her expectations) require a corporation. So it's the workplace at the center of her life. Husbands are so insignificant in the workplace. The wives do try to be faithful and enthusiastic, but the contrast (struggling young husband = failure, rich mature boss = success) is too cruel.

I've known brilliant professional men with salaries in the top five percent, who never married because they never felt able to support a family. It's the infinite obligations that castrate a man, the ten thousand dollar a day hospital taximeters and the big-target lawsuits, just waiting to nail you when you are vulnerable. Not to mention the many faces of family malice when it smells money.

She did not make this world. And strange to tell, she probably feels trapped too, whether she is clear about it or not—she would rather have love. This knowledge of enemy action does not show a way out, but it can lead to victory if the right moment comes. All those girls in their little glossy jails! It is almost like some exotic fairy tale.

And this leads to the final point—the one that hung me up for over a decade. There is no guarantee of a time. Frustration can be borne if there is some point to it, such as finding a bride. But there is no guarantee of that either. Unpeeling my white-knuckled fingers from the notion that I could somehow arrange a love life for myself was something I never did until age 30.

You have to give up. That is the secret of "cool". No pretences will do. The real thing makes you (in medieval terms) ready to "serve the fair" however circumstances dictate. The odds are actually rather great that something will happen. The years even of your youth are a long, ever-changing period: do not try to grasp the whole all at once.

Any serious writer on these subjects had better finish with some advice for the lovelorn. If even Gospel writers like St Paul can do it, I should not be embarrassed. The girls get their own list next chapter.

1. No putting down women

2. Ditch all porn and artificial sex

3. Leave off part way

4. Don't let them pay

5. A good old Catholic rule

6. Be polite to drunken mistakes!

7. Don't string along a girl

8. The "weakness" of women

9. Good books

No putting down women

Any man who takes advantage of a good woman's devotion or obedience to bully her is a man badly in need of a beating. This goes even for bullying talk. I do not mean using the word "bitch". I mean the verbal grinding down of women among men speaking together, the unfunny jokes that are really just a wad of spit aimed at anyone who loves.

The talk and the actions usually are a buildup for some other agenda, such as the man's catting around on some trusting wife or girlfriend. Tolkien wrote to his son about "the fair and false," about whether women had a tendency to be unfaithful to their men. "Very much the reverse," he said. The bullying just sets the stage for this grubby disloyalty—the oldest divorce story in the book.

Texts on the authority of a husband, like Ephesians 5:22-24 and Genesis 3:16, always imply love, as the texts themselves never fail to make clear. This is the prime example of "good use". He is magnanimous, he is to see her thrive, or his kingship is nothing but shit that feeds the fungus of feminism.

Ditch all porn and artificial sex

Step 1 to real manhood: destroy the dirty slides and movies, block the 900 numbers, toss every one of the dirty pictures and magazines (from *Playboy* on down) into the dumpster. It is not good for the man to be alone. That part of you belongs to a real woman, to a woman that you actually meet, to do *her* some good. No self-tweaking, no wanking, just lie fallow till then!

Artificial sex objects are "better" than the real and ruin the appreciation. Real women feel pimply and flat-chested because of these glossies: the first a pure lie (airbrushed), the second nearly so (all those silicone pump jobs). This is one of the worst things we do to them. What would you think of a mother who rejected her own child in favor of some ten-year-old actor whose trained gestures and murmurs of "Mommy" were more attractive?

This makes the real women wilt, or drives them in other directions, like status games. Our modern culture is actually quite sexless compared with a more normal time. Read a good translation of *Sir Gawain and The Green Knight*. Ask yourself why impotence clinics are so needed. Once in a while, in some odd place like a medieval choir, you will meet a real woman whose confidence has not been destroyed. The impact will rock you right back on your heels.

Leave off part way

Get it through your head that your single life is meant to be filled with frustration. Your twin reactions of lust and horror (at getting her onto a couch, and at introducing her to your mother and friends, for example) just mean that God means you to leave off part way. Take out the rest of the energy some other way: wailing music, heavy talk, hard useful work.

I'm not describing anything different from the reality you experience, of course. What I am saying is that it is not a mischance, a set of roadblocks or unlucky circumstances. It is the way things are supposed to work. And it is not fruitless: you are impressing the girl a lot more than you know. More on that below.

Of course, if it goes on until you are twenty-eight years old and finally get your thesis accepted for some advanced degree, this is a little bit inhuman! The aforementioned enemy action. There may well come a time when you have to catch your girl in defiance of the laws of economics.

Don't let them pay

Dates are a misbegotten notion. The companionship is wrecked by the one-on-one tension (a set of mutual friends would be better). And the thing looks too much like a commercial transaction. He buys her dinner, and in return, well?

When you do her a favor, you don't let her pay, even if it frustrates her too. Seize on impulse, or when she helps you (two favors the same way)? A real social occasion, with more than two people, is more fun. Fiestas and carneval balls with masks—southern cultures typically have moments when they actually make it easy for the young people to approach each other.

It really is a dance. There are months and years ahead of you. This is not like some economic "window of opportunity" that is guaranteed to go away if you do not grab it immediately. Women stay able to to be attracted, and you can pick up the thread again at some unplanned later time.

A good old Catholic rule

Mothers of teenagers hear from their moms and aunts: Forbid car dates! This is thirty years behind the times, of course. The latchkey party, in the empty house of someone's working mom and dad, is the up-to-date occasion of sin. The idea is the same.

Your good old energetic hormones like nothing better than a clear channel to pour themselves down. No obstacles, no surprises, victory assured ahead of time. The rest of your head knows all the good reasons why not. The solution (which will make part of you wail with frustration) is to let your ingrained habits and laziness defend you. Don't go.

There is a wrong feeling about these things: locked doors, shuttered windows. The "hostess" at such a party rarely tells you the whole story of her life. If you know it you are quite likely to curl up inside and not want any more fun. So trust your feelings of disquiet.

Be gentle with drunken mistakes!

If you've gone and done it, the last thing you want (starting from wake up the next morning) is to meet the girl again and deal with her. Throttle this flight impulse. Behave with the honesty of someone who, for whatever reason, has just signed a blank check with all accompanying commitments of honor.

It will be nothing but embarrassing, but you can at least *act* right. That puts her to the test, and you will know soon whether she is doing right by you. The matter then disentangles itself. You continue to owe her help and protection proportional to the original action. (It is the same principle that applies to ex-spouses after a divorce. They really are not "ex". A shared relationship and duty persist forever.)

Acting justly to her helps you act justly to yourself. The temptation is to consider yourself the drunken mistake, and to abandon hope in yourself, writing yourself off as just another slut. After that, drugs and worse trouble. This is typical devil stuff. Nip it in the bud: pick yourself up and plod back, enduring the reminders, the duty and embarrassment.

Don't string a girl along

If young, you think that it is all tilted in favor of the woman: "she has it, he wants it." This particular worm turns with time, as Genesis 3:16 and other ancient wisdom warns. A girl who accepts your attention, even with no sex, can soon come to be attached to you pretty desperately. This situation can sneak up on you.

It is not so sweet as it sounds. You may enjoy her company but want to hold her at arm's length status-wise. Is she good looking enough for my friends to approve? Up to my family's standards? An asset to my future work? It all sounds terrible when stated this way, but if you are honest you know the thought is there.

Tolkien, in his letter to his son (#43 in Humphrey Carpenter's collection), warned sternly against this danger. Either break off with her (accepting the loneliness) or marry her (however that disturbs your plans). Whether she ends up yours or not, you have made a terrific impression on her. Your genuine kingship breaks through, as it will many times throughout your life. See that it does her good.

The "weakness" of women

In all the old cultures from Christian to Chinese, women are presented as "weak". It cannot be their tenacity which is stronger than men's (they endure more and live longer). It can hardly be their physical strength which is not so much different from that of a man. A hefty woman is stronger than a small man. It could be their status and authority which in all enduring cultures is subject to men's. It could be, but I argue it is not: that is an effect, rather than a cause.

When the shells are falling, a man can scurry from place to place and leap over the rubble, while a woman is hampered. She is clumsy and slow because of the two-year-old clinging to her skirts and the older children that she is calling and shepherding to safety. Not so much feeble as weighted down. She survives by trust, by passing the power and warrior strength completely into his hands. That is why armies are made of men. Wars get ugly when women fight—so says Tolkien.

This is your male birthright of full and just kingship. Of course it carries with it the implication that you will lay down your life if necessary to defend the "weak" woman who shelters all your treasures. All lesser magnanimity is included in that implication, even opening doors for women. Your love rules in broad sweeps, hers completes the picture in detail. It works pretty well in practice, and it works better the worse things get.

Good books

There is not a single one of the above ideas that is original with me. It happens that the subject of sex and love is the most deeply treated subject of art and literature, in any and all cultures. Everyone has a father and mother; most people have a lover, and children. You have an immense smorgasbord of classic work that is good to read and good for your heart.

Anything not tainted with modern self-justification will do. (Other cultures' self-justification are easy for you to filter out.) Good mysteries like Sherlock Holmes or Father Brown. Romances and adventure stories: *The Black Arrow*, or *The Sire De Maletroit's Door*, or *Around The World In 80 Days*. Apocalyptic fiction like the Michael O'Brien novels. The space trilogy of C.S.Lewis: *Out Of The Silent Planet, Perelandra*, and *That Hideous Strength*, mostly because of the last book, which seriously addresses marriage and therefore embarrasses most critics, even good ones. All the great ones: the Bible, Shakespeare, Dante, Confucius, *The Arabian Nights*.

There is a very simple technique to get a mine of these works. Find some educational and literary surveys from before 1970. Compare their praised and recommended lists with those presented by current educators. The difference (the books and stories and cultural perspectives presented a generation ago, which are not found on today's lists) are usually good sources for thoughts about love. This is because the great difference between then and now is censorship by the feminists, and it is a rule of thumb that anything they hate is pretty good stuff.

Where did Red Haired Irishmen come from?

A good-hearted young girl will go to a war movie or a disaster movie and weep with love over the young hero who dies. She is permitted to love a boy who dies, but what if he goes on living in the real world? Then it seems there is no way for it to work. I need to offer a way out of such a deadly trap.

Start with something so obvious it ought to need no comment. Beauty is the primary reality of young women. Any story or movie or poem or song or work of art, from ancient times until the present, celebrates this fully and without hesitation.

The Song of Songs, an entire book of the Bible, celebrates beauty from end to end. Read on the literal and human level, it tells about a sweetheart who is so anxious to meet her boyfriend that she almost gets arrested for being out after curfew on the city walls. But it spends many verses— detailed, poetic, physical and erotic—to describe the charms of this beloved young bride. Read it, and never apologize for caring about beauty again.

A simple natural good like this is never satisfactory in the world of commerce. It must be turned into an engine of money, and therefore it can't be something you have—it has to be something you are going to get. The ever-receding carrot. This is so fraudulently false that a special breed of man, famously gay, has always been in charge of women's fashions. They are, in literal fact, woman-haters.

Nature gives them two places to insert their levers. The first is quite simple, that morning-after coldness of which any man is capable. Not Helen of Troy, not any woman alive can captivate a man who is out of the mood. But you are apt to assume it is some defect in your attractiveness. So then the clothes, the treatments, the creams and exercises and colors and all the other mighty money flows for which you serve as engine, when what you've got and he (in better mood) wants is 90% youth and health and blooms fully with no effort at all.

A girl in homespun looks just as good, probably better than a fashion queen to a man. This has held true all through history, from kings and peasant girls to that recent actor, Paul Grant, who preferred a hooker to his million-dollar model girlfriend. And don't be fooled by any romantic notions of "homespun". As produced by a peasant of common skill and wealth, it was just a step above burlap sacking. A normal man responds deep down to healthy signs of aptness to love, and royally ignores status symbols.

This leads to the second more subtle lever: evasion. This is not a misunderstanding but a kind of corruption. In thousands of words, the counselors and glossy rags are serving up ways to exercise the power of beauty while staying in control, without giving yourself away. The terrible thing is that men are as sensitive to *that* as women are to the quick grab artist. The happy compulsion is completely shattered. The joy of your youth becomes a woman-to-woman status game. Expensive tedium indeed.

The acres of print! The barking TV! Pounding on your ears and eyes so many of your waking hours, to keep you from realizing the meaning of something pretty near your heart. And that is that love is a great good, a mighty reason to toss aside minor questions of safety and conventional success. In the rest of this section I will follow that thought ruthlessly, to what may seem to be some rather grim places. But the conclusion is not grim at all, rather the opposite. It can bloom in fact, and without great effort, and without great good luck.

To be simply lovable be simply vulnerable, like Scheherazade. Live in trust that you will not be thrown away. What jars people about the forbidden verses in the Bible, like Ephesians 5:21ff, is that the sacred author is stepping down from his pedestal to become an advice columnist. The stern tone is embarrassment at the secret fatherly motive of wanting the young folks to be happy together.

It is pretty darn obvious to any parent or teacher that girls are more docile than boys. The American nature-hating way is to be ashamed of this. Ditch that false "sense of sin" and you are halfway back to love. Are you ashamed to be a passenger in a car? The driver, after all, is in total control. If he wants to fling you all to a flaming death, one twitch of the wheel will do it, and you can't do a thing to prevent it. So don't worry.

The husband's "head of the family" status is the foremost example of "good use" and is always a comedy. (If as often happens the wife has the better head for business or strategy, the solution is simple: she tells him which decision to make, and he makes it.) It may well bear fruit, like a citrus tree, ten years later. It literally can take this much quiet encouragement before a man knows his own hope: he spends years pursuing his notion of what his wife wants or needs without even realizing it. That even happened to me, despite my lifelong rejection of cultural imperatives. What is the point of marrying if your husband turns into something not himself as soon as he marries you?

Among my mother's Slovak relatives were several women who were pretty (shall we say) influential in their households. So when my grandmother told me the traditional qualifications for a bride— *pekná, pobožná, poctivá, poslušná, poriadna* (pretty, pious, faithful, obedient, neat)—I questioned the fourth one. She laughed: "Oh, that means sex." In *That Hideous Strength*, C.S. Lewis's character flatly states, "Obedience is an erotic necessity."

This of course turns the whole notion of success on its head. But it is natural. We have the commercial habit of comparing what we have with something unreal in the future, rather than something real in the past. A teenage girl who has a baby becomes an instant star among the other girls (to the consternation of their elders) because the baby is so cute! The others only have dogs or dolls or electronic pets.

The Mexicans have a custom (*Quinceañera*) of making a girl's fifteenth birthday into a great pre-bridal. It is loved by young girls and bitterly hated by United States social authorities, who are doing their best to destroy it, for instance by using their influence with Catholic bishops to delay Confirmation until after 15. One side of it is a big party, long prepared by the family, with dancing to celebrate the girl's beauty (it is also called the "Cinderella" party, and her special white dress may be speckled with tiny electric lights!) The other aspect of it is a church service in which the priest gives traditional instruction on the responsibilities of her womanhood.

Such a traditional instruction is more realistic than modern education, which vastly distorts the risks of love, enough to send you wrong for life. Abuse, for instance, is the least of problems if you are defenseless, for the simple reason that your man does not *want* to cut you up and leave the pieces in a garbage bag by the freeway. Marketing-driven lifestyles, on the other hand, can combine with the fact that the economy cuts the arms and legs off a young man, to box him in and define him as worthless before you even realize it—and then he may really break out into violence.

One that can really sneak up on you is a kind of despairing invulnerability. At age 18, on a student ship en route to Rotterdam, I saw this for the first (not the last) time. A Dutch girl (who did not believe in her own beauty—nice body, craggy face) got herself laid by one of the sailors for no more reason than that she was tired of being a virgin. This seems to be a big personality change in women who are used to being cool and in control sexually, compared with men. But it is only maturity.

Twentyish girls write letters to conservative journals like *Fidelity*, lamenting that they can never find a man. There was a fine young woman I met at Purdue when I taught there: I had to break off our acquaintanceship with a fiery letter, because she went to Washington D.C. and tossed away all her principles in this sort of desperation. You break something inside yourself in order to set things in motion. Movies like *Looking for Mr Goodbar* are pretty realistic. You can find yourself arranging to be passed around.

That brings up the next danger, which is rape. Oh yes, a man can speak with authority on the subject—a man who knows several women who have been raped. As I do. I present what may seem a strange way of dealing with this terror, but it is a way with a time honored history, in fact it is the way of our ancestors.

If "the child is father to the man," then the little girl is mother to the mother. Like the *Gasoline Alley* comic strip, a great many real family histories feature a "baby found on a doorstep", to the delight of little girls playing with their dolls. Has it ever occurred to you what that often really meant? Baby found on the doorstep—of the mother's body! A happy myth, invented by a strong foremother to protect her innocent child from horrible guilt, turns an adult tale of evil into a fairy tale clean enough to delight a child.

But it remains valid on the adult level as well. Where do you suppose red-haired Irishmen came from? Viking invaders got them started without a by your leave for their mothers. Ellis Peters, writing the very culturally accurate Brother Cadfael stories, had some fascinating observations about the low social status blond-haired children had in the times and places where that story was common.

The answer, then, is that the little girl is right. You have an absolute duty to protect your baby, any baby that comes your way, doorstep or otherwise. This is a center and core of your love, and the best way to grasp it is a thought exercise for the (unraped) girl. That certainly does not mean that you have to court rape or submit to it—on the contrary!—any more than a young man who imagines having to fight heroically to defend his family must thereupon go out and get himself killed.

Love is a ferociously demanding and absolute ruler, for man or woman. But what shouts in extreme terms in your mind comes through only as the quietest murmur to your neighbor. In about the right tone, in fact. Without vision, the people perish—says God. In fact they cannot even love.

And what of the girl who really has been raped? Is it true that she can never love? One such woman would scream during a sexual act as if she were being tortured, but was happy sitting teasingly on a man's lap, like a frozen teenager. She it was who still mourned the baby conceived by rape, whom the all-wise social workers had aborted: "They took away my baby," she said. And there is one step back toward love, in reverse time order, as I said before: baby first.

Even if no pregnancy came from the rape, imagine one, and a full and faithful life bringing up that child, like a woman of old. Is there an orphan in need of help? It is possible to enter into one of those missionary fostering arrangements where you support some child in a poor country—some child born around when yours would have been—and exchange the occasional letter.

There is a book I recommend for all women who have been raped: *My Thirty-Third Year*, by Father Gerhard Fittkau (Fidelity Press, 206 Marquette Avenue, South Bend, IN 46617). Yes it is by a man, in fact by a celibate Catholic priest—he is even a one-lunged priest. Nevertheless this is the book for you.

Despite its innocent-sounding title its subject matter is pretty grim. Those who love the stories of Tolkien may understand it as the destruction of the Shire by Sauron. As a young man I loved European history and languages, and am familiar with little countries all over the map. It gave me quite a chill therefore when thirty years later I read this book about

Ermland, a name I had never heard before. It and its memory were wiped off the face of the earth two years before I was born.

You will find details you did not expect. For instance, darkest humor cannot be suppressed—the frying pan *a la Russe*, and the priest too dim to give directions. You will watch the healthy die and invalids survive, and discover where the weak find strength. You will meet a Soviet theoretician of rape, and near the end you will meet a Russian doctor just after he tries to save two German girls. You will look in his eyes then and see that, once again, the feminists have lied through their teeth.

Life is not like business suits and resumes, but muscular and rather confused. Catch as catch can. The mighty family of which you are the center may have started wrong and without justice. The worm does turn, and may not take as long as you think. Remember those red-haired Irishmen kicked ass, when Brian Boru and his army threw their worthless fathers out of Ireland.

I have mentioned one thing in passing: the low status that comes from being raped, and attaches to the children of rape. It is rather horrible to present this as a consideration, but be honest—just as I said to the boy with the clinging girlfriend, in the last section. Worse things than low status will certainly punish your love, even if you have not been raped. It is best to think of them as a chance to show strength, devotion, even heroism.

For women of our time particularly, you have to think love = poverty. As a modern woman, you need to accept poverty as a precondition of love. Money is a rival of your husband, even if you have not found him yet. It is likely you have to send this rival home with boxed ears, before your husband will even approach you.

Money has the same function as a husband, protecting and providing for you and your children. Nowadays it seems money does it better. Ancient generations were saved from this conflict because the property was in the husband's name. The price paid was caring for widows like pensioners (see the many mentions of this in the Bible). Thanks to our financial individualism we now have a bare-knuckled conflict.

To soften yourself for the coming of love, you will have to abandon all grasping for monied self-assurance. Holy poverty is not normally a secular virtue but for this generation it is. That of course does not mean you refuse or waste money, your own or your husband's. It means you treat it as a guest that can leave at any time, without shaking your life or your hopes to the foundations.

Women are more attuned to this than most people think. My son's social justice teacher, Coach Bryant, noted that women suffer wage discrimination because women allow it. He seemed to imply that is a fault, but of course it is a virtue. Courteous young women, driven by need, take up minimal space in the economy, in the hope that what they decline to take will benefit heads of families. What I am saying is to carry this instinct to its logical conclusion.

The interesting thing is that it leads to a lifestyle quite different from the conventional. We made several house moves—always in a southerly direction—as we slowly realized this. More on that later! The mall life was rather empty anyway, and all the stuff they sell is the same. The compulsion is gone, so embracing holy poverty usually means you end up with *more* money and less debts.

And out of this holy poverty (with its odd earth-shaded accumulation of property) comes a new form of wealth. It happens because the gracious absolutes of family loyalty and hospitality send you out among family, friends and neighbors for the needfuls each time. Time is tremendously long—you cannot grasp how much of it there is. And information and personal acquaintance are real wealth. A chatelaine, a lady of more romantic times, this is what you become.

As promised, here's my feminine list of advices to the lovelorn. I cannot claim to have been through it—please talk to mothers and aunts!

1. Truly a social occasion

2. Don't kid or trap yourself

3. Beware advice

4. You do not have to pay

5. Trash all commercialism

6. Trash all social status

7. Your man is stronger than you think

8. In each other's danger

9. Good books

Truly a social occasion

They train you to feel guilty if you frustrate a man. That is a win-win alternative for them: making you either a slut or a heartless bitch holding out Dear Abby style for a better offer. But a man is sturdy under rebuff because his deepest desire is to possess *you*, and your heart should be out of synch with Dear Abby and in tune with that. "Write on me."

In fact a rebuff from a real woman (in a flowing dress, laughing) can be sweeter to him than going to bed with a modern mistress of investments. Just the talk that mounts on one of these near misses is unknown to the quick rollers. It's like hydraulic power that can lift your car, but not if someone drills a hole so that all the fluid squirts out where it "wants" to go.

The owners will try to shame you out of this conviction, as will any unthinking man who has a "line" to add to his true feelings. The only payment you may have to make to him is more modest dress (if the sight of too much of you is really bothering him). It is enough for him to realize you are really deep down willing to be carried away when the time comes. It will release him from the constraint of scoring and allow poetry and courtship—you could end up alarmed at your own beauty.

Don't kid or trap yourself

I already discussed this point above. They get you with a two-pronged attack. The feminists build up their ideal woman as coolly autonomous in wealth and emotion, controlling excitable men like an angler playing a line. Then when a little of the real woman begins to tug inside *you*, the sleaze rags tell you that you are some kind of nympho and may as well become a thoroughfare.

Well, guess what. You get to endure some frustration too, or you will soon find yourself used and hated. Those "nympho" feelings are just a faint shadow (you ought to take some steps in a young man's moccasins sometime!!) and sex for you is still 90% gift-sharing and cheerleading. Realize this and you will not need to manufacture orgasms (his will do for two for quite a while even after you are man and wife). To be calm while he is not is part of the nature of beauty.

Women are taught to rush away from their own nature as if it were proven bad. Some are grinding on themselves to raise an impulse that is not there yet. Others are tripping themselves up with drink and drugs and social traps: arranging their own rape, really. And all the protection. And of course once they are pregnant, instant violence against their own body which does all it can to protect the baby. Peace! Silence! Time! Even here and now you are not *that* doomed.

Beware advice

Women's natural defenses have a flaw. Your antennae quiver accurately to the secretest physical hunger in a man, however smooth his attempted approach. But you were not built to expect a two-front campaign. The disinterested advisor, the fatherly or motherly talk from someone who does not want your body, is past your guard at once, even though that someone may be nothing but an agent of the hungry one.

The most horrible sex education excesses are in all-girl high schools, like a recent case in Baltimore. In all-boy high schools the same authorities tread very cautiously: boys are more rebellious than docile, and what (for instance) gay promoters say can have immediate physical consequences on the promoters' bodies. All the advice columns and magazine articles at the checkout counters aim at a woman and approach, in a manner of speaking, on the other side of her from her man. Rich and powerful men take the time and trouble to arrange an attack from both sides.

Who am I to speak? Another advisor, indeed: but you will notice my side is hated and vilified by all the cultural powers, from Disney's *Nothing Sacred* to the international aid agencies. That ought to give you a notion who is honest. Also, as Jesus Christ pointed out, by their fruits you will know them.

You do not have to pay!

The old love stories tell the simple truth. It is one of the deepest wishes of a normal man to be affected overwhelmingly by beauty, and then to serve this beauty. The truest frustration is not sexual at all. It is helplessness: to be unable to do anything real for her. A valuable service really and instinctively is its own reward.

Therefore never pay. Not even if he reflexively parrots some demanding modern "line". Do not forget that the modern world is totally anti-love and anti-sex and worships nothing but money, of which orgasm cash is a variety. You need a little bit of courage to dismiss this false sense of shame. It will be richly rewarded, starting with the friendship of the man himself.

As in *The Sire de Maletroit's Door,* this mode of service could in theory become a trap: but in the real world (again as the story tells) it does not happen. An ancient father would solve the problem simply by *giving* you to him. There are modern equivalents. Young people worry too much about these incidental details which are Gordian in nature and susceptible to sword cuts.

Trash all commercialism

If you want to load yourself with a debt on behalf of your sex, try commercialism. It is as if you had to do public penance for all the TV salivators and mall robots. This is not really true, but it will do as a start toward finding a good man. You should explicitly bend over backward to assure him you do not need that stuff. The culture, with tremendous power, convinces him to take it for granted that you do.

The woods hippie with her plain cotton dress has always seemed the most sexual of women to contemporary men. No anvil here. But her image is not original, in fact it is just a resketch of a very old-fashioned frontier or medieval woman. The point of learning household skills (besides the fact that they are useful—more on that later) is that they provide a calming atmosphere. The woman with such a life can simply outwait a man, being patient until his "gotta make it" twitch stops twitching.

Being fearful in advance about practical details that have not arisen yet, like insurance for the children, is very effective at killing your rapport with your man, here and now. It creates an inhuman gap between sex (done right now with protection and quickly forgotten) and commitment (infinitely burdensome and possible only after wealth is achieved). Even if commitment happens there will be no more sharing hopes and dreams. Such fragile creativity is crushed like a bug under the weight of tomorrow's realism.

Trash all social status

According to Bill Cosby, women go in herds, even to the bathroom. You are going to have to be countercultural about this, because that herd is one thing that is most totally under control of the bad guys. Practice a level stare and a touch of acerbity—nice isn't everything! Think over just how ready they are to control you by putdowns, and you won't even want to be very nice.

There are compensations. You have to be anorexic to meet the status standard of beauty, but the real standard of beauty (to which men respond) is much more forgiving. Any pretty Tijuana shopping clerk would draw eyes away from poor Princess Diana. Let the herd torture itself with exercise and diets. They will resent your success, of course. You have to have the courage to face that.

And both you and your man will suddenly be much richer. Designer nothing! You can do what the best of rich people do and have a real designer (a human being that you personally talk to) make a special thing for you. We did it with bedsheets, of all things—after years of fruitlessly searching for the top fitted sheets that all the manufacturers had pulled off the market. It is surprisingly easy and inexpensive when you take the trouble. With this kind of approach you do not need status, because you are unique.

Your man is stronger than you think

Money may seem to provide better than a man, but wait until someone gets you at a disadvantage. The money life only works if you make sure that can never happen, which takes a lot out of life. You can never love your child, for instance—there are a hundred ways they can and do take that child hostage. The world finds a woman alone and slowly squeezes her into a narrower and narrower space, and there is no point where she can resist.

The notion of man as primarily a provider is bourgeois Calvinistic bullshit. He is foremost a warrior. Providing is one of the things he does to fill in the time when there is nothing more exciting going on. Think about his *real* personality sometime! My old boss even rallied to his ex-wife's support, when he heard that her house had been broken into and robbed.

Once you bust your cash flow requirements way way down, like a good countercultural woods hippie, you can encourage him to come into his own. Freeing him from chains is a slow, slow process of many tiny little adventures. Before it is done you may well find others gathering around you with a feisty and protective attitude: sons and even daughters. All together you find there are some things you can do very well indeed, freeing you from the universal American feeling of inferiority (that you never knew you had) to the "world class" people in the newspapers and television. Then you can lean back and grin at each other, because you have won.

In each other's danger

The all-American doom is divorce. 50% divorce rate. Among Mormons, whose marriages are sealed in heaven—the same. Among Catholics, who believe that marriage is indissoluble—the same. Among foreigners who come from countries like Afghanistan where marriage is firm—as soon as they move within our borders, the same. You can't get away from it, with one exception—one group of Americans with a 2% divorce rate.

They are the couples who refuse on principle to use artificial contraception. These are found in organizations like the *Couple to Couple League*, and some consider them a far fringe of the anti-abortion movement. Nevertheless, this stunning success. It was only two generations ago that almost everyone shared their view that protection was a kind of perversion. Interestingly, it was only two generations ago that almost all marriages were solid as rocks.

It seems that love requires adventure and danger. A couple who lie down together in each other's danger is a couple in whom the blood continues to flow. It is always a lively topic of conversation, is it not—when some little happy impulse, like my wife's fear after the woman was raped across the street, can overturn our lives once again? This is a scary requirement for those who thought they could find safety, but according to my reading of the evidence there is no other possibility, none at all.

Good books

The same ones! Yes, I insist on an adventure story. A love story has to be an adventure story. Security is corruption. Reject certain romances, not because of the oversexed nature of the embrace in the foreground, but because of the overpriced nature of the palatial residence behind.

There are adventures like Christopher Stasheff's *Warlock* books that follow the stories of a whole family. The best series authors, like Dorothy Gilman (*Mrs Pollifax*) and Ellis Peters (*Brother Cadfael*) obviously love their main characters and the details of their work, so that though the romances may seem incidental the affection is central, and therefore it is all real. Escapism is great! You sure do not want those steamy "realistic" novels with their bloated power brokers and their harems.

Escapism is the only thing that makes sense, because the dominant culture is such a tormented bag of pus. And here is the secret hiding inside all those good books: You have great power to make them come true. As wild as that may seem! You with your espoused ally and those children of yours, who esteem your mind and desires above all the world besides (if you would only accept their fealty)—you who have incredible oceans of time at your disposal—you will be more than surprised how much creation is within your power.

Chapter 6

Heroes

I have spent many of my free hours speaking in favor of my betters. My own grim and unfriendly personality has little place in this work. It does shed light on the topic of this chapter, though.

Vance Packard applied the term "other-directed" to those people who imitate and adjust to the preferences of those around them. They detect changed fashions and quickly change their own; they perceive which walk and talk is approved, and that is the way they walk and talk. I was so far from responding to others this way, during my youth, that I could not even understand why anyone else would want to do it.

In 1980 for the first time I met Afghan students and refugees, the Seattle compatriots of the man on the cover of this book. Now, suddenly, it was important to me to dress and act right. To behave as expected in the presence of *these* people was an honor and a privilege. For they are the heroes; they uphold mercy and justice no matter the odds; they spend their lives as a lesser man would sign a check, and they prove that a human being can be more than slime.

It is no surprise then that they attract the best people to themselves. These want to know how the great deeds are done. There is even a story like that for this book's cover picture. The young author Debra Denker travelled at great risk to write the *National Geographic* cover story about Afghanistan (the one with the famous picture of the green-eyed girl). Though she was not the photographer, the heroic reality so gripped her that she made her own photographic record on the side. It included this *mujahid*, cheerfully inviting the travelers to share his meager goods.

The Afghan Help Organization (our little aid group) bought the rights to sell several of Debra's pictures, but this one, "Hospitality", was by far the most popular. And no wonder! It is living evidence that somewhere,

143

even if far away, there is something right in the world.

Are you with me? How much better to be that man, who out of the grains of his poverty finds enough to share with the tired strangers, than to be some billionaire Bill Gates clone who defines himself by "eating the lunch" of whoever he can get at a disadvantage. I know America glorifies the latter kind of character. Whole magazines are filled with worshipping articles. All that means is that America has fallen very low, but my good news is this: the world has better to offer.

The Creed of Unyielding Will

The hero sets himself against a darkness that is greater than he is, and does so without hope. You cannot understand the hero without the darkness. If it were not for that he would merely be a speculator, sensitive to the newest wave as it begins to form. You could buy stock in him on the Over-the-Counter Exchange, and make a mighty profit after he was listed on the NYSE.

Heroism is the opposite of commerce, because commerce goes with a winner. The good money is made by dealing with the slave owner, not with his victims. Trade with the rich tyrant, not with the poor oppressed, and that way the resources will be allocated in your favor. Do not dawdle around mourning over the grave of justice, when you can anticipate the victory of amoral violence, and be first on the road to profit.

Tolkien studied and revered the reverse of that coin, the mighty man who chooses not to walk away from those left behind. In his essay, *Beowulf: the Monsters and the Critics*, he says:

> ... the theory of courage ... is the great contribution of early Northern literature. ... I refer rather to the central position the creed of unyielding will holds in the North. ... 'The Northern Gods,' Ker said, 'have an exultant extravagance in their warfare which makes them more like Titans than Olympians; *only they are on the right side, though it is not the side that wins. The winning side is Chaos and Unreason'*—mythologically, the monsters—'*but the gods, who are defeated, think that defeat no refutation.*'

But the hero has a reason to spend it all. The focus of Tolkien's entire essay is on that unavoidable conflict:

> He [the author of *Beowulf*] makes his minstrel sing in Heorot of the Creation of the earth and the lights of Heaven. So

excellent is this choice as the theme of the harp that maddened Grendel lurking joyless in the dark without that it matters little whether this is anachronistic or not.

And again:

> A light starts—*lixte se leoma ofer lands fela*—and there is a sound of music; but the outer darkness and its hostile offspring lie ever in wait for the torches to fail and the voices to cease. Grendel is maddened by the sound of harps.

The light and the harp are not some abstraction like Culture and Civilization, puffed up by mere size. They are homely and small. The song of creation is sung by a young couple. The human being, the lover, the neighbor *makes* this music on his or her little patch of land.

We see the Mexican neighbors hanging the colored streamers for their *fiestas*, and listen to their song and dance late into the night. We eat the *koláče*, the sweet biscuits made carefully according to our ancestral peasant recipes, and attend a wedding in the old language.

I have travelled in little old-country peasant villages, and visited the home overhanging the shop in an old town. The wood of walls and the handles of tools are rubbed smooth, as by decades of use. Spaces are small, things are few but each has meaning. Cheerful in adversity, a family curls up around a hot stove in a single room, and goes out with the morning to grace the customary hillsides with gifts of food, light, and music. According to Ursula LeGuin, love, like bread, has to be made anew each day.

Death is always close to them, closer than it appears. Among the most evil of Solzhenitsyn's stories in *The Gulag Archipelago* is that of the uprooting of those people, whole villages of peasants torn away from their homes and their humble tools, hurled onto a frozen wasteland and mockingly told to do their earth magic. Of course they withered and died. The warmth of home is an infinitely fragile thing, even if it has carried on unbroken for hundreds of years.

A kind of tenderheartedness is central to the creed of unyielding will. The hero does not turn his face away from the scenes of horror, as for example in *My Thirty-Third Year*:

> ... Another woman, from a village just three miles away, had removed the covering from the sled on which she had packed her three children. She had wanted to feed them. But she found all three frozen to death. She had to bury them quickly in the snow by the roadside because another sled with the rest of the family was already a hundred yards ahead of her and she had to catch up with it.

The hero objects to this; he wants to stop it happening, and he will throw all his mighty strength against it, against the inevitable march of power. At the heart of the hero is pity.

There is nothing alien or dated about this theme, because pity is alien to the masters of the twentieth century. That lamp and that harp were in millions of homes throughout the world. I happen to know Eastern Europe, but what of Africa and China? Let me speak my history; theirs will be no different. Whether they were Jewish families out of *Fiddler on the Roof*, or the village Christians with their village shrines so lovingly described in Father Fittkau's work, they were driven out to die, and their light was extinguished.

All the powers of the world—Nazi, Soviet, British, American—were maddened by that light and that music. It made them furious that remnants of old independent love-centered life were still hanging on all over the place. *All* of them liked to see ancient town and peasant communities crushed, driven out, sunk and drowned on refugee ships. Kick the nonsense out of them, drag them into the twentieth century!

They all collaborated in the death marches, our own best and brightest shoulder to shoulder with the tyrants. If that shocks you just check history, from the starving Ukraine in 1932 to the broken earth of China now, with its fifty million dead baby girls. Every one of these mass murderers has had a hollow storefront of an operation, and has been completely dependent, economically and especially financially, on us. If our progressive leaders didn't love it, they would pull the plug on it.

In World War II, when they sunk the warship *Bismarck*, the Allied forces rescued its sailors. By contrast, when they sunk the refugee ship *Wilhelm Gustloff*, they left over 7000 civilians to drown in the icy Baltic. The express purpose of the firebombing of Dresden, an ancient cathedral city of no military value, was to burn refugees alive by the hundreds of thousands. (Kurt Vonnegut was inspired to his literary career by witnessing this.) After the war, British and American leaders ordered the forcible return of millions of refugees to Stalin to be raped, sent to slave camps and slowly starved to death.

In the last case in particular, code-named *Operation Keelhaul,* our leaders could have frustrated Stalin with a snap of the fingers. But they did not. The only explanation is that they enjoyed what they did. Scum rises.

Hitler only seems to be an exception. He posed as a friend of family values, and our leaders mistakenly believed him. They mistook which side he was on. If they had realized how happily the Nazis raped Polish girls and murdered priests, they would have found a way to support the Nazis too.

The powers of the world are Grendel—the grinder. They love the inevitable, as it takes over the lives of people and turns them into a slurry that is pumped through big pipes to nowhere. First racial, then political, now economic reality: that is their name for it, though none of it works to bring human happiness. Each "reality" crushes what is left of the happiness of actual human beings, and our masters cheer every step of the way.

The racial thing covered the earth in its day, built up over years, and (as we now forget) there was no hope of stopping it. The political Soviet thing later reached over the earth, and (as we are already forgetting) it was truly unstoppable, liquidating millions who stood in its way. Now it is the economic grinder, and we have to feed our own babies into the garbage disposal, starting with us and the Chinese, but in the end even the fundamentalist Islamic nations will be forced to submit. Whoever survived the old purges will be crushed by economic forces. At the moment of this writing, Jay Hoffman informs me, these are ruining the Irish countryside, putting out the last light of good cheer and friendliness in postwar free Europe.

Against every such massive trend, poor and hopelessly outclassed and jeered at, stands the figure of the hero, motivated by some personal pity. He will probably not stand for long; he, with his dead loved ones, will probably just end up as a bloodstain on the road of progress. Yet he by himself is worth more than all the indistinguishable droplets in the victorious wave put together.

A child will eagerly listen to his story in years to come. What child ever cared about the life history of a corporate winner?

The Darkness

I am writing in the late 1990s. The crushing advance of the racist evil is forgotten by all but a few aging survivors. Even the bitter feel of a world overshadowed by the Soviets is fast fading from memory. To adolescents today it is an item of history.

The trouble is that we look back after the heroes have set the world right. We take that rightness for granted, and forget how wrong, how hopelessly and permanently bad things were for them. It is necessary to recreate, if possible, that gloom. Such a recreation will turn out in the end to be a foundation of hope, not of despair.

One word picture, of one such time, will have to suffice. The Soviet empire in 1979 was history's greatest winner. America had been defeated three years ago in Vietnam. The world had watched America's supporters being led off to death camps. The muted and weakening cries that were allowed to trickle out of the new Vietnam added up to one long drawn out gloat.

In Cambodia, the killing fields blossomed. One third of the people were exterminated. This was a kind of research laboratory for low-cost genocide. To save on consumables (bullets), people were clubbed and buried alive by bulldozers. This hell was off limits to aid, and we were all helpless.

Because of the nuclear balance of terror, there was no hope of putting an end to the Soviet system, which could bring the world down with it if threatened. The events of the 1970s made it clear that there was also no escape for any countries that were marked for absorption by that system. They had to be abandoned to their destiny, in the hope that the rest of us could maneuver within shrunken borders to avoid the same fate.

Under the Brezhnev doctrine, the Soviet empire was like a black hole: once fallen in, no country ever escaped. Many of us had relatives condemned to that national life sentence. And just as in the realm of astronomy, this black hole was gradually but inexorably growing at the expense of the light. Even America's near neighbors were slowly bending red.

Not only could we not do anything but lose ground, we were not even *allowed* to struggle. Effective resistance was always, for one reason or another, immoral. Our best and brightest were permitted to work to advance the Soviet empire (Hanoi Jane's American troops chanted "Ho Ho Ho Chi Minh, the NLF is gonna win!"), but those with family and friends going into the darkness were ostracized as "cold warriors" or "McCarthyites" if they proposed to fight it.

On occasion a popular uprising would bravely catch fire: Poland, Hungary, Czechoslovakia. The end of each such story was the same. Tanks, slaughter, and then after a decent interval our commercial and political leaders would cozy back up to the butchers. Realism always meant shoveling the dead heroes into a mass grave of futility. Not surprisingly, each episode of resistance was more feeble than the last, or so it seemed.

There were those in the "Free World" (as it was then called) who, in their hearts, still wished the chains struck off their unlucky brethren. They learned to keep quiet about it. By 1979 it was not even a point of contention any more, merely an opportunity for mockery if anyone unguardedly made such thoughts known in the presence of realists. There were two pleasures for the realists: joining with the oppressors in crushing and starving the slaves, and detecting and dousing any feeble flame of hope remaining in those who sided with the slaves.

The Soviets had long since been legitimized in diplomatic forums and, more importantly, in commercial partnerships with our most wealthy corporate interests. Ford Motor Company was a partner in technology for the Kama River "truck" factory, which made military vehicles used to attack countries like Afghanistan. A West German firm even made instruments of torture for them.

It was the world-wide privilege of the Soviets to lie about those they were strangling. Everybody had to sit still and keep a straight face while they went on and on slandering their victims, who even if they had friends in the West could rarely muster the money or influence to answer. This miasma of lies made winding down the Cold War *on Soviet terms* seem the only rational course of action.

Do not misunderstand me. Voices of outrage (of which I was one, in a small way) were not silenced. It was not necessary. Ever since the *New York Times* orchestrated the coverup of the artificial famine in the Ukraine, with its eight or ten million dead, the lie machine always had our pathetic peeping well under control. We were never a threat. It is true that most of the American voters had a vague and visceral hatred of the Soviet system, gleaned from subconsciously remembered details—that is why the Cold War continued—but in "serious" forums, the well-funded academic advocates of Soviet inevitability easily made fools of any third-generation descendants of peasants who dared to debate them.

In the same manner as feminists today, Marxists took up influential positions in the educational system. Such teachers often required their American pupils to write papers praising the Soviet system. Dissenting points of view were punished with low or failing grades in required courses. This happened to my wife in Seattle's Lincoln High School. The lie had infinite free speech rights, though schoolchildren did not.

There was a double standard that protected the Soviets from censure. An example was Vietnam. South Vietnam was roundly condemned for things like minor restrictions on the political rights of Buddhists. North Vietnam was permitted to get away with disembowelling hundreds of women (that was the starting gun of their revolution, as Dr Tom Dooley remembered) and burning everyone alive in a village. This kind of "real man" dictatorship is what pleases our elite, and possibly turns them on sexually as well. They still favor Hanoi as a provider of slave labor.

The moneyed interests were always heavily pro-Soviet, because Soviet bloc powers could be trusted to lie consistently and effectively. After all, only the lie is totally under the control of the powerful. The truth is a "loose cannon" or a "bull in a china shop" that can have an unpredictable effect on investment portfolios. It cannot be bought in any case, and very often it is infuriatingly dug up by low-budget stringers and freelancers who have to be dealt with before they make waves. Such truth-telling gets you a career on the moneyless fringe where you can keep squeaking till you starve. Fame, cash and promotion go to those whose outrage points in a safe direction.

This was the world of December 27, 1979. In the last section of this

chapter, the third of my stories of heroism, I will carry the story beyond
that evil day.

The White Rose of Germany

Despair reaches into the Twentieth Century by many means, and in many
different times and places.

In 1969 I spent time in the little Swabian village of Ergenzingen, at the
home of my girlfriend's parents. A beautiful and homelike place, surely a
thousand years old; a big tall house in a rambling yard, where I taught
her little sister the trick of turning a "Hula Hoop" into an earthbound
boomerang. The friendly fields were a short walk from the houses, all
perfectly fitting Inge Scholl's words:

> We sniffed the odor of moss, damp earth, and sweet apples
> whenever we thought of our homeland.

And yet there was a heaviness in the air, a sense of going through the
motions, a broken mainspring of the heart. When you cling to a girlfriend
even across a gulf of language you learn these things. She recalled how her
parents hated fireworks because they brought back the reality of war. This
was Germany the twice-caught world sinner, convicted of ruin. It is as if
anything good started there, any duty faithfully carried out, must always
fall short and fail.

I always have sympathized intensely with them. In 1990 I wrote a
furious letter in answer to some chauvinistic gloating in a local paper:

> ...Before sneering at the German "national character", Mr
> Saville should read about Operation Keelhaul and learn of the
> filth at the base of our own. At least the Germans are repentant.
>
> I once spent a year in Tuebingen and learned about the
> German national character in the most realistic way of all—by
> falling in love with a local. (It will be a warm day when America
> produces human beings who are as nice to marry as the average
> German.) Their problem is not evil but self-doubt, magnified to
> self-hate. Like a pool without an outlet, Germany has concen-
> trated the whole world's poison, and Germans think it is their
> own taint. Which is worse, their despairing self-awareness or
> our mindless hype?
>
> It is not too late for us to repeat the German experience.
> Since we closed our frontier by retreating from the moon, our

children's hearts have rotted. Wealth and power and corruption
are worshipped here...
[*San Diego Reader*, 15 February 1990]

But between 1969 and 1990 I had discovered a new facet of German
history, a secret flowering as it were, a song against despair: the White
Rose. They lasted two years (1942-3), but I don't think their country
would have stumbled through another generation without them.

The elder sister of two of them, Inge Scholl, wrote the primary source
about them: *The White Rose* (1952; translated by Arthur R. Schultz, Wes-
leyan University Press, Middletown, Connecticut, 1983). Quotes here are
from that work.

Everybody wants to forget it now, but Germany fell in the first place
not because of some alien savagery but because of legalism and overcivi-
lization —faults writ large upon us right now. The resilience of the human
family, still powerful everywhere else between the World Wars, had been
sapped early on in Germany by Bismarck's pioneering social security system. So many people there learned already, *in the 1920s*, what it is to be
human garbage, dependent on a money income that was suddenly valueless.
Elderly retirees became prostitutes.

Into that morass of purposelessness the light of Nazism entered. Suddenly there was something for the younger generation to belong to, a vision
to look forward to. Inge Scholl's picture is brief:

> ...And Hitler—so we heard on all sides—Hitler would help
> this fatherland to achieve greatness, fortune, and prosperity. He
> would see to it that everyone had work and bread...But there
> was something else that drew us with mysterious power and
> swept us along: the closed ranks of marching youth with banners
> waving, eyes fixed straight ahead, keeping time to drumbeat and
> song. Was not this sense of fellowship overpowering? ...
>
> We entered into it with body and soul, and we could not
> understand why our father did not approve, why he was not
> happy and proud...But Father's words were spoken to the wind,
> and his attempts to restrain us were of no avail against our
> youthful enthusiasm.

It is easy to pass over that part of the story, though it embraced a
greater part of the young people's lives than did their rebellion. But every
word is important. It is the second part of the denaturing of man. The
legal authority takes the slurry of helpless individuals, the human mush,
and *reconstitutes* it according to its godlike will. Banners, drums, songs

—they sound silly, unless everything else in life is leveled. "But Father's words were spoken to the wind..."

And then the change began. It was the finger of God. It was the arms of His children, reaching out of the dark abyss toward Him. It was based on nothing in the calculus of power.

> ... a friend—a fifteen-year-old girl—said quite suddenly and out of the blue, "Everything would be fine, but this thing about the Jews is something I just can't swallow." ...
>
> ... Why should he be forbidden to sing these songs that were so full of beauty? Merely because they had been created by other races? ...
>
> "You don't need a banner of your own. Use the one prescribed for everyone."

The day came when the real king's words were no longer spoken to the wind:

> "Father, what is a concentration camp?"

That is how children of privilege, the offspring of the Master Race, become children of God. Now the tools of civilization, the vine-grown university buildings, the chits of commerce, even the wheels of war, need to be turned to a new purpose. It's a lonely existence. You mustn't let them know that you have a heart.

> During their transport to the front their train had stopped for a few minutes at a Polish station. Along the embankment he saw women and girls bent over and doing heavy men's work with picks. They wore the yellow Star of David on their blouses. Hans slipped through the window of his car and approached. The first one in the group was a young, emaciated girl with small, delicate hands and a beautiful, intelligent face that bore an expression of unspeakable sorrow. Did he have anything that he might give to her? He remembered his "Iron Ration"—a bar of chocolate, raisins, and nuts—and slipped it into her pocket. The girl threw it on the ground at his feet with a harassed but infinitely proud gesture. He picked it up, smiled, and said, "I wanted to do something to please you." Then he bent down, picked a daisy, and placed it and the package at her feet. The train was beginning to move, and Hans had to take a couple of long leaps to get back on. From the window he could see that the girl was standing still, watching the departing train, the white flower in her hair.

And while Hans was at the front, Sophie returned from college to a home that could at times be a holy refuge.

> Now and again nurses from Schwaebisch-Hall, former friends of our mother's, came to visit. In that city there was a large hospital for mentally ill children.
>
> One day one of the nurses called. She was despondent and distraught, and we did not know how to help her. Finally she told us the reason for her grief. For some time past her wards had been carted off by the black vans of the SS and sent to their death in gas chambers. After the first contingents failed to return from their secret journey, a strange disturbance agitated the children in the institution. "Where are the trucks going, Auntie?"— "They are going to heaven," replied the nurses in their helplessness and confusion. From that time on, the children mounted the strange trucks singing.

Now you can understand the formation of these young people. But at their University they found a strange thing. *The machine of civilization was not wholly in the service of Hell.* From some ancient backwater of Teutonic scholarship a Professor Kurt Huber was found who specialized in theodicy. Theodicy is "the vindication of the justice of God, an important and complex area of philosophy".

I never heard of theodicy until I read *The White Rose*. Did you? Would you have expected to find it ensconced in the ivy halls of Nazi Germany?

There they were, enjoying the higher sweetness of their ancient culture, a bottle of wine, a nightlong philosophical discussion, a boat ride on the quiet river. (They had those boat rides at Tübingen too, I remember, on the Neckar River.) And from their duplicating machine flowed the fruits of civilization, thoughts a thousand years deep, brilliantly clear and true, written in the blood that they would soon shed.

I still stand in awe of the words of the White Rose. Maybe those words are the highest point ever to be achieved by Western civilization, reaching back to all that went before. Reaching back to the very roots in a city that is aptly named München, which means "Monks"—the founders of Western civilization.

The words are as true, and as cutting, now as they ever were then. Here I can offer only a sampling. Get more: buy the book and read all the leaflets.

> ... If the German people are already so corrupted and spiritually crushed that they do not raise a hand, frivolously trusting

in a questionable faith in lawful order in history; if they sur-
render man's highest principle...then, yes, they deserve their
downfall. ... Offer passive resistance—*resistance*—wherever you
may be, forestall the spread of this atheistic war machine before it is too late...Do not forget that every people deserves the
regime it is willing to endure.
[White Rose Leaflet I]

The words have a certain sting, do they not, when you begin to apply
them to a "lawful order" closer than Germany?

It is impossible to engage in intellectual discourse with National Socialism because it is not an intellectually defensible
program...At its very inception this movement depended on
the deception and betrayal of one's fellow man; even at that
time it was inwardly corrupt and could support itself only by
constant lies.
[White Rose Leaflet II]

In legalistic and overcivilized America, I substitute the pro-choice movement for National Socialism, and I get a perfect fit. Remember the fraud
recently exposed in the *Roe* and *Doe* decisions.

...since the conquest of Poland *three hundred thousand* Jews
have been murdered in this country in the most bestial way.
Here we see the most frightful crime against human dignity,
a crime that is unparalleled in the whole of history...Someone
may say that the Jews deserved their fate. This assertion would
be a monstrous impertinence; but let us assume that someone
said this—what position has he then taken toward the fact that
the entire Polish aristocratic youth is being annihilated? (May
God grant that this program has not fully achieved its aim as
yet!) All male offspring of the houses of the nobility between
the ages of fifteen and twenty were transported to concentration
camps in Germany and sentenced to forced labor, and all girls
of this age group were sent to Norway, to the bordellos of the
SS!
[White Rose Leaflet II]

This is the kind of thing that brought chivalry back to life at the University of Munich, and ended up causing an anti-Nazi riot there.

He [the German] must evidence not only sympathy; no,
much more: a sense of *complicity* in guilt. For through his

apathetic behavior he gives these evil men the opportunity to act as they do; he tolerates this "government" which has taken upon itself such an infinitely great burden of guilt; indeed, he himself is to blame for the fact that it came about at all! Each man wants to be exonerated of a guilt of this kind; each one continues on his way with the most placid, the calmest conscience. But he cannot be exonerated; he is *guilty, guilty, guilty!*

[White Rose Leaflet II]

Every law-abiding conservative may want to think that one over clearly, or then again, perhaps he may not want to?

. . . A victory of fascist Germany in this war would have immeasurable, frightful consequences. The military victory over Bolshevism dare not become the primary concern of the Germans. The defeat of the Nazis must *unconditionally* be the first order of business. . .

[White Rose Leaflet III]

So much for the lockstep superpatriotism of Germans. Would we have the guts to apply such thoughts to our own nation? It's a pretty lonely place to be in.

. . . Man is free, to be sure, but without the true God he is defenseless against the principle of evil. He is like a rudderless ship, at the mercy of the storm, an infant without his mother, a cloud dissolving into thin air.

[White Rose Leaflet IV]

Well, the Afghans would agree with that. But I don't think it plays any part in the New World Order, the *Pax Americana*, the World Bank. What if the wisdom of the ages turns out to be right after all?

. . . Freedom and honor! For ten long years Hitler and his coadjutors have manhandled, squeezed, twisted, and debased these two splendid German words to the point of nausea, as only dilettantes can, casting the highest values of a nation before swine. . .

Our people stand ready to rebel against the National Socialist enslavement of Europe in a fervent new breakthrough of freedom and honor!

[Last Leaflet]

The debasement of words by dilettantes: it does not fit our self-satisfied notion of Hitler as other, does it? It actually gets pretty close to our very own blow job leadership cadre, our mass media and so-called education. *I do not think we really won the Second World War.*

The White Rose had its whiff of success, even in the middle of the German war mobilization. During fall 1942, the first four leaflets spread around the University of Munich and farther, causing a new attitude among the students. Then came the speech of a crude *Gauleiter* who insulted the honor of their women. They rioted on 13 January 1943, but they didn't riot enough. If only they'd had Herat to show them how—another overcivilized city, but there the kindling wood was dry!

After that the tragedy approached its destined end. Betrayal, arrest, a trial presided over by a Doctor of Laws, and execution. Their end was clean; the Munich Nazis could not employ Pittsburgh police to sexually assault them. The accounts of their last words and gestures still bring tears to the eyes of some of us, two generations later.

> The police guards reported: "They bore themselves with marvelous bravery. The whole prison was impressed by them. That is why we risked bringing the three of them together once more... It was just a few minutes that they had, but I believe that it meant a great deal to them. "I didn't know that dying can be so easy," said Christl Probst, adding, "In a few minutes we will meet in eternity."
>
> "Then they were led off, the girl first. She went without the flicker of an eyelash..."

The resistance spread nevertheless to other cities, leading to more executions as the Nazi monster entered its death throes. But more. This story was there new-minted, like the only book in the rubble, for ruined Germany when the dust settled after the war.

Later Inge Scholl even apologized for this circumstance:

> This book was written in 1947 for use in the schools, for adolescents from the age of thirteen to eighteen. It was addressed to the young people who had grown up in the Hitler Youth and had experienced the great disappointment of their lives as a result of the Second World War...

As if such an audience made the work less serious! Without the blood of the martyrs the prostrate people could not have been washed. They would have choked on their unrepentance and died, and probably dragged down a sickened Europe with them. Look at the history of Communist East Germany, factory of dead babies, home of reborn Nazism.

But with someone clean to mourn, they put aside the insane nihilistic Nazi propaganda that had soaked their minds for half a generation. Everyone now takes this amazing transformation for granted. They performed the great deed that is misnamed "the Economic Miracle", rising from the center of the rubble and pulling ruined Europe back to life with them.

The miracle was far more than economic. The Adenauer Germans used papal social theory—the exact views of the White Rose—in opposition both to the Marxists *and to the free-market capitalists* to save everyone from starvation and rebuild their country. This free but non-capitalist regime was far more successful in bringing prosperity to everybody than any of the recent free-market revolutions in the Third World or the former Communist states.

Just like the White Rose, it was rooted in civilization and it was guided from above. While the elite of other countries, such as our own, always leads the way to selfish degradation, this German elite was different. *Noblesse oblige*, familiar to us from the story of the Trapp family (*The Sound of Music*), was often seen in Germany.

The Scholl children remembered the hectographed letters from Count Galen, Bishop of Münster, who risked his privileged position to tell the truth against the Nazis. How great he looks compared with American bishops who agree to any official demand from the United States cultural authorities.

Only Germany responded to the fall of Communism with generosity, accepting the *Ostmark* at par and going into debt to bridge the gap. I remember an American company in San Diego (General Atomics) gloating over how the ruble's fall enabled them to pay top Russian scientists only ninety dollars a month.

Only in Germany did the Supreme Court, heir to Professor Huber's theodicy, strike down a newly passed law *allowing* abortion. It violated the universal right to life and due process written in reaction to the Nazis in the postwar German consitution. This happened just a few years ago.

Poor Germany! That gesture now looks to be their last clean one. They are being taken over by the same human swine that we are so familiar with in the U.S.A. And once again the resistance is a day late and four marks short: instead of a last ditch stand the old theodicists have reached a compromise with (if you can believe it) the East German point of view. It's like old King Baudouin of Belgium, who flinched and let his parliament legalize abortion, when he could have plunged the whole country into a constitutional crisis, and maybe brought all Europe back to life politically.

The German birthrate is plunging; poor foreign workers are taking over the cities; the old peasant farms are being shut down to make way for the "free market"; famous businesses that were bywords of German quality, like Daimler-Benz, are going to marketeers of the Disney/Eisner stripe. The country is dying, and to me it is unutterably sad. They get so close and then blow it. I could yell at them. Depose the moneychangers! Trash your soulless careers! Make babies and go East—it's so huge, so needy, with such good odds of generous adventure!

German congressmen and leaders were among the greatest supporters of the Afghan Resistance. They were quick to recognize their better selves. If only they could have learned more from them.

The Diplomatic Service of the Lithuanian Republic

My second tale of heroism is a *eucatastrophe* straight out of Tolkien's essay *On Fairy-Stories*. Acted out in our real world with its sadly deficient cast of characters, it achieved a happy ending that would have been judged incredible in a romantic fantasy. Even more incredible to some is the fact that our own tainted national leadership was a steadfast and worthy part of the noble story. Something can go right, even this close to home.

Two disclaimers are called for before I embark on the history. First, except for one interesting digression, I do not rely much on personal knowledge, which in my case concentrates on my own nearby roots in Slovakia. I rely mainly on three sources. Bronis J. Kaslas' book *The USSR-German Aggression against Lithuania* (Robt Speller and Sons, NY, 1973) provides documentary background. Anatol Lieven's book *The Baltic Revolution* (Yale University Press, New Haven, 1993) offers in-depth history and interpretation of the events for all the Baltic nations. Richard J. Krickus' book *Showdown* (Brassey's, Washington, 1996) is a passionate and involved recounting of the Lithuanian story and its consequences.

Second, my focus on Lithuania is not meant to devalue the equally noble struggles of its neighbors, Latvia and Estonia. These nations are quite distinct and even dissimilar, but power politics threw them into the same trash bin and they climbed out shoulder to shoulder. Much of what I recount here applies to them too, but my personal encounters have been with Lithuania. Nor is it meant to ignore the great power of *Solidarity*, or devalue the poignant but different stories of other captive nations like my own Slovakia. Lithuania whose fate was most extreme will in a way speak for them all.

The three Baltic countries, Lithuania, Latvia and Estonia (south to north) are packed into a chilly, forested backwater of northern Europe, on the east shores of the Baltic Sea, along borderlands of powerful Russia, Scandinavia, Poland and Germany. Lithuania had a big empire for a few medieval centuries, but other than that, it has been the usual story of pious peasants being beaten up rather frequently by invading foreign powers. On the dotted line labeled "Sphere of Influence", the usual entry has been *Russia*.

Images of Lithuania usually feature tall blonde girls in lavish national costumes, singing folk songs and leaping through traditional dances. This could create an impression of an Arcadian race of natural heroes, destined to be better than the rest of us. Not so. They are earthen vessels like ourselves.

Lieven points out that under Soviet pressure their marriages failed as frequently as our own, and their abortion rate was astronomical, as elsewhere in the old Soviet Union. He mocks at the refusal of Lithuanian women to concern themselves with feminist issues, and thus completely misses the real source of women's misery. He dismisses as "naive" the far more realistic judgement (at her 1975 trial) of dissident heroine Nijole Sadunaite, the mirror image of our own Joan Andrews, who skewers more than her Soviet judges:

> ... What remains after your victory? Moral ruin, millions of unborn fetuses, defiled values, weak debased people overcome by fear and with no passion for life. This is the fruit of your labors. Jesus Christ was correct when he said, "By their fruits shall ye know them."

And now after liberation comes a wave of pornography.

Nor have the men escaped deformation. Under Soviet tutelage, some Lithuanian Jews worked with the Reds and fingered their compatriots for deportation. Under Nazi tutelage, some Lithuanian Gentiles avenged themselves by massacring thousands of Jews, men, women and children. (Let's you and him fight.) By 1993 many of the parties were having trouble admitting guilt, even though a magnanimous Jew, Alexandras Shtromas, has shown them the way. So the last Jews are leaving what once was a world center of their culture, and many Gentiles do not seem to realize what an impoverishment such a "purification" will be.

At times too an air of thuggishness is noted. On his cattle car to the Gulag in 1945, Father Fittkau was displeased to make the acquaintance of

> [o]ne of our bully boys, a Lithuanian bricklayer named Antonas, [who] kept chewing at a big piece of bacon he had stolen at Insterburg Prison. He was strong and hard-hearted enough to

brush aside the request and then the threats that came from those who thought he should share it with his hungry neighbors. ...all of us were forced to keep on good terms with this unpleasant character because he owned the only knife in the car...

Nevertheless the actions of this Antonas seem to be constructive, such as bringing in water, locating them on the map and lighting a fire. It could be that the short and frail Father Fittkau reacted disagreeably to the Lithuanian's mere size. That is another national characteristic. Their country may be tiny and defenseless, but individual Lithuanians can be quite impressive.

During my childhood, a very tall Lithuanian woman lived across the street with her husband and family. Her son Loren Lailer grew to be a giant (to be sure part of that was from his father, a mighty sailor). Unlike many men of his size, he was not spindly or gawky but had the proportions of a man of average height. He was taking the air at midnight in Coos Bay, a rough Oregon port town, when he noticed local toughs harassing some Japanese sailors. Misjudging his height in the distance, they paid no attention to him as he advanced, until he approached closely and they looked up—way up. Then the gang took to its heels. The grateful Japanese feted him with strong drink for the rest of the night.

In any event, the Lithuanians were giving no trouble to their neighbors when they were secretly condemned to be wiped out. First Nazi Germany took back the Lithuanian analogue of the Polish Corridor. Then on August 23, 1939, Nazi Germany and the Soviet Union formed a secret alliance (the Molotov-Ribbentrop pact) and agreed to divide the lands between. After some subsequent trading, Lithuania was given to the Soviet Union. When war broke out, the USSR invaded Lithuania. The Soviet ambassador formed a committee that agreed to incorporate Lithuania in the USSR, and later an "election" was held, with one candidate per position, to produce a legislative body to request this. On July 21, 1940, the puppet legislature requested incorporation in the USSR.

Britain, ally of France, was at war with Germany, and America was in sympathy with Britain. However much their elite wished to favor the Soviet Union, they could hardly condone its open collaboration with their enemy. Lacking an ulterior motive to do otherwise, they—and countries everywhere in the world that were not under the gun—reacted with sympathetic outrage against the Soviet action.

The United States, for example, responded by freezing all gold and credits held by Lithuania in the US. On the day of incorporation, the U.S. Minister of Kaunas, Norem, was called by the provisional Foreign Minister of Lithuania, Miss Avetenaite, to receive the formal protest against this. She handed it over and then

> added very quietly: "Please disregard all of our protests. We do not act independently any more. We appreciate what Washington is doing more than we dare tell. People are listening and I cannot say any more."

Norem responded with chivalrous anger:

> While the Lithuanians would prefer to have their investments held safe until better times return, the Bolsheviks apparently are much annoyed and a trifle perplexed. They desire so earnestly to make the whole business of the transfer seem spontaneous on the part of these poor people. ... [Another official] called informally also and explained that "advisers" in the Foreign Office could not understand our inability to accept the invitation to attend today's meeting of the Seimas. He himself expressed deep appreciation of our Government's understanding and treatment of the whole procedure.
> [Kaslas, document 143.]

All around the world, on that day and the next two weeks, Lithuanian diplomats appealed officially to their host countries to refuse to recognize the incorporation. The host countries agreed, and committed themselves. The masters do not understand how dangerous it is to let justice triumph in the hearts and actions of people like Norem. Not so easy, after that, to spin things around the other way as circumstances change!

Seizing this gift of moral authority, the Lithuanian diplomats from all around the world met in September 1940, to take upon themselves the duties of their vanished government, and to organize the Lithuanian emigres (especially in the United States) as their people. By not constituting themselves a government in exile, they avoided becoming a puppet of the Allies and being betrayed like Poland. [Kaslas, document 156]

Then the deportations began. Many of those taken away would die in exile. It was devastating for these simple peasants, thousand-year homebodies who knew every stream and tree of their own good earth. In *The Captive Mind*, Czeslaw Milosz poignantly captures this heartbreak in words I remember reading as a child.

In Kaslas document 160, *Instructions Regarding the Procedure for carrying out the Deportation of Anti-Soviet Elements from Lithuania, Latvia and Estonia*, there is a section labeled PROCEDURE FOR SEPARATION OF DEPORTEE'S FAMILY FROM HEAD OF THE FAMILY that is worthy of our modern social workers. It says that

it is essential that the operation of removal of both the members of the deportee's family and its head should be carried
out simultaneously, without notifying them of the separation
confronting them.

Detailed advice is then given as to how to accomplish this.

Soon (June 1941) the Soviets fled the advancing Nazis, taking care to
deport or massacre their prisoners before leaving. The Lithuanians took
the country back before the Nazis arrived, but the Nazis suppressed their
government, renaming the area *Ostland* in preparation for a German colonization drive. The former Lithuanian Minister in Berlin, Shkirpa, who
was still in residence there, refused to accept this situation and ended up
in a concentration camp.

The Lithuanian minister in Washington, Zhadeikis, immediately protested the German takeover. The response from the U.S. Government
(Berle) was vague about the status of Lithuanian independence [Kaslas,
document 177]. Not surprising, considering the USSR was now a belliger-
ent against Germany and would soon be a U.S. ally. But the U.S. leaders
were caught! Even though they recalled Norem from his diplomatic post
and never again reassigned him, they could find no legal grounds to reverse
course on the 1940 policy of nonrecognition.

When the Soviets returned in summer 1944, a new wave of refugees
escaped Lithuania, and the Diplomatic Service protested that the Soviets were not behaving according to international law. Despite their ruthless pro-Soviet actions elsewhere, the Western Allies still had to insist on
Lithuanian sovereignty. How it must have annoyed them!

On the spot in the refugee camps after the war, the Diplomatic Service
and its supporters pried an important concession out of the Western Allies:
refugee Lithuanians were not included in "Operation Keelhaul". They were
spared the horrors of the Gulag, and could remain in the West as displaced
persons, swelling the constituency of the Lithuanian National Committee.

A nation, incarnate in its Diplomatic Service and barred from its homeland, had to be kept alive in the community of exiles. Thus the Lithuanian
emigres (fresh and fluent still) took very seriously their national culture.
There was an air of unfinished business. They could not assimilate in their
host countries, anymore than the Afghans in Peshawar. They even passed
this attitude on to their children, who worked to become fluent in Lithuanian, hoping against hope for a chance to get involved with their homeland.
This was an exceptional reversal of the usual second generation American
immigrant attitude of leaving old roots behind and getting ahead in the
new world.

As wave after wave of deportations chewed up the Lithuanian countryside, a spirited resistance took to the spreading woods. The "Forest Brothers", as they were called, fought on for ten years in total hopelessness. They knew the West had abandoned them. Every country that fell into the Soviet orbit, from Hungary to China, was irreversibly gone, now that the Soviets possessed a nuclear arsenal. Frequent if short-lived popular rebellions were left to be cut down by the Red Army. How much deader was a nation that was not merely in the Soviet orbit, but actually absorbed into the Soviet Union itself.

I remember reading a self-published book, in the 1960s, that celebrated a fictionalized resistance in Slovakia. (There had in fact been some resistance there in the 1940s.) The idealistic, agrarian, religious tone was laden with everything that I favored, but seemed hopelessly out of date and doomed for a country that could be crisscrossed by Soviet warplanes in a few hours.

The grim fatalism of the Cold War preserved the worldwide status of the Lithuanian legations, as if in formaldehyde. Year after year went by, and nothing happened except words like the law of 1959 establishing Captive Nations Week in the United States. These words appeared to have no effect. Because obstinate nonrecognition could outlast the lives of diplomats, host countries like the United States recognized the right of the homeless Diplomatic Service to appoint successors to themselves. The aging Stasys Lozoraitis, Chief of Lithuanian Diplomats, appointed his son of the same name to head the legation in Washington, DC.

Meanwhile, the Soviet Union shuffled workers and farmers around to sovietize the tiny homeland, which is only two hundred miles across. This was happening in all the absorbed nations of the USSR. Social scientists employed by the American government agreed that the digestion was working well, and within a generation or two the whole USSR would be a homogeneous Russian-speaking modern power. Holding the candle for the doomed little nationalities was thus an exercise in futility.

The liberalization and opening to the West led by Khrushchev and Brezhnev had two effects, one good, one bad. The Prague Spring (actually led by a Slovak, Dubček) left an aftertaste when crushed, and dissidents throughout the Soviet empire began secret publications, called *samizdat*, based upon freedom of thought. Among the earliest and most important of these was the *Chronicle of the Catholic Church in Lithuania*.

On the other hand, some governments began to trade away their Lithuanian legations for Soviet favor. As far back as 1958, Pope John XXIII tried to close the elder Lozoraitis' legation in Rome for this reason, but there was an outcry by the Lithuanian diaspora. Once again exercising their weapon of moral authority, they forced the Pope to back down. As the years went on, however, the Diplomatic Service began to lose ground, being shut down in countries like Australia.

In Lithuania, surviving Forest Brothers were secretly held in honor by
the community. Parents needed heroes for a new generation growing up
in the drab, soulless Soviet world. It was an amoral world of pilferers,
informants and abortionists, and the parents struggled against the state to
present their Catholic faith to their children as an antidote.

In the United States, young idealists like Victor Nakas, Ginte Damusis
and Rita Dapkus attended Saturday language classes given by their elders.
Roots indeed! I remember that passion, mail ordering my Slovak language
materials from the St Cyril and Methodius nuns, and later visiting their
girls' school, St Cyril Academy in Danville, Pennsylvania, to encourage
them to keep on. I had just visited Slovakia in the strange stealth year of
Dubček, before he entered Prague, when he ruled only the Slovak territories
to the east. We still have a colorful bilingual yearbook of St Cyril Academy,
and a vinyl record of Slovak Christmas carols that they made.

We Slovaks, like other captive nations, had some free arbiters: in our
case, the Slovak Institute in the Vatican. Over against that was a living but
enslaved government in the homeland itself. The Lithuanians had nothing
at all at home to compete with the authority of their Diplomatic Service.
This was true of those in the USSR as well as emigres. That more clear-
cut reality created a unity between homeland and diaspora that nobody
understood. To paraphrase Gandalf, why should we expect to understand
it, until the hour has struck? Saturday language classes would shake the
world!

The Soviets, like the social scientists, assumed they had won, and allowed communications to reopen. Saturday class graduates could visit
their cousins. Father Casimer Pugevicius began receiving and translat-
ing into English the samizdat *Chronicles*. The outrageous 1970s case of
Simas Kudirka, a Lithuanian sailor who defected in U.S. territorial waters
and was handed back in a mini-Keelhaul, struck fire on both sides of the
Atlantic. They had him out of jail and into America in four years—that
mighty moral authority again—but before he left jail he had become acquainted with dissidents from all over the USSR.

These were the darkest days for freedom. Saigon fell. The earth of
Cambodia was filled with the victims of genocide, buried alive. Cracks
appeared in Latin America, and red flowed in. Afghanistan and Ethiopia
were occupied. The elder generation of Lithuanians began to die off, and
with it memories of the days before absorption in the USSR. Publishers of
the *Chronicles* were jailed or killed, but it persisted.

Under the strain of Afghanistan and the pressure of *Solidarity*, the aging
leaders of the Soviet Union died off, one after another. Finally Gorbachev
took power and decreed *glasnost* (openness or truth-speaking). In particular, ordinary Soviet citizens learned of the Molotov-Ribbentrop pact. The

social scientists could go on and on about economic forces and inevitable trends. Here was impacted injustice for everyone to understand! Whatever their ignorance, all Soviet citizens understood perfectly well the evil of Hitler, and therefore understood at once the meaning of the Molotov-Ribbentrop pact.

Suddenly everyone in Lithuania, even Communist apparatchiks, could see that independence had to be, even though it was geopolitically impossible. So did Russians, when the Lithuanians looked them in the eye. Gorbachev and Bush did not understand it. Armored in realism, they calculated the fluid dynamics of a political liquid that reaches its level in the pipes and basins of power, and did not believe in human beings who can charge uphill. The jockeying for position began.

Communists and academics (Sajudis) soon agreed with the old dissidents that independence had to be. The only question was when and how. The young firebrands from the Saturday classes quickly leaped onto airplanes and hustled over there to start building the new Lithuania, before the old Soviet Union even knew it was threatened. They swapped riches for poverty, freedom for tyranny, safety for fear, a world power for a tiny marginal country—of course! The Beloved calls. Did you know that the Hero and the Beloved are just two different appearances of the same human being?

A music professor, Vytautas Landsbergis, stumbled into the limelight. He was out of his depth, of course. His grandparents had had much to do with codifying the Lithuanian language. He was on the phone with Stasys Lozoraitis, the hereditary Lithuanian diplomat in Washington DC, and together they misread the signals from friendly low-level State Department people as being from George Bush. The independence questions, when and how? were answered. Right now, and openly!

This happened on 11 March 1990. The tiny Baltic tail began to wag the mighty Soviet Union. The inexperienced Landsbergis proved a master of intransigence. Gorbachev's pressure failed, and he began to lose power to Soviet imperial hard-liners. Separatists from all over the USSR came to Lithuania to watch events. The young American emigres brought in loads of equipment like fax machines, and wily young Lithuanians like Lionginus Vasiliauskas got them past customs.

Gorbachev believed he had no choice but to depose Landsbergis or be himself overthrown. In January 1991 the troops moved, like a replay of Hungary, Poland, Czechoslovakia. The puppet front (National Salvation Committee) was set up. The tanks rolled.

Landsbergis appealed for the people to surround and defend the government and TV buildings. According to Lieven, who is politically no ally of Landsbergis,

his tone was quite different from normal: clear, hard, incisive
sentences replaced the mumbling academicism as he promised
to resist to the end and called on the nation not to bow to
tyranny. As he himself told me afterwards, he had at the time
"no plans for personal survival".

There they stood, at 1:30 AM on the freezing winter morning of 13
January. They were unarmed. They did not attack, and they did not
run. The tanks rolled forward at the Vilnius TV tower and crushed a
few men, then they turned toward a hill and crushed a girl. Then they
started shooting into the crowd. Ambulances were taking people away.
They took the TV tower by another route and moved on to the parliament.
Throughout all this, the people did not attack and they did not run, but
stood there singing—*singing!*— religious and patriotic songs, "beautiful,
haunting" (Barnabas Wyman, quoted by Krickus).

They would have had to massacre thousands to get to the parliament.
The tanks called for orders. The Red Army flinched, and the tanks drove
away. It was the end of the siege, though nobody knew it then, and the
people would stay on guard for weeks.

This was "Bloody Sunday", and its signature photograph is the one of
the tank crushing the girl (Loreta Asanaviciute). Her feet are sticking out
from underneath, and half a dozen men are trying to push the tank off her.
Her uncle was there, and when they were driving her, mortally wounded, to
the hospital, she asked, "Uncle, are my legs too crushed to get married?"

On the monument in Vilnius to the dead of Bloody Sunday, Loreta's
name is listed first, because the Hero and the Beloved are the same person.

The other Baltic countries used the same tactics of surrounding their
buildings with crowds, with the same result. There was some bloodshed,
and Soviet beating and murder of border guards continued for months.
America was preoccupied with the Gulf War, but some of us were outraged.
We too remembered Hungary.

At that time I was a member of the anti-communist John Birch Society.
Its local leader Dave Swanson, an old Afghanistan project associate, and
I appealed to the national leadership of the JBS to seize the opportunity,
and campaign for the Baltic countries against Bush's policy of inaction.
To our surprise the national leadership refused. Landsbergis and the rest,
according to them, had tainted associations!

The Soviets were equally ineffectual. They couldn't even shut down
the TV transmissions. Various local and emigre technicians jury-rigged
a transmitter at the parliament building a week later, and were back on
the air. They broadcast a videotaped interview of the squirming National
Salvation Committee, and admitted to the reporter (John-Thor Dahlburg,

Los Angeles Times, 19 January 1991) that they were a little worried about an imminent Soviet assault.

All President Bush's efforts were aimed at preventing Gorbachev's fall, but he was forced by a popular outcry to cancel a summit meeting. Time wore on, with Landsbergis surviving and not flinching, and the Soviets unable to dislodge his government, despite occasional murders. At last on 19 August, the imperial hard-liners seized control in Moscow. Boris Yeltsin defied them from the ironically named White House, which was defended by surrounding crowds of supporters in just the same way the Lithuanians had done.

Remembering Vilnius, the Red Army refused to storm the White House. Soon the coup unraveled. This was just in time to save the Lithuanians, who had gathered around their parliament in Vilnius again. The tanks were rolling down on them when news of the failure of the coup arrived and they were called off.

Soon after that, Yeltsin took over and Communism fell. Gorbachev still did not get it, and clung to his position until the Soviet Union was dissolved that Christmas. His fall was ordained as soon as he decreed that the truth be spoken. Such an honorable cause of defeat could be envied by most of the victorious powers which have survived his.

Now at last, Russia and the rest of the world recognized independent Lithuania. The newly empowered government received back its gold, and duly appointed Stasys Lozoraitis as ambassador to the United States. They granted him the position he already held from his father, finishing an unbroken succession reaching all the way back to the long-fallen Republic, and in residence in the same legation on 16th Street.

Thus beyond all hope, a perfect bridge was completed at that place, fifty-one years wide, over the bottomless abyss of national death. Not once had that flag been struck. The United States for all its faults stood taller than countries such as Australia that cut it down in exchange for a few wretched trade concessions, enriching a privileged pig or two. Like some romantic signal scorned by all practical men, here it flew and was in the end more real than their realism.

How vital was the seamless web of honor that included that flag and everyone that loved it? It may have saved the world. As Krickus documents, it was the memory of Vilnius that inhibited the Red Army from storming Yeltsin in his White House. This means that the heroism and wild confidence of the Lithuanians not only brought down the USSR rapidly, but brought it down *almost bloodlessly*. This was a disintegrating empire with thousands of megatons of nuclear weapons, massive conventional power and millions of hungry and embittered troops. Not only the rest of the old Soviet Union, but everyone else on earth, has a lot to be thankful for, I think.

How to thank them? As soon as the great days were over, they fell to ordinary partisan bickering and the usual post-Soviet economic problems. But that is not the worst. In all their discussions of the future, a new despair is palpable. It is as if the Beloved that they saved, their little singing national culture in all its heart-catching beauty, is now doomed with all other such cultures to dissolve swiftly in the acid of the West— global commercialism.

We are at the center of *that* monster. Nobody knows it better than we do. Why not reach for the impossible again, on their behalf as well as our own? Once more save what is dear to us, by bringing down the last and strongest evil empire, the one right here?

The Afghan Warriors of God

In 1992, a San Diego girl, Jamie Earnest, started a kind of anti-abortion insurrection among the fellow students of her high school. She was distressed to find how many of the parents were furious at her for telling the truth to their children. I talked to Jeanne, who had had a similar experience twenty years earlier, and the two of us wrote a letter to her. We knew the lonely odds she was facing in an America where money isn't everything, it's the only thing.

To encourage her I hit the almanacs and constructed the following table to show the odds that the Afghans were facing on that snowy winter day of December 27 at the ragged end of an evil decade.

Comparison, ca 1979:	Soviet Union	Afghanistan
Population	19	1
Land Area	33	1
Per Capita Income	13	1
National Income	250	1
Status	Superpower	Third World
Weapons	Nuclear; Rockets; Jets; Tanks; Gas; Land Mines; Bombers; etc	Single shot rifles; Knives; Pits in the road

At the time of the letter, we and Jamie could still observe the dust settling from the fall of the Soviet Union a few months before. And the Afghans were just taking back their capital city. Communist Kabul fell *after*

Communist Moscow, just another tribute to the tenacity of this nation of warriors. A tremendous sea change, a tectonic shift had occupied the decade preceding, and when it was done the mighty superpower was history and its battered victim was staggering back to life.

Mind you, this was no halfhearted toy war with "rules of engagement" like our failed effort in Vietnam. The Soviets were absolutely not inhibited by moral or political considerations, with the lone exception of nuclear weapons. They threw all their weight into the struggle, killed Afghans by the millions, and devastated the already poor and arid country.

And the Afghans beat them into exhaustion, into collapse, and changed the world for all of us. It is the greatest deed of the Twentieth Century. It stands there like a giant on a ridge line, thundering in the night. If we ignore it or are already forgetting it, then surely we are fools. How, how were they able to do it? How can we be more like them?

Read one or more of the many great accounts of the Resistance from the inside. I hope you can still find them in your bookstore; but if not there, then in your library. Each one of them is written by a heroic adventurer risking his or her life to bring out the truth (and you may be surprised how often it is "her"). Here's an incomplete list which I have referenced for this section:

In Afghanistan, by Jere Van Dyk (Coward-McCann, New York, 1983). *Caught in the Crossfire,* by Jan Goodwin (E.P. Dutton, New York, 1987). *Sisters on the Bridge of Fire,* by Debra Denker (Burning Gate Press, Los Angeles, 1993). *Night Letters,* by Rob Schulteis (Orion Books, New York, 1992). *The Wind Blows Away our Words,* by Doris Lessing (Random House, New York, 1987). *Afghanistan, the Soviet War,* by Edward Girardet (St. Martin's Press, New York, 1985).

This is wealth of vibrant detail that I cannot match, though I have personal knowledge from activism in Seattle and San Diego, and a trip to the Peshawar area in 1984. So what I offer here will be mostly a kind of character sketch. We need to know that character, because this is a story that started out like so many before it, started out in the darkness I described above, doomed to come to a sad ending in a few months like the others. There was something about Afghanistan that made this story end up different. Perhaps Rob Schulteis puts his finger on it:

> The original name of the place, Yaghistan, means "Land of the Unruly", "Land of the Ungovernable", or "Land of the Out-of-Control" . . .

They love great tales, great boasts and rollicking practical jokes. Schulteis goes on to describe some of these, like the trailside motivational seminar for camels, and the modified Biblical precept of a foot for a beard. The other authors tap into this vein too; it's a pretty rich one, especially at border stations. I won't spoil the stories for you—read them yourselves.

Even my family got in on the fringe of this. Jeanne remembers the women at Faizullah Kakar's house in Seattle, giggling as they slipped the eyeballs into my rice. They looked just like raisins, and I scarfed them down without even noticing. Another time, when Jeanne and I were inside a San Diego hall helping with a presentation to some students, our little son stayed outside and played with some newly arrived Afghan refugee children. The game was "Hide from the Russian", and of course Tommy—tall, pale, without a word of Dari or Pashto—was the Russian.

Jeanne and I were involved from near the beginning of the Resistance, and we can claim some prescience. On the day of the invasion, Afghan emigres were out demonstrating everywhere, including far-off Seattle. We, who were then married only a few months, gleaned a phone number from a newspaper article. Soon we were in touch with the young epidemiologist Faizullah Kakar, who wrote the article "Afghan Blood" to explain the peoples and their flinty resistance for our little magazine *November*.

No one who gets acquainted with Afghanistan is ever after free of the fascination of it. It is the size of Texas, but gives the impression of being a whole other planet, more than able to hold its own against our homogenized masses. Not some protected tourist park with old-fashioned folkways prettily displayed live for vacationers to see. It stands on its own, and seems limitless.

I often toy with the idea of a simple mathematical transformation of the globe that would give a map of the human spirit. On it Afghanistan would be huge, and cover more than half the world; all the rest of us would be squeezed into space equivalent to the pettiness and sameness we so eagerly embrace. Afghanistan is border country. All through history, empires have pushed part way into Afghanistan and petered out short of conquest. And yet they all remain alive and vibrant today in their descendants, who form not a melting pot but in Susan Aronson's word a *mosaic* of so many wild and beautiful colors.

There are the ancient, wearily civilized Persian (Dari) speakers whose cities like Herat and Balkh are thirty centuries old and more. Zoroaster started the religion of the Magi there, a thousand years before Christ. These city folks are dominated by the tribal people, the Pathans, whose code of honor, called *Pushtunwali*, is as ancient as the cities. The Pathans are the ones who give outsiders such a feeling of the Wild West in Afghanistan. Even today, many are nomadic cattle drivers. There are people of a European cast (Nuristanis) in the eastern woods. There are Orientals (Hazaras) in the center, reputed to descend from Genghis Khan's troops:

they liberated their inaccessible mountains before the Soviets came, and kept them that way through the whole occupation. There are Turkish peoples in the north, and desert peoples, such as the Baluchis, in the south. There are no railroads and few paved roads.

What united them, as Dr Kakar wrote, was *Jihad*, the so-called holy war—the fight for the right. The Western image of millions of screaming Khomeiniacs is distorted. It is more like the Christian ideal of chivalry. As Peter Kreeft points out in his book *Ecumenical Jihad*, it is just as valid for Christians and everyone else as it is for Moslems. It is not so hard to distinguish a right from an abominable wrong, if you are willing to think straight.

Let me illustrate this point. Debra Denker poses a question:

> ... Commander Mohammed Naim lies shivering in a hospital bed [after] an artillery shell ripped off his left leg and broke his right leg and left arm...
>
> I tell Naim that everyone in Jaji, from every party, admires what he has done. His dark, frank eyes meet mine. It is perhaps one of the few times he has looked at a woman directly. "Everything I have done, I have done for our faith."
>
> The faith of this young warrior echoes the faith of another warrior I have met, Mother Teresa of Calcutta, the relentless warrior against poverty. I reflect on the certainty of these two, and wonder if they would understand each other and allow the differences of dogma to be submerged in a sea of faith.

I can answer that question with an unequivocal yes, though it would be clearer to substitute "trust" for "faith" in the last sentence. I am an old-line papal Catholic and have always worn that on my sleeve when dealing with the Afghans. It never created a barrier. Instead, it led to a quicker meeting of the minds. When I interviewed Gulbuddin Hekmatyar, the feared leader of the most extreme fundamentalist *Hezbi Islami*, he even told me that Muslims were permitted to violate their own rule against wine to extend hospitality to a Christian or Jewish guest.

As for Mother Teresa, I never spoke to her, but I share her faith, and we know how well-beloved she was among people of all religions in India. Out there, all the extremes get close together, not because of mushiness but because of clarity. Clarity about what is loved and what is evil.

This clarity creates a brilliant sophistication that has astonished more than one guest of the *mujahideen*, when he found it in some illiterate peasant on top of a mountain peak. They all listened to the BBC, and their savvy questions about politics half a world away could surprise the visitor.

But it came by arrow-straight logic from knowledge of reality in their own back yard, plus familiarity with human nature and the twists and turns of language.

That is why they shut down the land reform program by refusing to accept stolen land. That is why modern, educated *girls* were the first to hit the streets in protest in the capital city of Kabul, in the teeth of the Soviet program that was supposed to liberate women. That is why Afghans stormed the U.N. compound in New York, going up the wall in waves, trying to burst in and kill the Soviet leader Kosygin with his lies still on his lips.

Such clarity could lead to decisive and fierce action. It was March 1979, the year before the Soviet invasion. In melancholy, worldly-wise Herat (so lovingly depicted by David Chaffetz), people mulled over a decree that had come from the new Afghan Communist government. It harmlessly required them to send their daughters in for "education", but they were sensitive enough to smell what that really meant, what later proved true in Nicaragua and other places. The little girl who was happily tugging her rag doll around their home (and her mom and dad knew every detail of her bright young personality) was to be pulled out into the cold world and trained as a sexual toy, a semen spittoon for atheists in power. And they objected violently! A hundred thousand rioters surged through the city, slaughtering the resident Soviets and their Afghan sympathizers, and hoisting their heads on poles.

Authority in an Afghan family or village or province comes from within. No demand from outside is any more than a proposal, until the village men sit in a circle, a *jirga* or a *shura*, deliberating as armed equals with power to veto any tyranny. No man's traditional dress is complete without the well-kept, shining gun, but the women dress in bright colors so they can be seen and never harmed in a battle. The gun is an effective sign of every man's authority, should he find sufficient reason, to decree a fight to the death. Afghans and all who deal wisely with them are very polite.

Here is one reason why the Afghan story had a different ending than the others. Afghans have centuries of experience herding many species of domesticated animals, from camels to sheep. But the people themselves cannot be herded. It was not possible, as the Soviets discovered, to crack the whip around the fringes of the crowd and get them all moving as you wished. They just didn't get the point. The ones you hadn't yet hit would ignore you. You had to beat down every single one of them.

Edward Girardet observed:

> While traveling through Paghman province in late May, 1982,
> I came across veritable traffic jams of weapons caravans of Uz-
> beks and Tajiks weaving their way through the Kohistan moun-

tains, only three or four minutes flying time from Bagram airbase [the main Soviet airbase near Kabul], to Kunduz and Takhar
provinces to the north.

Similarly, Jere Van Dyk's escorts would simply ignore helicopters that
were leveling nearby villages exactly like their own. It is not "fatalism" but
a sublime courage and faith that faces a power that can easily destroy you,
but may not get around to it in the time provided.

Here's another reason. My sister Rose is always relaying pathetic stories
of acquaintances who cannot function or do right by their families, thanks to
some trauma or other, bad parents, discrimination, addiction. The Afghans
solved that problem. No social workers or counselors are needed. Just snap
out of it!

If you think I am kidding, try out these traumas: Burying the burned
or crushed bodies of all your children, after a bombing attack. Having your
young wife or little sister raped and then thrown naked out of a helicopter,
to be smashed on the village square below. Or (you are a young woman
teacher in Kabul) being tortured and then locked in a room full of pieces
of women, including a friend whom you recognize.

Afghans are not made of stone and steel. These things tear you apart
inside, just as the artillery shells rip big pieces off your body. Of course now
and again you go down, blind and shaking. The *mujahideen* understand
and give you space and time to recover. When the flashback is over, you
stagger erect and start putting one foot in front of the other again. You
are still breathing, so one way or another, you will get the job done.

A third reason the Afghans endured was the fruit and consequence of
the first two. They could appeal for help. They could take on a task that
was far more than anyone could really do (but it had to be done). Then
they could look you in the eye. Whether you were Arab or Pakistani or
American, you knew that you were not going to get off the hook. If you
did not help, they might fail and go down; but they would never bow to
worldly reality, which counted up their pitiful per capita income, around
one hundred fifty dollars a year, and decreed them helpless.

The help came only in a trickle from foreigners afraid to be linked to
a loser. Each year (1980, 1981, 1982, 1983, 1984, 1985, 1986) the Afghan
resistance was judged to be reaching the end of its strength. Each year, it
was estimated they could only hold out one more year. They themselves
spoke of winning a "moral victory". A moral victory is what you win when,
like Poland in 1944 and the Hungarian patriots of 1956, you all get betrayed
and slaughtered, leaving only a memory like a fishhook in the minds of your
betrayers. One more year, and then one more, and then one more... Your
endurance turns out to be more than you expected, maybe more than you

wanted.

The Afghans thought their appeals were making no impression, and so it appeared, from the mainstream media. The title of Doris Lessing's book is part of a quote from a *mujahid* commander in 1986:

We cry to you for help, but the wind blows away our words.

Much of her book elaborates on this theme. And so thought most of the other reporters. They sweated and bled and pleaded, and it was all wasted on deaf ears, it seemed. Yet in the end it turned out, despite all the powers of darkness, that they were heard. How was this? Here my own experience offers some answers.

After we moved to California, Jeanne and I were angry at this very inaction, and we determined to try to start something. In Poway, the San Diego suburb where we then lived, we hung up copies of a crude poster that said

THE BAD GUYS
DON'T
ALWAYS WIN.

This message of hope
is brought to you
by the people of Afghanistan.

At great cost to themselves.

It caught the eyes of Susan and Dennis Aronson, a Peace Corps couple who had worked in Afghanistan. You could describe their family by saying that for them, JFK has never died. Soon Susan, an efficient organizer, had taken our project in hand, and word was going out to thousands of other Peace Corps alumni in newsletters.

She introduced us to Elaine Brantingham, a conservative political activist, and she passed the word to her friends. After Dr Robert Simon spoke at our meeting, we were stunned and happy when a Mr Bob Hunter was so touched by the story that he dashed off a check for five hundred dollars to Dr Simon on the spot. We didn't even know then that Bob's son was Congressman Duncan Hunter.

Beyond our horizons, many other networks of people were forming the same way, apart from the mainstream, moved by the truth as if privately. The Afghans had their emigre groups and newsletters everywhere, and everywhere they found one or two who would listen. Soon there were the French doctors, and the West German congressmen, who visited personally at great risk. There were honorable Jews who really meant it when they said "Never again," and had already been shaken by the fate of Cambodia. There were elements of Hollywood, old Western actor Loren Greene for one. Debra Denker consulted in the making of *Rambo III*, which (don't let the reverse hypocrisy fool you) was deliberately pitched to help the cause.

There was a group of Congressmen like Duncan Hunter who had an honest and old-fashioned belief in America, expressed by his "Western Barbecue" campaign fund-raisers with their traditional themes. They influenced the better side of Ronald Reagan, who had the same feelings at heart; and in the end the President flung aside the professional advice and ordered real arms, like Stingers, to be sent to Afghanistan.

It was great to see genuinely wealthy and powerful people, movers and shakers, circulating among Afghan cultural exhibits and listening to the slide shows of Dr Simon and other IMC doctors and nurses. It brought out the best in them. One time I was invited to say a few words to the assembled dignitaries. I told them that America was used to giving foreign aid, but in this case we were *receiving* foreign aid from the Afghans. By giving everything they had, they were hauling the whole world out of its despair, showing us that right and justice had a chance, that the good fight was possible, that there were heroes.

I remember Mrs Aronson, who had been around, as she warned us there was a difference in how women were treated in male-dominated Muslim societies. She loved Afghanistan but disliked Saudi Arabia. The Saudis' attitude was bullying, while the Afghans were chivalrous. Jere Van Dyk tells of a teahouse on the arms smuggler's road:

> Two boys, about seven and eight, in dirty pajama-clothes, skullcaps, with pudgy hands and bare feet, walked around the mat, pouring tea, collecting greasy Afghani notes. ...I asked Mallem where the boss was. He asked one of the kids. He looked at Mallem and said that he was.
> "How old are you?"
> "Eight, I think."
> "Where is your father?"
> "My father was killed by helicopters. My brother and I are now in charge. We have two sisters and our mother. We must support them."

Nobody who has dealt with the Afghan cause can fail to notice how many women are among its supporters. Not just reporters and writers, but also doctors and nurses and leaders of aid groups. No traditional shrinking violets, these are very modern Western independent women from half a world away. I mean really independent: ready, every one, to dress up as a *mujahid* and go for a hike in a free fire zone, so you can imagine how unkindly they take to *purdah*, and how they sympathize with the Afghan women who are stuck with it. Their sharp prickly opinions are all over the spectrum. And what attracts them to this antithesis, this most masculine of warrior nations? Each story is different of course, but it is not difficult to discern a common theme. There is such a thing as love.

The experience of the *Jihad* teaches how much the economy of heroism is like that of love. You plunge ahead without counting; and when you are in need, you cry for help. It is as if reality itself becomes moody. Personal encounters like comradeship and betrayal become much more important than abstract security and long-range financial planning. Each new day is a whole world unto itself.

My wife still remembers how the freshly-returned Afghan warriors entertained our one-year-old son in the basement of Faizullah Kakar's house. These people have heart, so much heart that they could do amazing things with next to nothing. One ten-year-old boy watched grieving as the tanks which had just killed his father stormed through his village. He prayed to God to be able to do something, but he had no weapon. He stood there while the tanks rolled by him onto a bridge, then took off his jacket and jammed it in the treads of one of them. The tread stalled and the tank swerved, falling into the gully. The one behind it swerved to miss it, went off the other side of the bridge and was also destroyed.

When Jay Hoffman heard that story, he said, "Imagine what he could have done if he'd had a rock!"

The Soviets had to pull out all the stops. Their main weapon was starvation and "migratory genocide": the destruction of thousand-year-old irrigation systems, for instance. They distributed toy bombs to blow the hands and feet off children and so force their families into exile. I still have a graphic poster labeled *Disarmament Soviet style*. Anthropological experts sought the weak points of Afghan culture; its sexual shyness, for instance, led to the tactic of helicopter rape I mentioned above. Chemical weapons were used in remote areas. Carpet bombing leveled ancient cities like Herat.

Afghan boys, however, take as naturally to weapons as American boys take to cars. The experts scoffed at the romantic notion that these primitive warriors could handle a modern weapon like the Stinger. Their eyes bugged out of their heads when the first reports trickled back: the warriors were achieving an early kill rate of 80%, until the Soviets learned to fly high out of range. The best trained American troops reached less than 50%.

The Stingers appeared at the end of 1986, but it was still a long hard slog for the Afghans. It became clear at last that with contested air power, the Resistance had effectively taken back the land. On the imperial level, Reagan stared at Gorbachev, and Gorbachev blinked. The Soviet withdrawals began, and were soon complete.

And did this lead to the happy ending at last? Not so easily. There was layer after layer of bitterness to work through, and they are not through them all even now. Our advisers, hoping to finish the war quickly, persuaded the *mujahideen* against their better judgement to try for a decisive victory, a Dien Bien Phu. This was the siege of Jalalabad in 1989, which ended in disaster.

So the warriors went back to their Afghan wisdom. The Kabul regime quickly abandoned Communism and terror, becoming just another warlord struggling to survive. Inch by inch, in complicated detail, fighting and making deals, the Afghans took back their towns, until provincial capitals began to fall. It took three years. Finally in 1992 Kabul itself fell into their hands, and the long holy war was over.

Other wars were not over. I spoke of clarity above. The Afghans live clarity; and there were some unresolved issues beyond the demise of Communism. It infuriated Western agencies that they could not be set aside once and for all, locked in the cellar by some formula of legitimacy, so that they could deal with one all-powerful Afghan Government. But that was not the way it was to be—and in this I am on the side of the Afghans. Long live the mosaic! So what if it makes the accounting a little more complex. That is what you hire the accountants for.

Hekmatyar's Islamic fundamentalists held out against the moderates, who held Kabul with the aid of a northern warlord formerly associated with the Communists. Now the swollen capital city began to lose much of its population, because paradoxically most of the countryside was at peace while Kabul was regularly shelled. The refugee camps of Pakistan eerily emptied, the people returned home despite the mines, the devastation, the total poverty—as soon as it became obvious they could set one stone upon another without being bombed out.

In typical Afghan fashion, his own soldiers tired of Hekmatyar and his endless, pointless shellings. They simply set him aside in favor of a new force, the *Taliban* (it means something like "Students of religion" or "Theology majors") which had recently arisen and was taking over towns in the south. Now another of those Afghan-style elections took place, people simply transferring their allegiance *en masse* in large areas. Islamic law was enforced and women went behind the veil. Kabul fell, once again with little fighting, and the last traces of Communist rule were erased. Najib, the former Communist ruler, was killed, his body hung on public display.

And so it stands now, with most of the land under Taliban rule. Not all! That would be too easy! The Panjshir and much of the north are still

in the hands of the moderates. So there is still no unified government for
the foreigners to deal with. And anyway they do not want to deal with the
Taliban, with their veils and their scary Islamic ways, their killing of adul-
terers and their cutting off of thieves' hands. The land is unreconstructed,
not even agriculture has recovered, thanks to the mines and the ruined irrigation. The people are bitterly poor and endangered, still dependent on
a trickle of aid shipments. This information comes through Zia Waleh, a
San Diego Afghan activist and restarauteur.

So does that mean it is all a waste, gone for nothing? I say not! There is
an undercurrent that I have long followed in this history, and all the events
conform to it. If I am right—and I do not think that God will abandon
His best and wildest nation of heroes so easily—then there is a secret sense
behind it, that will take some time to unfold.

Never forget Afghanistan's extreme poverty. The whole country could
be bought and sold as an afterthought by any Western economic power.
The standard Third World pattern—the end of independent village life,
the gigantic capital city, the ownership of all roads to the future by a tiny
moneyed elite to whom most of the people are useless, no matter how
anyone kids himself about education programs—came last in the world to
Afghanistan, and was interrupted by the Soviet invasion. With that over, it
was once again all ready to be set up, and still is, *by people with the best of
intentions.* But it still has not jelled, with too many shells flying, too much
land changing hands too often. If any stones have been set upon stones, it
is Afghan hands that have done the setting, and in their own way.

I may be called presumptuous, expounding my theories about a faraway
injured land filled with millions of people, most of them my betters. But
I can only shed light with my own lamp. It appears to me that this time
of anarchy has saved Afghanistan from slumping into the melt, a term I
will explain in the last chapter; from sinking into the final despair and
a hopeless servility that is eating all the rest of the world. It could be
critically important not just to them, but to all of us. It could be the key
to the millenium.

Are old-fashioned nomad caravans picking their way through the rubble
again, even if for no better reason than that they have no option? Are mud
houses going up, donkeys and bullocks cultivating any strips of unmined
land that can be found? Is there anyone left who knows how to make blue
tiles, so that the ancient cities can be rebuilt, wall by wall?

If I am right, then the best days may lie ahead. In the meantime, my
childhood memories of the board game *Risk* may offer some comfort to
tired *mujahideen.* I was always struck by how huge "Afghanistan" was on
that game board: it was a great slice of Central Asia. But now it seems
to have come true. Look at any new map of Asia, at the layer upon layer

of new countries (old Muslim nations) that lie to the north of Afghanistan. All broken from the atheistic empire, all freed by Afghan valor. Space for caravans to navigate by the stars. The ancient Silk Road, and the call to prayer heard again in Samarkand.

Chapter 7

Do Not Despair

You do not know what part of your victory is small, and what part is great, until you have won your whole victory and lived it. I am here to tell you not to give up even on the "small" parts. Reach for what the heart desires! It says in Scripture that even the least of our prayers will be heard.

It is a trick of the defeated mind: What appears small is really just pushed aside, because there seems no hope of winning it. The gate to freedom may be only a small part of the encircling prison wall. What could be smaller (in a world context) than your own son or daughter? This measuring of hopes is really a concession to despair. We have been trapped in changeless despair for long enough. There is no need to accept anything less than a world of color and beauty.

When the poetic mind delights in something, it is because that something is a great good. Trust your instincts, and do not despair. How epic, even in the twentieth century, to have genuine caravans threading the mountain passes and navigating the plains. How beautiful it is that not only did the Afghan resistance win their war, they won it *with camels.*

In this final section of my book, I will just begin to show how some things inevitably lost from modern life are not only good and beautiful, but necessary. And our children, your children can reach them. I include your troublesome children, your bad children, your children who are booked and condemned and lost.

Life is rightfully a comedy. Those who sell despair may squeal with horror at some of the mighty effective suggestions to follow. Just roll over them! You have the power to abandon what they find necessary and revive what they want dead. There are secret weapons, from a forgotten punishment so gentle that it is practically a blessing, to a little-known monkish vow even more radical than chastity. There are allies so near at hand it

181

will scare you to meet them.

In case you do not think I am serious, I will go into detail about some wretched modern realities that nobody can do anything about. It turns out we can solve them. Easily. By dynamiting those mental prison walls.

Yes to the Underclass

Being part of the underclass is a consequence of poverty. In America, poverty is a result of having a heart, of letting your children live and caring for them, and of speaking the truth, or of refusing to speak lies. Shame, guilt and punishment are all a consequence of poverty.

If you are poor and find a notice from the police in your mailbox, it is guaranteed to wreck your day, or worse. But if you are rich or important, no problem. You did not inhale.

This book is aimed at the underclass. If you are happy with your prosperous future, I haven't got much to say to you. If you are poor but kidding yourself (I'll be an executive someday!), I haven't got much to say to you either. But even if you are rich, if you balance it on the tips of your fingers, if you know it can be gone tomorrow—then you are ready for this message, and I ask you to listen.

I have to answer an objection. In taking an axe to law and civility, have I rejected old friends and allies, who have done nothing to deserve it?

There are Congressman Duncan Hunter and his family: he tries to make good law, his mother spent her last strength working to help the Afghans. What about good assemblymen like Bruce Thompson who fight the persecution of poor motorists? Good judges like Clarence Thomas who have whip weals on their backs because they insist on judicial honesty? Antique and honorable officials like the 1991-1992 San Diego County Grand Jury who wrote Report #2, *Families in Crisis,* exposing the infamies of the legal kidnapping establishment, and were later vengefully persecuted by the establishment for doing so? I met the head of that Grand Jury one time, when my son was visiting a polling place with the Boy Scouts. He was like a citizen leader of the Roman Republic.

I do not reject them. They plow their field, and I plow mine. They deal with law and therefore with its owners: the wealthy and powerful. They have an uphill struggle, in the great universities where the lie dominates all teaching, in the executive associations where mention of anything restraining the personal will of the powerful shows an embarrassing lack of good taste. They have to deal with a master class of Clinton wannabes, whose hope is to get sucked like their hero. Occasionally something with new shock value (like partial birth abortion) can make momentary headway against the suction, but it is an uphill battle, an exhausting one. Certainly I honor all my legal friends (and I take the trouble to vote too), because each temporary victory, every iota of rhetoric and delay that breaks the flow of corruption, is of value to so many of the poor and downtrodden.

But I am too tired to go on shoveling that bog. And I have children, who need to be introduced to a better class of people. It is my job to turn my back on the upper class and speak where there is more hope of being heard. Connie Youngkin, the anti-abortion crusader, recently passed out pamphlets at the doors of various San Diego County high schools. She got a bitterly hostile reception in the upscale neighborhoods, but the underclass high schools, the ones with the drugs and gangs and race problems and dropouts, were more friendly to her. As they value her, so I value them.

Here and now. Just as they are. The beaten-down elders, as well as their fierce children.

This not an empty formula of encouragement. We really have no other hope. Just as anti-Communist activism went nowhere until *out-of-control* Afghans entered the picture, so honor will achieve no victory in America until the morally upright underclass enters the picture. By "morally upright" I do not only mean the underpaid working people who support the whole inverted-pyramid economy on the backs of their pickups. I also mean the welfare mom who is more generous than the well-paid career woman; the street corner gang members who care more about right and justice than powerful lawyers and police; the unemployed boy who is more ready for honest work than the climber on the corporate ladder; even the herb grower or drug dealer who by self-restraint can come closer to honoring the Hippocratic Oath than does the American Medical Association.

Do I surprise you by including you among the morally upright? Take it to heart! They've got you feeling dirty because their feature writers and social workers vent your troubles in public. I'm telling you that you are cleaner of heart than they are. I want this book to spread around the welfare housing, the decaying cities and the country towns that are falling apart. In those places the people speak the truth more often, so in those places there is hope.

Moral Decay — *Jihad*

Everyone fears for his children's souls in America, but there is nothing inevitable about it. Moral corruption comes from the culture of wealth (if you doubt me, examine the supermarket checkout counter headlines) and is cut down to size as soon as you deny that culture of wealth its primacy in your life. That means be yourself, even if it is your tired and heartbroken self, and do not dream of being like those glamour sluts. That tired and even heartbroken self is loved by your children.

This is only a start. Each self has the deeds of a lifetime written upon it. I am speaking to people who do not use lying as a way of law and life. Instead of velvet glove language, phrases like "killing my baby" come from their lips. So there is no avoiding the dark side. What if you—or someone close to you—are guilty of what you admit is really bad? That makes "morally upright" seem a mockery, if you are upright enough to admit the truth. Does this commit you to serve the devil, or at least to serve the feminists?

Let me start by making it hurt worse—like scrubbing the dirt out of a wound. Follow the very same example. They try to lift the load from you by offering the new abortion pill: it's so little, and not bloody. It merely sends the embryo away without nourishment so that it starves. But that is poetically an even greater offense. Like the "Little Match Girl" your child is driven out into the snow to die. There is no escape: nothing short of a heart of fire will do. There is no choice but hospitality.

Poetry makes the fiercest conscience. I am not only talking about abortion, or to women, believe me. You can fill in your own details, as can I; you know where you have added to the ruin. Fill them in poetically, and they will bite their sharpest. You have to bleed to get the poison out. This is the opposite of mushmouthed counseling and weaseling excuses. You may have to think of months or years of your life that you have blanked out, because if so, those times have blanked you out, and turned you empty and bland.

I deny that this pain is despair. This is where my religion shows through. To a Catholic it clearly points the way to a confessional (in Lincoln, Nebraska if necessary). I will strike a blow against Feeneyism though, and offer a path to the others. The Faith is offered to whom God wills, and only to them the confessional; but there must be a way to justice for everyone else too.

The penitent unpeels his or her fingers from the goal badly grasped at; lets the American Dream float away down the stream. To take its place I suggest a pilgrimage. Mecca, Fuji, Compostela, the Ganges: whatever your tradition is, it is sure to offer something better than our money righteousness, which sees greed as the greatest virtue. If you are too poor for the physical pilgrimage there are pilgrimages of the spirit, all taken slowly, on foot, using much time, in the company of other pilgrims. The world may find this odd, but your children will not, they will love the story.

If you are not guilty of such a great offense, you may as well take the pilgrimage too. Who can map his future nights?—your only assured way to the American Dream may lie through the same evil. So let it go ahead of time. Back in the 1950s when our way of life was innocent, the American Dream could be blameless too. Now we have only the two choices: determine to fight for the right, or consent to sink into the blood.

If you have children, you cannot teach them to be at peace with the new America, or with the World Bank world, with its crushing of the poor and friendless, and its worship of ruthless wealth and power. That would be more evil than any personal misdeeds in your past. And you know that your kids cannot just slip by on the way to a career. The "politically correct" power geeks occupy all the educational passes, and they require the children to bow down and kiss their dirty idols.

The only escape from our moral decay is to abandon the peace and embrace the *Jihad*. Of a time similar to our own, the prophet Ezekiel said "they have misled my people, saying 'Peace' when there is no peace" [Ezek 13:10]. *And this is good news!* Abandon false hope, and see how the truth makes us free.

In war we have enemies and we have a right to fight them. Bring them crashing down without a single qualm of conscience: The school officials who fine a poor family $500 for a single day of school missed. The free marketeers who take away your man's job. The media fountains of lying and moral corruption. The secret informers and secret counselors who destroy your child. They are enemies and your warrior's job is to ruin them.

We can rightfully aim for the *utter destruction* of evil institutions. No need to flinch, just wipe out the "Child Protective Service" and all its surrounding laws. Lay waste everything from enforcement tools to international lending agencies and leave nothing in their place. It's a myth that anyone needs them. We get along without them in Tijuana.

Obliterate the false universities (start with the weaker ones, like the turncoat Catholic colleges that support abortion) and leave nothing at all in *their* place. And what about the Fortune 500, aren't there some companies whose ruins would be more beautiful than their living reality? Then use your voting dollar to make it happen (it doesn't take much blood, in the investor sharkpool), and do not feel any obligation to pick up the pieces.

Young men! Do not be ashamed to enjoy destroying the enemy in such a just war. They fill your heads with the false commandments of civility, requiring you to be "constructive" when opposing the powerful. (The powerful never feel any obligation to be constructive when they legally wreck you and your families for the most petty offenses or for no offense at all.) Under their system, you end up blowing holes in the kids down the street. No, no! Chop down the real bad guys!

Here is another liberating truth: In war, you are going to take casualties. That means they cannot control you by guilt. You can wipe out the CPS, even though they are crying that the CPS saves one genuinely abused child a year. That child qualifies as a casualty (if we don't save him by other means), so we don't have to flinch as we achieve the much greater good of crushing a perverted tyranny.

All the media, newspapers, TV, magazines, work overtime bringing "hard cases" in full color to prevent you from threatening the powerful. They show the abused child or the crumbling school or the unhappy spouse or the burst of intolerance. It's to make you swallow your rage when you are tormented, and your children are wrecked. It's to make you leave their enforcement tools untouched. But now you are free. Just call each lurid plea a casualty, and go on smashing the enemy.

Think of yourselves as like the people in wartime Afghanistan. You mourn those who are lost, men, women and children; and you avenge them where possible. But it does not keep you from utterly rejecting the occupying powers, and gleefully doing everything you can to grind them to powder. *You can make a better world than this.*

Slumping into the Melt — Poetry

The free market system offers your children a constructive role. Like bulbs or tendrils hanging from a kelp plant, they are permitted to hang from a TV set or other marketing device, connected by cables through eyes, ears and brain. In response to the demands of compound interest, their legs and arms and mouths pump more and more strongly, thrusting gas pedals, banging keys, signing credit slips, talking nonsense, and creating an income flow commensurate with investor expectations. As age slows their responses, they are moved by degrees to a passive position in an income pump made of high priced medical devices.

By contrast I counsel destruction. Because of technology's very great excess economic efficiency, on the order of six *times* what is needed, we can bring much of it crashing down and still not be threatened in our needs. It is fun to wreck what is ugly. When a war needs to be fought, everyone can find purpose and employment. And young men love it. The nagging moral question remains: can it be justified?

When the Nazis were massacring whole halls full of Jewish people, and the Soviets were hauling trainloads of unfortunates off to starvation, the flaming sword was clearly justified. The fact that it was justified was good news, because otherwise the whole world was tainted by compromise with such heartless evil. The other side of the coin appears here and now. If market atheism does not offend enough, then we can't fight it. And if we can't fight it, nothing can stop its paving the world and reducing all human lives to futile twitching. This is real despair and I have to answer it.

In a way it answers itself. View the world it offers our grandchildren. The market can only function with rapid economic growth, real growth of five or ten percent a year, much greater than population growth. (It has to stay ahead of compound interest or it will implode in a depression.) As long as there is something constructive, or destructive, to be done to feed this fire, it works. War, cold war, space race, run-up of real estate values, drug research, making a telephone for everyone: our economy has been running through the options at an ever-increasing rate.

The big wave of the 1990s is to expand the boundaries of the market economy in a world that used to have big swathes of traditional or communist territory. That "making up for lost time" provides a spur for growth far beyond local population growth, as is needed. But there is only so much world and we've pretty much swept it by now. Stock markets and dollar convertibility: all but a few holdouts show the signs.

Well? What is left when the dollar bestrides our entire earthbound human race? Then there is nothing more than to bring them all to a level, to make every place a new California. We now have hundreds of countries and languages and cultures on this earth, each unique and beautiful for thousands of years. When all of them are done slumping into the melt, we will have nothing anywhere on earth but freeways, housing developments, glass, steel and cement, and cars honking in a worldwide eternal traffic jam. And, of course, some well-tended parks.

Once it gets underway it won't take long. I would guess less than a decade. The financial giant has never yet flexed its muscles in a truly united world. It will need a worldwide building boom to take up the economic slack, and no place will be too distant. If the dollar is king, do you suppose that they won't hear of it in Outer Mongolia? Or that they will consent to be left as living fossils so that the rest of us can have a picturesque place to visit?

In the long run I don't even think the languages will survive. Who needs anything beyond commercial English, the native language of the dollar? Even China has become a servant farm for the dollar economy, and has abandoned its ancient ideograms to come closer to the English language look and feel. In international executive suites English is spoken.

And once this is over, we will enter a phase of absolute desperation trying to keep the growth going. There will be nothing left but ever more frantic marketing. Get a new car! A new computer! Bigger! Faster! Prettier! Cleaner! Longer hours! More returns! Be healthier! Be sexier! Have it all! Keep it all for yourself!

But another trend will go into panic speed (already has gone into panic speed) behind the building boom. That is technological improvement. Efficiency can still get you market share, though the returns are slimmer and slimmer, so the effort put in is greater and greater. Believe me, I know it!

That means the percent of the people needed to keep the economy going, already disastrously low, will crash. More desperate pursuit of educational chits. More clawing for position. More people downsized and marginalized, pretending that someday, somehow, they too will be executives.

In the *Wall Street Journal*, they praise the new workfare programs that send welfare mothers to earn \$5.50/hr eight hours a day. The day care costs \$10.00/hr ten hours a day. They carefully squirm out of the absurdity by calling them "entry-level jobs". Everybody knows that is a pretense: for all but a lucky few, they will be "forever-level jobs". It is even more senseless when you realize day care is a second best: a mother's presence is worth more than \$10.00/hr to her children.

Unless, of course, you cut right through to what the free marketeers are really thinking. Which is that the mother and her children are all garbage.

As soon as growth begins to die of exhaustion, and the culture of self-ishness pits the strong against the weak, we will see how long they will continue to fund these pleasing pretenses. They are forced to be ruth-less against even their favored productive workers. I worked for a company where a highly paid consulting programmer had preceded me. He had some kind of digestive trouble that had him going to the toilet a lot. They stood over him with a stopwatch and docked him for his potty breaks, and soon turfed him out. Well, the project was behind schedule, and the sharks were closing in on the boss too. You must never show weakness, never get old, never get sick.

If this is how they treat their best contributors, how much meaner will they be to the millions of poor sloggers left in the dust of progress?

Jay Hoffman asks, "What if drugs are better than life?" I think there will be an awfully high percentage of drug use. Both among the insiders and the outsiders, the rich and the poor, those frantically keeping up and those hopelessly fallen behind. Strain, strain, harder and harder, longer and longer, your neck tendons standing out, your eyes bulging, your head throbbing; try harder, and maybe earn your piece of cement!

It is already mostly this way. The essence of slumping into the melt is to put an end to any hope of escape anywhere. That will be the picture for our grandchildren, forever and ever, for all eternity, like a planet of *Nazgûl* preying on the less competitive. In reality I doubt if it will last long before the tenting comes.

There is only one answer. The old-line humans must enslave the corpo-ration. Total war is justified against this literally subhuman enemy. The corporation is the true orc, for if any corporate leader acts upon a con-science, the laws of competition insure that he will be swept away by one lacking that scruple of conscience.

Whoever flinches at dishonest marketing loses to one who does not; whoever refuses to employ slave labor is undersold by one who cares not. There are rare exceptions, always where the corporation is dominated by one individual with a personality (like Adolph Coors, Sam Walton or Carl Karcher). The next generation usually lets even these corporations subside into the soulless mold.

Take up the weapons of economic destruction with glee. The landscape will be littered with dead companies, before the others learn their lesson and bow to the yoke. This gives you and your children an element of worthy purpose. Every deed you do to wreck the enemy is a good deed. And they are trapped in the investor's world of compound interest. Just by not listening, just by not buying, you will soon strangle them.

Think of destroying the corporation as our masters think of drug interdiction. They are willing to destroy everyone's rights and to ruin countless poor families to pursue that goal. Turnabout is fair play. It is good for us to topple many a glass and steel tower to interdict the mental drug of finance-driven marketing and meaningless motion, which enslaves far more souls than any white powder that ever was made.

It's a new demand, a demand for a world worth living in, a world where all the best parts are not cut away by "economic necessity" or "progress". Whether we prefer fantasy or adventure or historical romance or science fiction, we have up till now accepted defeat without a fight, we have all taken for granted that the real world has to be this gray shrieking rat race to nowhere. But we cannot accept it ultimately, unless we are willing to slump into the melt, and totally abandon the love of life.

That is liberation. We are driven now into a corner. Defeatism has to stop at last, because otherwise our descendants are condemned to flailing lifelong in this worldwide mosh pit, driven by an eternally mounting crescendo of marketing to dance five percent faster each year. We have no alternative except to fight for a world based on poetry: we must, and therefore we can.

And poetry can win—because poetry is not based on compound interest. The marketeers' mosh pit is inhuman and will suffer a final nervous breakdown. If we wait passively for that victory, everything good will be lost before it comes. Our job is to save what is lovable by killing the mosh pit before its time. It really is possible to offer our children a world of color and beauty.

Poverty — Beasts of Burden

Let's start by busting the international problem of poverty.

The free market doesn't do it. The free market is a wrecker. That is proved by the impoverishment of the post-Soviet nations. Revisiting Lithuania, our authorities mention just in passing that GDP declined by *more than half* in the two years 1992-1993 (Krickus), and "the purchasing power of the average family dropped 44 percent during the first months of 1992" (Lieven). And this was not some cushy deal for Lithuania that was being corrected on behalf of other parts of the former Empire. All the post-Soviet nations fared alike.

It is as if a sluggish aircraft were refitted with a new, more powerful engine that occasionally cuts out and lets it plunge ten thousand feet. This ought to worry people especially if flying at an altitude of nine thousand. But our writers seem to be hypnotized by an uncritical herd instinct since the Cold War ended. They (including Krickus and Lieven) report these facts but do not notice the implied problem.

Remember we are comparing the new system's performance with the Soviet Union, one of the most efficient engines of poverty and corruption ever invented. And yet the free market does worse! These drops in GDP are quite capable of killing people, when income drops below a subsistence level. The free market evades the blame it deserves when these millions of deaths by starvation fail to happen, because of families supporting their members, or little suburban potato plots yielding a saving harvest. The free market tried to cause a famine; ancient feudal and tribal remnants prevented it.

Here's another telling fact. The end result of the free market in most ex-Communist countries is an *increase* in the lead that the former Communist managers have over their people. They, like the rich and powerful in the West, are in possession. The free market rewards possession far more than it rewards all those much advertised virtues like honesty, competence or initiative. It also frees the possessors from all moral responsibility. Even Communism didn't do that.

Socialism is no answer. Socialism is merely a parasite on the money economy. It expects personal, national or international freebies to flow in response to rhetorical pressure, to those who never take the trouble to earn the goods or (what is even worse) to suffer the uncertainties that productive people have to endure.

Socialism (or liberalism or clintonism) is political manipulative behavior, exactly equivalent to a drug addict wheedling money out of working family members. It can only be destructive. As can be seen, those strata of society, like workers and minorities, that have most listened to the socialists, are now relatively worse off than ever before. They are paid peanuts and are utterly at the mercy of the managers and social workers.

The moneymakers and the money milkers are both wrong. This leaves only one logical possibility. The solution must devalue money itself.

Financial capitalism is, from an engineering point of view, a terrible design. It results in a wildly swinging valuation on the worker's services. When it is up, he gets income he does not need, which in real life is NOT saved, but is dissipated on luxury goods of little value. When it is down, he is dispossessed, degraded, starved. The dry period can always outlast his pitiful savings, which are quickly devoured by his massive obligations.

Some engineering equivalents: A car with springs but no shocks, which bounces upwards just fine, but crushes your spine on the way down. A child's swing nailed to a wall, good for one half swing up, and broken bones on the way back. A boat moored atop a reef in a storm, lifting with the crest of the swell and crashing to ruin with the trough. A designer would be strung up for any of these monstrosities, but the effect of the money economy on ordinary working families is exactly the same.

The answer has to be independent of the vagaries of finance, which can withdraw its favors from any of us for any or no reason. It must devalue money itself. And there is logically only one way to become independent of money, as the post-Soviet peoples have all discovered. In Lieven's words:

> ... The collectives were originally mechanisms intended not to increase production but to guarantee procurement. This is connected to a key truth about peasants [which] is that peasants will simply cease to produce for the market in circumstances in which the terms of trade are rigged against them or in which, due to this or to inflation, their products will not bring them real money or real goods. The urban worker has to continue working in these circumstances because he has to eat. The peasant does not. Instead of taking his grain to market he will feed it to his pigs, and eat the piglets himself.

This notion of not being a slave is so creepy it almost seems sinful.

The practical details are summed up in the Idea of Prokhorykh, presented by Panin (p 146-149) and later put into action in millions of Russian private plots and even American pea patches. A small family, according to Prokhorykh, needs only a half acre intensively cultivated by hand with modern agricultural methods. Those peasants who refused Lenin's loans in the 1920s, and did not run themselves ragged in land greed, were also more likely to survive the famines and purges that followed. The small private plot, which saved them from Communist starvation in Soviet days, also saved them from capitalist starvation in post-Soviet days. Many inflation-devastated pensioners need all the output of their suburban gardens, reached by long bus rides, as a recent National Geographic article on Russia describes (ca 1995).

The Idea of Prokhorykh is the engineering completion, the shock absorber or backswing space or water depth that makes participation in the money economy possible at will and without devastation. Notice that the only class of people really favored by the free market are the independently wealthy: those who have enough cash or possessions to take care of their needs for life. They can operate without terror, because even when their investments fail, they bounce back. Some insurance fund or institutional investor or small risktaker always takes the loss. With access to the Idea of Prokhorykh, through a cohesive family or circle of friends that has rural connections, every worker can achieve this status.

The Idea of Prokhorykh is a form of the economic system called autarky, which means producing what you need for yourself. When you combine it with the other half of the design—some participation in the money economy to get exotic needfuls or desired items—you get partial autarky, the correctly engineered answer to the money-centered market system. As the quote from Lieven shows, there is really no other choice, unless you consent to being helpless, driven slaves for all your generations.

See how many problems it solves at a stroke.

Now your essential economic conversation is with the good earth, not with human weasels who wreck you senselessly at will. It is true that you must avoid monoculture and learn good agricultural methods. Russians or Mexicans or library books are available to get you started. Also, you must make arrangements to stay in touch with good medical care. Often only the worst can be found in unstylish rural locations.

Currently, education is an infinite regress. The market atheist must cull his own mother (or daughter) if she scores low on the standardized test. God does make junk and the Stanford-Benet test reveals it. Once again autarky provides the only answer. So-called "slow" (that is, artistic) people are plenty fast enough to keep up with the seasons, and more apt to function well in friendship with the earth.

During my youth, in the mid-70s, I purchased a few acres of raw land on Vashon Island, near Seattle, to try to span rural and urban life as my parents had done. I bought them from an unlettered middle-aged couple of the kind you would expect to have straws sticking between their teeth. That man could do things like build a swamp drain of buried logs. My development plans foundered after the first heavy rain swept part of my poorly drained road onto a neighbor's land. The brilliant Princeton PhD had to be rescued by the old landsman, who found another and better suited buyer for the land.

We have always patronized restaurants, even while rejecting the commercial media. The arts of hospitality and service are better than loud mastery by what Jay Hoffman calls the "clever cowards". Only the dignity conferred by autarky can set this balance right. As John F. Bolek says in the Autumn 1980 issue of my magazine *November:*

> What is owed by the high to the low is impossible to describe, for if it were simple enough to describe it would be simple enough to command, and so would be a tax not a gift. Since the gift is beyond telling, it it not spoken of and thus is taken as nothing. The Inklings [a literary group including J.R.R. Tolkien, C.S. Lewis and Charles Williams] do not make this error. The King of the West is grateful to an innkeeper: "*He* says your beer is always good." [Tolkien]
>
> ...Pride of place and pride of folk, with their reverse, the love of manifold foreign lands: we hunger for these in the computed sameness of Instant Communications. Ten thousand rooted communities are replaced by one electronically reproduced Image. The redundance of most human beings would by now be undeniable, were not the Image so obviously low in quality. But the real thing cannot exist without the "steady unnoticeable nourishment and repose" [Williams] that is given only from below.

Only autarky can restore the family to its true value. Under the financial free market, the family has negative value. Your parents would be $145,000 richer if they had killed you. Now go back to the land and find out how good it is to have teenagers! Good care for every motor; for every horse its groom. The earth (so much of which is being abandoned in America) is generous to a muscular young family.

Only autarky can set us on the way to enslaving the corporation. Victory can only happen if life outside the corporation's world is possible. That establishes labor as a gift at least equal to money. You can actually benefit employers of whom you approve, by offering your labor *only* to them. No more need to worry about quotas or other desperate, dishonest, humiliating techniques for getting first in the employment line.

Finally, only that deep, slow connection with the land can ever make the world huge again. No longer just junk land you whiz past or over when going from city to city. The amazing reduction in velocity even goes so far as to bring back beasts of burden. Their speed is appropriate to the job at hand.

Beasts of burden! If they seem a pure step backward, ask yourself this. Why were they essential for the victories of Afghanistan and Lithuania both? When the Soviets, in their last anger, cut off petroleum supplies to separatist Lithuania, the "primitive" farmers just plodded on with their horses. Just as animals made the Afghans immune to standard military superiority, they made the Lithuanians independent of economic pressure and senseless, destructive "change".

Real autarky is not possible without beasts of burden. You have to pay for manufacture of machinery and fuel supplies, all controlled by alien powers or huge corporations. Beasts of burden are fed by what grows everywhere, and they make little beasts all by themselves.

So there's a reason why a few places have preserved such a life, and with teeth too, like Afghanistan. A sane world has to have a seed from which to grow back. But here is the interesting thing: *you can have it both ways*. The autarky is partial, and you can (and should) have a foot in both worlds. The "pea patches" found in many cities are exactly right. But the country cabin (once sheltering sharecroppers) is also right, and you had better ditch any lingering prejudice against it.

Remember the engineering model. Working for money without being a slave is only possible when you are backed by the land. It actually makes the free market theories come true, which will be a thing the world owners will be horrified to see. It even helps technology, when the many independent customers are not driven by marketing monopolies and fear of lost profits to accept junk, but can tinker with what they feel is the best, like academic hobbyists.

It opens up life, even in the city, to true comic values that few would have looked to see. Let me finish with just one example.

It is the automobile. Polluter, freeway clogger, it is nevertheless the vehicle of knighthood for city youth. So all power to the car culture! An engine hoist in every backyard! Good, greasy handed boys making those valves just hum. Side by side with farms and horses, you just watch, they will be able to make the move with hardly a hitch.

The zoning regulations, we smash those. Remember, we have devalued money. Up with the engine hoist—and down with property values! It's the best thing economically that we can do for our children: take the hit as we slither towards the death of our failed elder generation, and leave them everything to be bought up cheaply, without eternal slavery to the moneylenders.

The Jihad against property values: what freedom from oppression its victory will bring! No sneaking calls from neighbors to bring reluctant cops to harass shade-tree mechanics. No dirty little covenants to turn you into a secret criminal for acting like a free human being in your own house. Neighborly courtesy instead of legal one-upsmanship biased against generous families.

And those glossy cars, huge, colorful, works of art from under the hands of your own sons. Hundreds of little shops (repair, don't replace!) to spread real prosperity every way. Pride that builds and does not wreck. You can have thousands of monster mobiles, flowing from inner city and stump farm to slowly cruise the suburbs and corporate business parks. And corporate executives, newly enslaved, can line the sidewalks kneeling in the cement dust in their three-piece suits, touching foreheads to the ground in obeisance to their superiors.

Gangs — Lordship

Youth going bad everywhere! What about the graffiti, the packs of young criminals, the school wastelands, the terrible streets, the senseless drive-by shootings?

That one is actually pretty easy. Stop hating our own children.

America hates teenagers so bad. We provide a special indulgent diet to make them stay tadpoles until the adult economy needs them, which may be never. One touch of youthful rebellion, and we bring in the big guns to crush the teenager: counsellors, threats from the legal kidnappers, psychiatric "help". *All* normal societies are indulgent toward youthful rebellion, which is universal and healthy. But we treat any such self-assertion as a threat to the American way of life.

And so it is, but so what? That is normal too. How about us being man and woman enough to be on the side of our own children? There is nothing a boy does so well as help his own father. Or a girl so well as helping her own mother. It is your job to figure out what they are ready to help you with. If it does not fit your heretofore conventional and respectable life, then so much for that life. Your children commit you to things. It's an adventure. Cross half the world if necessary, or become a flaming outlaw, but do not betray your own flesh and blood to the legal trash compactor. No other nation was ever so evilly sure of itself as to abandon a large part of its own younger generation.

Dr Laura Schlesinger says young people must have a "dream", or they will go bad. I say they all have a dream, or want to. But what if the world kills it aborning? What if, for instance, the dream is love? Teenagers are shy about what is closest to their hearts. How easy it is by adult example to puncture their hopes without ever a word being spoken. Then the rebellion gets bitter.

After that, standard operating procedure takes over. It matters not what was in the child's mind in the beginning (and children's minds are infinitely various). Authority casts the child into the standard mold of a criminal drug addict, even if nothing along that line has happened yet. Warning lectures and films amount to training courses. Soon the poor kid probably will forget what motivated him in the first place. The counsellor (to whom the cowardly parents immediately abandon all responsibility) says "Stop that rebellion or you will end up as a drug-sodden jailbird." And the child hears "To continue your rebellion you must now become a drug-sodden jailbird."

My young relative, an eighth grader, has just gone through this in the course of less than a year. What started out as romantic sympathy with the homeless ends up, in months, in a crime camp, and her mom has to get a second mortgage to pay for the camp. I was agonizing with my wife over what creates such self-destructiveness in a youngster, whatever the pressures. My wife told me that Elizabeth after a few hours or days of dark thought about this, as is her way, had come up with a judgement.

"It is the fruits of divorce," she said. "Didn't Jesus say, 'By their fruits ye shall know them'?" Horrifyingly apt. In the child is written the love of her mom and dad. If that love dies, there is a certain logic if the child self-destructs. This logic is not absolute and can be fought.

Young people are pushed to go bad (and many that go bad do not do it so openly) for the same reason that even younger people are tossed into dumpsters. Their elders (and I don't mean just mom and dad) have a filthy agenda which they ruthlessly advance over the bodies of all our children. Is it any wonder that these children take counsel with each other? It is pure self-defense; hapless and doomed, mostly. Things get their minds from behind. The little coteries of children are guided to self-destruction by all the *impersonal* adult influences, like education and marketing, that they accept without thinking.

I'm here to talk about gangs. In themselves there is nothing wrong with gangs. They have a tendency to go good with time. The Hells Angels becomes a club of middle-aged nonconformists happily showing off to their little kids. Here in Tijuana, there is an annual all-gang conclave of motor-cyclists, thousands of them, thundering in hordes across the border to aid a local orphanage.

Gangs are a gesture in the direction of something good, and we need to take that gesture up constructively. After all, one obvious answer to family disintegration is neighborhood cohesion. And most of our children do try to keep their gestures of rebellion as harmless as they can: graffiti after all are just parodies of advertisements, street corners don't suffer from being hung around on, nor do roads suffer from cruising. Our vicious authorities respond to this harmlessness by making the laws ever more stringent, so the youngsters will at least harm themselves.

Youthful energy, gathering of friends, defense of the neighborhood: they all sound generous to me. Once you realize that your son is on your side, then a small but muscular army shoulder to shoulder with him has to be even better! It is mighty nice to have them around on moving day, for instance.

It is the poisonous culture that poisons them. So it is your job, at whatever inconvenience to yourself, to kill the culture before it leads them wrong. It is as if you are a rejected rebel, just like them. In fact the whole neighborhood needs to get that way.

When we first moved into Mexico, it took us a while to get used to grandpa and grandson clambering around on the same building site, hammering to the rhythm of the same popular music. Age segregation has no reason to exist. Even in America, some neighborhoods have gotten wise: graffiti become mural art when encouraged by the older generation. "Protection of the neighborhood" has a fine ring to it when, as Jeanne has seen in Tijuana, roving gangs rough up criminals whom they catch preying on women.

This is where neighborhood elders are needed, elders who are with their people and not clinging to the approval of the masters. Their experienced judgement must rule the gang, before it can rise to the status of a just militia. It just takes that basic knowledge of the rules of evidence to avoid being manipulated.

An example is babyraping. Obviously no clean neighborhood can harbor a babyraper. On the other hand, it is a standard false accusation in any modern divorce custody struggle, so how do you know? The wise elder is aware of corroborating evidence, like possession of pornography and knowledge of one's "rights", and can help to set up a trap where the compulsive geek will give evidence against himself right on the spot.

Any self-respecting gang will be at its roaring happiest in some ugly crusade like this, but what about the times between? That is where they go bad. They listen to the media, which are all for money and heartless sex and willing to wallow in them while you remain locked out forever. After a while some of the young people begin the struggle to gain the approval of the money masters and be granted these things in time. Others take the direct route of traditional gang or organized crime activities. They can equally be considered lost.

So here is an elder duty more important than rules of evidence. Young people, not yet corrupted, know that partying is really a second best. The greatest (and most inaccessible) thing is to be able to *give* love. Oh yes, inaccessible to a pretty girl too: casual sex is more like giving hate, as she will soon find out if she tries that route! The shooting does not usually start until after some of that.

Something for the empty hours of your teenager, whom the economic world has conspired to lock out of constructive work? It is frightening, but you can do it. Let them build: cars, pea patches, the livelihoods and businesses of neighbors. There can be whole weeks on a farm, if your life is family-centered and no longer career-centered. Young people are mighty strong, and soon become skillful—in ways you never pursued yourself. You will find you can lean on them.

And much of the responsibility rests on the young themselves. There is never any need to get stupid on drugs, or to thieve. I don't care if your family is the unhappiest one in the world. You have a responsibility to the rest of us. This kind of thing only gives greater power to the rotten lawmakers and the haters of teenagers. Stop sucking up oppression for all of us!

There must not be any hope of big money. You should get rid of all the tags of the consumer society, the brand name stuff and the expensive fads, and trash your TV and your slick magazines too. You are draining your family to help evil people when you patronize these. Also, it is the love of money that leads people into organized crime stuff like drug running. In the end your friends get killed, for what?

No big money, but big accomplishment, yes! The elders of your neighborhood, those elders I am calling for, will show you where you are needed. You can help neighbors get on their feet—and see their new business patronized with the money you did NOT spend on fancy sneakers. It is still a rebellion and an adventure, because your first loyalty is to your neighborhood and to your elders, not to the rotten law.

It is the nub in America. You cannot both be with the young and with the law. Logically I am calling for the alienation of troubled inner city neighborhoods from the regime. Practically speaking, of course, this has already taken place. I am asking for the good effects of alienation as well as the bad.

But it is a partial alienation, just as the previous section asks for a partial autarky. Mostly you are allies with real-life authorities. I think the average good cop might even be happier to gain the allies and lose the territory. And even this side the law, a whole neighborhood speaking as one is a political power. It can convince state legislators to take immediate action to relieve an evil of law—which is the best solution for all concerned.

You are no longer restricted to the corruption of our legal authorities. Your elders have much more grist for their mills. Minority Supreme Court opinions are often a source of justice when the majority lied. Dig them out of a law library, study them, quote them: they are not so inaccessible. Ancient traditions of your people (literally handed down from grandpa) are another source of wisdom. What fun for the elders in an ethnic neighborhood, now that they have the guts to make it stick, and a loud army to help them!

The important thing is to uphold a higher standard than our masters, and to be proud of it. Here is an example: drug dealers. By following the ancient rule of "do no harm", and like a good bartender making no sale to the person who obviously has had enough, a drug dealer achieves moral superiority over the American Medical Association, which will do anything for money. When polls showed that most people hate the idea of sucking out a live baby's brains, the first priority of the AMA was to protect the doctors that do it. Even if the process itself is outlawed (they propose), please make sure the killers are tried only by an AMA panel, not by a real judge and jury.

Of course it does not take much to be better than the AMA. As a drug dealer you are still making a rich living off the compulsions and weaknesses of others. Even if you act with restraint, you have risen only to the level of a marketing strategist or advertiser. The world holds better—actual healing perhaps? Happy hunting!

The most important ones to uphold a higher standard are the elders themselves. They have a following of young people. They cannot be your standard Clinton slimeball. It is true that hardly anyone escapes the sexual and marital misadventures of our time, but keep it down to a dull roar. You know the difference between a crotch-grabber and one who really is protective of women, protective of the weak.

The *lord* (for that is what he is, in historic terms, as will become even clearer next section when I place him in a rural setting) is a naturally sociable fellow, gathering lots of followers and hangers-on wherever he pitches camp. His parties are huge! His hospitality is of the stay-for-a-year variety. His yard is large and cluttered. When he wants to, he can organize something pretty big, maybe bigger than local authority likes. He is honest and generous and fair, and will go to great trouble for a friend.

In *Women in the Days of the Cathedrals* (Ignatius Press, San Francisco, 1998, translated by Anne Côté-Harriss), Régine Pernoud examines the life and charters of the great twelfth-century lady Eleanor of Aquitaine. She concludes:

> Furthermore the object of these charters may be surprising, as they invariably consist of donations. Their form varies, their content also...But the constant thing was the gesture...Anniversaries, wills, pilgrimages, stages on the road or in a life; everything in those days was an occasion to make a donation. It was a specific trait of the time and did not survive the advent

of a new society that was more preoccupied with acquiring than with giving. This love of gain came to dominate and was not slow to supplant the generous habits of the past. But that is another story.

This whole section is getting a medieval flavor, and for good reason. It is what we need. By great good luck, I know the medieval world personally, through an accident of birth. No, I was not born in a time machine, nor am I eight hundred years old.

In fact, I was well acquainted with my grandmother and my great-uncle Tom, who came from Slovakia around 1900. I learned some Slovak from them. And Slovakia around 1900 was a pious European backwater, tilling its soil, faithful to and happy with the ways of seven hundred years before, which had never changed, and too poor and remote for anyone to care. That is all there is to my time warp. So out of personal acquaintance I can assure you that the dark stereotypes are exaggerated. Though there was pain and evil and occasional disaster, medieval people are traditional, skilled, artistic, opinionated, dutiful, affectionate, hospitable and moderately prosperous. And they love to sing.

And lords too? No, I knew no lords through my grandmother. That is an even stranger story. Here in modern California, over the last fifteen years, I have watched (in awe) as a personal friend has *reinvented* lordship before my eyes. I doubt if he realizes it. I never told him, and I don't believe he reads medieval romances or Brother Cadfael mysteries.

Ever since we met him at the modestly illegal party he gave for two hundred people in old Poway, I had this odd feeling that he cuts too wide a swath for a mere citizen. It became more pronounced when he moved to the country. The hangers-on now became so rooted they approached the status of crofters or serfs on his land. And, like life imitating art (*A Morbid Taste for Bones* by Ellis Peters), he takes on the exact ancient prerogative of a Welsh lord, who has the right to hire a harpist. Once or twice a year a band sets up on his land, attracting people from around the county to his traditional Mountain Fest.

So I know the right personality for a lord. He can't be the only one. The time has come for this particular color to return to a gray world. There will be someone like this in your neighborhood, or someone who can be encouraged to become like this: you might be surprised how low a value he puts on himself. What may encourage him is to know how much good he can do by taking his place. Well led, the gang becomes a force for good and a source of pride, and the hood stands up for itself and is transformed.

Drugs — Serfdom

Don't idealize the drug addict. Try this one: a divorcing wife is filling the house with vicious tattooed gangsters. They are fed by 1 AM withdrawals from the ATM machine, and if that runs dry she sucks them off to pay for the unidentified bags of drugs that she gulps down wholesale. When the husband comes to pick up some of his machinery, she is sitting, raddled and hideous, in the garage, where she curses and reviles him for two hours straight, except when she is demanding some favor as if by right. All of this is his fault, none of it her own.

This kind of human garbage litters our streets. Many of them have children. And we propose an answer even for that? Actually it is not far to seek. We have (as they say) the infrastructure all ready to go. While we are at it we can solve the problem of welfare (and not by the ugly mockery of "workfare", with the absurd day care explosion it requires).

The source of the problem is manipulativeness. This person is never in the wrong, never owes anything, always has the right to collect from people around her. All alcoholism, drug addiction, prostitution and similar irresponsibility are the consequence of the willingness to manipulate. Without that, it just becomes sad love affairs or physical sickness, like a headache.

This person refuses to be more than a child. But reverse that, and a child is just like an addict, and yet we deal with children without any trouble. The catch is that an addict has the freedom and powers of a responsible adult. So take those away. This is the minimum necessary to stop the damage.

If you act out load shifting, if you are never at fault, and are good at causing guilt in others: you can consent to live unfree, like a moral child. In your better moments you know you are a good-for-nothing. Turn yourself in and accept serfdom—become a homebody.

The druggie's little kid wants to drag her mother around like a huge limp rag doll. Let it be that way. Toss Mommie in the corner, but love her. We will imitate blessed Bolivia, where children remain with their mothers even when the mothers go to jail.

But where can we put them, better than jail? Again we design to make the little kid happy. Nothing pleases children like being on a farm, in rural places with their absurd profusion of growing things and junkheaps and wilderness. And lots of adventurous little kids like themselves. We can guarantee that. Remember the human garbage littering our streets? They have children too. Take a lemon, make lemonade.

The social workers insist all children of dysfunctional parents are doomed. I have seen how the wretches try to protect their kids from their own fate. In their vicious pit of freedom that is not possible, but unfreedom makes it possible. An unraped younger generation will make a step up, at home with their broken parents, loving and pleasing them as God intended.

Serfdom is a punishment, not to be imposed without a conviction, but those who know they need it can accept it voluntarily. As long as you are a homebody (this variety of serfdom which I will soon define), you can live behind an unlocked door, and you can be there to see something better take shape for your children. So many of those addicts and prostitutes were raped early and often, they were more done to than doing. For these, the restrictions will be a blessed relief, giving them the years they need to heal up inside.

Serfdom for the male is much like being drafted. It is imposed on those boys who pretend they have a right to do violence because someone in their family tree was once oppressed. Just as in a healthy military, those who are incorrigible end up dead. This does no net damage. They were going to end up dead on the streets anyway.

Some will protest that this revives the worst kind of medieval backwardness, long left in the dust of history. They are kidding themselves. Serfdom is already a modern reality, though not under that name. As a punishment, in forms rather similar to what I am suggesting, it goes on in drug rehab camps and reform schools, although they don't do it right (see below). But I don't just mean that.

They abolished medieval serfdom in Russia in 1906, but revived it in the United States only ten years later. I mean the income tax, where we have to report our innocent economic activities to the master, and give him his cut off the top. We did not flinch at that type of serfdom, so they have introduced others. The master forces us to pay for offenses we have not yet committed (liability insurance). And the master now has the right to demand an accounting of our family life, and to confiscate our children. Christian medieval serfdom never went so far as that.

To be quite precise, my proposal of homebody serfdom as a punishment should include a release from these modern varieties for all those *not* convicted of irresponsibility. It would result in a decrease in the total sum of serfdom. What is rightly a punishment should not have become a normal state of affairs for the citizen.

Homebody serfdom is founded on stability, that little-known monkish vow that roots you right here until (shall we say) your term expires. There is a wrong and a right way of doing this. Las Colinas Jail, a women's jail in San Diego County, housed a friend of ours for a few months once. No visiting except through glass panels. An extremely restricted list of things you could give the prisoners. It used to include books, but before long even they were forbidden (drug-soaked pages?) and practically the only thing you could give was money.

They have that exactly backwards. Here's the right way: open door, books allowed, hugs allowed, picnics and even parties allowed—but money absolutely forbidden. Seize all possessions and accounts and forward to Aunt Susie for safekeeping, put Social Security number on blacklist, see to it that the homebody's signature does nothing and can open no accounts. No money or equivalent like jewelry is allowed to be earned or spent except with the lord's permission (like a child with parents' permission). If found in violation, simply take everything and send it to Aunt Susie.

That should take care of the drug trade, even better than glass panels and body searches. No drug dealer wants to be paid with loads of potatoes.

If there are welfare checks, the idea is that they go straight to the lord, before the boyfriend can get his hands on them. It is the lord who provides food, clothing, shelter, parties; he will need help from roving medical charities and the like. The boyfriend, cut off from his source of income, may as well join up too. Together they can provide a little inefficient help around the farm, or (who knows?) they may do better. Not just irresponsibles. Decent people down on their luck can become homebodies too, letting their fortunes heal in a space without money or worry. In the end you eliminate money welfare completely.

I've told you that I've seen the natural evolution of crofters or serfs on my friend's property. Therefore I know what to expect: Good hard simple work of the woods hippie or Amish type. This is something that brings peace to the mind and emotions, as the Benedictines long have known. It is surprising what pride and skills a little slowness of life can bring out, even in the saddest emotional wreck or addict. There will be good crops, cooking, restaurants, sewing and artwork, machine shops, and the best pack animals and custom cars.

The lord has a right to protect all his people. Rock salt should normally suffice. Any prostitution with a serf is treated as seriously as child prostitution. Possibly the Taliban can advise us on the punishment.

Of course the lord must not exploit the serfs personally. This is not as much to expect as you might think, with the right kind of lordly personality. It is as if these sad cases are not fair game. The danger is more in the other direction. No manipulation—do not suck up more oppression! And it is only right to ask the homebody to show a little pride in doing a good job for his or her lord. This kind of farm is not any route to rapid wealth, but try to help him at least break even.

There is no inheritance of serf status. That is where the medievals went wrong, trying to set up a stable economic base for the lords (like the "fee for service" system tries to stabilize the medical economic base, as contrasted with charities like the Hospitallers of St John). We have to take the chance of 18-year-old kids being wheedled by their irresponsible parents.

There is no reason the lord cannot be a relative, maybe an aunt or grandfather. This should be encouraged, if the serf will behave honorably. We want people moving away from degradation and toward normal family life, not the other way.

So let's have none of these crime farms where they send incorrigible children, soaking the parents with the cost of a second mortgage! There is no age segregation among homebodies. Salt each mix with more old souses than flaky kids.

But it will take a lot of tolerant lords with sturdy and loyal free helpers. It would be too wearing for each of them to have to deal with more than one or two irresponsibles. The prohibition of money is the key to stabilizing each serf. It brings him back to the meal table. Of course, I can hear the howls from the corporate marketeers: I am taking their best customers out of the money economy.

Once established, this way of life has its good side. Even now, people burned out on the corporate fast track are overcrowding the guest rooms at the various Benedictine monasteries and convents hidden around the U.S.A. There will be the crofter—the volunteer homebody—who will choose the quiet life out of preference, giving support to a lord he likes, and enjoying the interesting characters that drift in and out of the serfs' cabins. This will take the pressure off the lord in dealing with the irresponsibles. And the parties will be better!

Much the same will be the position of those free workers who remain after their punishment has expired. For those badly hurt in the world of manipulation, or those whose children are growing happily there, it will be natural to stay. And there is also devotion to a good lord, as in Charles Williams' poem *The Departure of Dindrane*. These are all motives which are hardly remembered in our willful modern world, but are well within the human range, and were once quite common.

So in a while the better lords should have good thriving kibbutz-like establishments. The poor raddled drug addicts can hide from their weaknesses and watch their children grow strong. In a unique environment, they are capable of the unique role of culture seeds—see next section! That is a totally new function, not available at all in today's society. Only the slowness and stability of the good lord's farm can make it possible. Thanks to the unfreedom imposed on them for cause, they and their children can save what otherwise is lost forever.

There is no evil or sadness, including that of addiction and dysfunction, that cannot be the seedbed in which something good can grow. Just bring it within the range of the people involved. Remember: long ago it was the children of corrupt and lying Rome who built the honor and chivalry of the Dark Ages.

Nationalism and Mass Destruction — The Beloved

Mass destruction? Expose the mother of all forms of mass destruction, and then cure that one too.

We take it for granted that nations will unite, seek for dominance over other nations, and end in bloodshed. Croatians killed Serbs in year A, and Serbs killed Croatians in year B. Yorubas versus Ibos, Tutsi versus Hutu, Japanese versus Chinese, Chinese versus Tibetans, English versus Irish. Europe colonizes the world. The Americans sell smallpox blankets to the Indians. A hundred little Student Prince duchies melt into a united Germany and then fight war after war, trying to dominate all the other nations neighboring them.

Is this inevitable? Nowadays it sure seems to be: such struggles are getting an air of ever greater desperation. When they get nukes, we are all likely to end in fire. But there was a time when nations were not nearly of such importance. You had many kingdoms in a nation, like the Germans, or you had many nations in an empire, like the Austrians. They all rubbed along together without much friction. Everyone in authority spoke Latin anyway.

In fact when nations were neglected and ignored, they all throve and flowered. You could hike down the road and pass through half a dozen different languages. It was still true in 1967 when my family visited the area around Subotica in then Yugoslavia. If the wars haven't ruined it, it should be true yet. Each village spoke a different language: Serbian, German, Hungarian, and one of them (Selenča) my own Slovak, from far to the north. They had all been settled by Empress Maria Theresia.

The very idea of a political nation is wrong. A nation is a language. The Latvians have millions of folk songs, more than one for every ethnic Latvian. That is their nation. You learn the much-loved mother tongue at your mother's knee. Nationalism is a form of filial piety, surely blessed of God. Why then does it express itself so hideously?

The nations are melting away in a kind of acid rain.

Maria Theresia's empire produced no acid. There (at least till recently) the nations prospered side by side. Similarly, in Baja California and Argentina and such backwaters, settlers from many parts of Europe formed their villages and live on even now in their variety of mother tongues. America used to be that way: Pennsylvania Dutch, Louisiana Creoles, New Mexico Spanish. But more recent ethnics have dissolved in ferocious acid, "the melting pot", as it is called. Generic English in one generation, most of them.

Wherever nations are thrown together in a political unit, acid eats away the weaker ones. That is the new rule. Thus the nationalist desperation of the Scots or the Welsh or the Tibetans. And when many political units crowd next to each other, they struggle for dominance. It's the future they fear, when the units will coalesce into larger ones, and then who will survive? Even for the Germans with their historic culture it was basically terror. Our future is past! No empire! English is coming!

After two dreadful wars most of Europe has given up. With sad nostalgic sounds its nations are dying, the smallest first. They won't be speaking English for a couple of generations yet—languages like French and German have some momentum—but after a while their shrinking generations will have to ask themselves, why bother? Life is TV and jet planes, so why not speak world language all the time? No space for folk dances on the village green.

They felt it coming, you know. They've felt it for hundreds of years. They feel it coming even in Africa and India. Tribes get thrown together in a political unit and know the cold breath of economic change. Mom, Grandma, my people's sweet history and all my pride of ancestry, it's to die soon. Who will live? The fighting is desperate and ugly.

There is a grim sex change here. People treat nationalism as a masculine thing, really hyper-male, Germans goose stepping over their prostrate neighbors, ravaging tribal armies seizing the capital city. But every nation is feminine. She is the mother tongue, the mother's song. This is the deep dark secret. If you admit your nation is a woman, she will be raped.

All the horror and cruelty comes from an honorable love, the wish to protect my mother. That is what makes it so incredibly strong. Every Mexican in Tijuana insists that *his* grandmother speaks Spanish right.

The thrust for domination was never really natural. It is like that scene in *Star Wars* when Princess Leia and her friends are trapped in the shrinking garbage room. Climb on top or you are crushed. A political unit was the shrinking room. Now it is the whole world.

In a way it is good news. There is no more need to struggle to win. All the wars are in vain. All nations are equally doomed. Without exception they will slump into the melt. Not even America, the source of world language, is exempt. Whatever is loved or distinctive about America, the cowboys and the caucuses and the Mark Twain stuff, will dissolve, is already fast dissolving. The country towns are bled white; they are not populated by rooted natives anymore but by economic prisoners, suburban mall and freeway commuter wannabes.

The beating heart of everyone's national love, all the beauty, was created hundreds of years ago, mostly by farmers in the winter. The last two hundred years have been nothing but destruction. The commercial culture needs only fifty people to maintain it. Villages grow to duchies, to nations, to one world, but this number does not increase per unit. Everyone gets crushed closer together in a shrinking room of the soul.

This reality is rooted in dishonor. People laugh at the Student Prince, at little German kingdoms of two hundred years ago. What if every one of that prince's ancestors was true to his salt and loved his land and people, while the great and growing empires are long since built on robbers and impious liars with crowns? The true prince tenderly protects *all* the Beloved, not just the part that makes money and power.

Where people are mighty in honor, the great mosaic lives on. Postwar Afghanistan, the ultimate in demobbed military force, all armed to the teeth and at strife in civil war: why have they proved so comparatively sane? In the recent earthquake disaster in North Afghanistan, when foreign aid was slow in coming, the Taliban Army stepped in to send help to their enemies. Not for the first time. The Herat city people aided their enemies, the nomads, when they were brought low by famine in the early 1970s.

It makes sense as courtesy to someone else's Beloved. The Student Prince would understand that.

There is a French video about the Afghan resistance which has the heart-catching title *Valley against an Empire.* The valley won. It was the Panjshir which never fell to the Soviet empire despite a dozen massive invasions. The Panjshir in its tens of miles, about the same as the Soviet Union in its thousands. That's the kind of victory we want.

Tolkien was onto something when he railed against the airplane, because compression of distance is a great evil. It is the shrinking room. It is as wrong in its fullness as Genghis Khan finding ten thousand and leaving only one alive, or only one meaningfully alive. The global village is an abomination, a world suicide. What a noble task it will be to reverse it!

Others fought and won the first two battles, the one against racism and the one against the political leviathan. Each of those was hardly a century old. We face the final opponent, the one that has been grinding the sweet singers of creation for five hundred years, the enclosure movement, the economic monster, the acid of the West. It is unused to being opposed at all. Let us oppose it, so that the many loved and victorious valleys cannot be known without being crossed slowly in a journey like Marco Polo's that takes years.

Why does the mosaic still exist, even at this last gasp? Why are the Celtic languages, Welsh and Irish and Breton and Gaelic, still alive in tiny backwaters? When science fiction authors like Poul Anderson conjure an improbable historical fantasy to fill a future planet with speakers of such a tongue, they reach for a deeper truth than they know. Not a single Beloved needs to be lost. If she is still alive, it is because we can save her.

Nations were once being created and not destroyed. Only the land and the monkish virtue of stability made that possible. And now we have the need for just that. What a beautiful creative future for addicts and rejects and the heartbroken. The homebodies who are compelled to the land have one great act of freedom to make on behalf of their children.

In a new Subotica of cultural lords, choose some fine root in your tradition, whether Welsh or Ibo or Ainu, and make it the speech of your children. It is not hard when the skills of the land and of animal husbandry fit the many many tongues of the land, seeding in with the same human treasure teaching both. It works! We did it with our Alice! Even if the parents hardly speak the new old tongue, what do the little children know of that? They will grow up speaking it, like Jews reinventing Hebrew in Israel.

Nothing will do it but stability, the land, the long quiet years of a child's growing up—the very things we need to stanch the bleeding. Heavenly Silence, required to keep the wound clean and the compulsion turned off, also opens the door to the silent seeding in of an ancient alien culture. No more despair for the wretched! They save what was lost and despaired of, a work of art that is theirs alone to bring to fruition.

Can art really be a foundation for a world? Already it is. Your favorite music is already close to your heart. And from the sixfold surplus, most other things are art too: advertising, entertainment, visuals, packaging. Only it is usually bad art, both in its quality and its effects.

According to Hilaire Belloc in *The Great Heresies,* the Arian generals of the falling Roman empire ruled their satrapies in sublime assurance of legal supremacy until there was nothing left to rule. The people simply turned elsewhere. As citizens of the world empire of modern times, we can do likewise. We can thank Afghanistan and Lithuania by throwing open the back doors of the world to the spread of their image.

Not a camel, nor a folk song nor a blue tile nor a grandmother's accent needs to be lost, while there are thousands strong and young and ready to uphold their Beloved. Honor can defend each valley in the countryside, and put different lights in the windows of each neighborhood of the rejected city. We quietly eat into the heartless rings of steel and concrete and glass, the suburbs and malls and money towers that come in one unvarying flavor worldwide. We eat into the enemy's territory from both sides. In the end their commands will echo from empty cement, like the Soviet Navy shouting in deserted Kaliningrad.

As slowly as a tree or a child grows, as quietly as the feet of men or animals tread a long journey, as fiercely as a poet makes a song, the human being, leaning hard upon dear family and neighbors, *makes* the world that shows under the light of his hand.

Bibliography

This bibliography adds some resources beyond those detailed in the body of the text (which see). I also omit repeatedly cited works that everyone is expected to be familiar with, like *The Hobbit* and *The Lord of the Rings* by J.R.R. Tolkien.

[1] *Catholic World Report* (magazine). P.O. Box 1328, Dedham, MA 02027.

[2] Chaffetz, David. *A Journey Through Afghanistan: A Memorial.* Regnery, Chicago, 1981.

[3] Collier, Peter, and David Horowitz. *Destructive Generation.* Summit Books, New York, 1989.

[4] Confucius. *The Analects.* Arthur Waley, tr. George Allen and Unwin, London, 1938, 1971.

[5] *Culture Wars* (magazine), formerly *Fidelity* Magazine. 206 Marquette Avenue, South Bend IN 46617.

[6] *First Things* (magazine). Institute on Religion and Public Life, 156 Fifth Avenue, Suite 400, New York 10010.

[7] Greer, Germaine. *Sex & Destiny: The Politics of Human Fertility.* Harper & Row, New York, 1984.

[8] *HP Palmtop Paper* (magazine). Thaddeus Computing, 110 North Court Street, Fairfield IA 52556.

[9] Jones, E. Michael. *John Cardinal Krol and the Cultural Revolution.* Fidelity Press, 206 Marquette Avenue, South Bend, IN 46617, 1996.

[10] Kreeft, Peter. *Ecumenical Jihad.* Ignatius Press, San Francisco, 1996.

[11] Lafferty, R.A. *Past Master.* Ace Books, New York, 1968.

[12] Milosz, Czeslaw. *The Captive Mind.* Jane Zielonko, tr. Vintage International, New York, 1953, 1990.

[13] Neuhaus, Richard John. *The End of Democracy?* Spence Publishing Company, Dallas, 1997.

[14] O'Brien, Michael. *Father Elijah.* Ignatius Press, San Francisco, 1996.

[15] Orwell, George. *Keep the Aspidistra Flying.* Harcourt Brace, New York, 1956.

[16] Packard, Vance. *The Hidden Persuaders.* McKay, New York, 1957.

[17] Panin, Dimitri. *The Notebooks of Sologdin.* Harcourt Brace Jovanovich, New York, 1976.

[18] Pernoud, Régine. *Women in the Days of the Cathedrals.* Anne Côté-Harriss, tr. Ignatius Press, San Francisco, 1998.

[19] Peters, Ellis. *A Morbid Taste for Bones.* Mysterious Press, New York, 1977.

[20] San Diego County Grand Jury, 1991-1992. *Families in Crisis.* Report Number 2, February 6, 1992.

[21] Shakespeare, William. *Complete Works.* Garden City Publishing, New York, 1936.

[22] Solzhenitsyn, Alexander. *The Gulag Archipelago.* Harper & Row, New York, 1975.

[23] Stasheff, Christopher. *Starstone.* Ballantine Books, New York, 1995.

[24] Tolkien, J.R.R. *Beowulf: the Monsters and the Critics.* Folcroft Library Editions, Folcroft, PA, 1936, 1972.

[25] Tolkien, J.R.R. *Letters.* Humphrey Carpenter, ed. Houghton Mifflin, Boston, 1981.

[26] Vonnegut, Kurt. *Slaughterhouse-Five.* Delacorte Press, New York, 1969.

[27] *Wanderer* (newspaper). Wanderer Press, 201 Ohio Street, St Paul, Minn. 55107.

Index